WESTMAR COLLEC O9-ABH-028

FACTS AND FADS IN BEGINNING READING:

A CROSS-LANGUAGE PERSPECTIVE

Dina Feitelson

School of Education
University of Haifa, Israel

ABLEX PUBLISHING CORPORATION
Norwood, New Jersey

Copyright © 1988 by Ablex Publishing Corporation.

All rights reserved. No part of this publication may be reproduced, stored in a retrieval system, or transmitted, in any form or by any means, electronic, mechanical, photocopying, microfilming, recording, or other wise, without permission of the publisher.

Printed in the United States of America.

LIBRARY OF CONGRESS
Library of Congress Cataloging-in-Publication Data

Feitelson, Dina.
    Facts and fads in beginning reading : a cross-language perspective
/ by Dina Feitelson.
        p.   cm.
    Bibliography: p.
    Includes index.
    ISBN 0-89391-507-6; ISBN 0-89391-531-9 (ppk)
    1. Reading—Cross-cultural studies.   2. English language—Study
and teaching.   I. Title.
LB1050.2.F45 1988
372.4—dc19   88-4119
                                                                              CIP

Ablex Publishing Corporation
355 Chestnut St.
Norwood, NJ 07648

To Jehuda, Eran and Dror

CONTENTS

Preface

A sabbatical from my home institution, the University of Haifa, enabled me to undertake the initial research on which this book is based. The comradeship and gracious hospitality I met with during my sabbatical in the Department of Psychology and Social Relations and the Reading Laboratory at Harvard and the Department of Educational Psychology at New York University, were instrumental in providing the framework in which I could pursue my quest.

I am deeply grateful to Jeanne Chall, Courtney Cazden, Marjorie Martus, Lenore Ringler, Trika Smith-Burke, and Catherine Snow for encouragement, help, and stimulation over many years. Discussing ideas with them helped clarify my thinking and set me on the way.

Repeated opportunities to discuss my work with Isabelle and Alvin Liberman, Richard Venezky, Robert Calfee, Harry Singer, Jay Samuels, Irving Sigel, Joyce Morris, Marie Clay, Carol Chomsky, Barbara Tizard, Micha Razel, and Joseph Shimron provided fresh insights and new angles.

My indebtedness to Eric Wanner is beyond words. He shepherded me along during years of writing; his enthusiasm and quick understanding was largely responsible for bringing this book into existence.

Roy Freedle and Charles Perfetti read the entire manuscript. Their generosity in giving so freely of their time, and their substantive advice is deeply appreciated.

Crucial aid was provided by a personal small grant from the Ford Foundation. Access to the exceptional library facilities of New York University's Bobst Library during my sabbatical and subsequently on repeated visits enabled me to undertake the present task despite the handicap of living abroad.

I am grateful to Gary Feldtmann of New York University who, with constant good cheer, found solutions for the many small and large problems which beset visiting scientists. Steve Levine helped with the English in several chapters. Irene Eshwege patiently typed and retyped undecipherable scribbles. In the process she became a close friend.

This book is lovingly dedicated to my husband and sons. Without their interest, understanding, and forbearance it could not have been written.

PART I

Points of Departure

CHAPTER 1

Introduction: Facts and Fads on the Reading Scene

In 1956 UNESCO published an international investigation it had commissioned William S. Gray, Professor of Reading at the University of Chicago, to undertake.

Chicago was at the time the undisputed center of scholarship on reading, and William S. Gray the eminent authority who had made it so. The fact that Paris-based UNESCO had chosen him was in a way an acknowledgement of Gray's status on the reading scene and his worldwide reputation. The aim of Gray's study was to document the most recent attainments of research on reading and writing instruction with a view to formulating an overall policy UNESCO would be able to recommend for adult literacy campaigns. Due to Gray's personal prestige and the cross-language aspects of his investigation, *The Teaching of Reading and Writing an International Survey* turned into a landmark among publications on reading. Here was an authoritative, research-based summing up of the state of the art in modern reading instruction. Gray's book soon came to stand as a consensus of enlightened opinion, and collective endeavor in the field. Was it the secret workings of the irony of history or no more than a mere coincidence that a year before Gray's book appeared, Harper & Row published a small volume which was destined to become a bestseller and to challenge the tradition Gray and his colleagues represented?

Rudolf Flesch, the author of *Why Johnny Can't Read—and What You Can Do About It* (1955) was neither a professional educator nor a reading researcher. Yet he ushered in a period of uncertainty and discontent with American reading instruction which continues to this day. Nor was Flesch's book the first time education in the United States was attacked by an outsider. A series of articles published by a New York pediatrician (Rice, 1893/1969) more than 60 years earlier had had a comparable impact. Joseph Mayer Rice was commissioned by the publisher of a periodical to report on educational practices he would encounter during a tour of schools in different parts of the country. A major part of Rice's descriptions of the school systems of the 36 towns he visited dealt with reading instruction. Rice criticized the insipid, mechanistic, rote-drill kind of reading exercises he encountered during many of his visits (Rice, 1893/1969; Mathews, 1966). Cremin (1961) sees in Rice and his message a forerunner of the movement towards progressive education which soon afterwards gained foothold in parts of the United States. This was the time of the shift from subject-centered to child-focused instruction. Formal teaching was considered outmoded. According to Dewey and his followers, children would acquire the art of reading incidentally. Above all, reading would always be linked to some purpose and would therefore be meaningful right from the start. In time the approach which developed according to these criteria came to predominate in the United States. Called Look-and-Say, it was espoused by the leading experts of the day, among whom Gray was perhaps the most prominent.

Flesch's (1955) book was in turn a call to arms against Look-and-Say. However, what he proposed instead seemed not unreminiscent of the old rote-drill routines Rice had so roundly criticized more than half a century before.

It is precisely this problem which continues to plague the reading scene to the present day, and which is at the source of much of the controversy, dissatisfaction, and confusion which characterize it.

On the one hand Look-and-Say has, after long popularity, lost favor with large sections of the general public as well as with some well-known members of the academic community. On the other hand, proponents of alternative approaches have thus far been unable to dispel apprehensions that systematic introduction of decoding skills will require young children to engage for lengthy periods of time in abstract exercises instead of enjoying meaningful experiences with reading. Nor do many of the proposed alternatives seem to have withstood the test of time. Aukerman (1971) catalogued about 100 mostly newly developed beginning reading programs in the early 1970s. When he set out to prepare a new edition of his book 10 years later, he found that more than half of these programs were no longer in use (personal communication, 1981).

In this context a remark about the educational scene in general, written many years ago by a distinguished professor at Columbia Teachers College, unfortunately, still seems to apply to reading—"a kaleidoscope of changing fads and fancies, each guaranteed to solve the problem of education until the next appeared" (Kandel, 1969, p. 308, Originally 1926).

Several widely publicized studies which seemed to show that little of what occurs in schools substantially affects chances for success in adult life (Coleman, Campbell, Hobson, McPartland, Weinfeld, & York, 1966), and more especially that differences in methods of beginning reading instruction have no lasting impact (Bond & Dykstra, 1967) contributed to the spread of feelings of futility and discouragement in regard to what organized education in general, and reading instruction in particular, have to offer. Maybe the answer is to revert to teaching in the home as in the days of old. Flesch addressed his book to the parents rather than to professional educators, and he not only suggested that parents teach their children themselves, but also provided a detailed curriculum to show them how to go about it. Other recent proponents of reforms in reading instruction (i.e., Kohl, 1973; Bettelheim & Zelan, 1981) seem to think likewise.

The trend away from schools as purveyors of reading instruction is based in part on a feeling that schools are not effective enough. Downing (1973) suggests that the concept of "teacher proof" materials, which gained acceptance in the United States, in fact expresses contempt for teachers' abilities to perform their job. His study of reading instruction in 13 countries showed this stance to be unique. By contrast English educational policy "reflects a high degree of respect for the teacher's professional judgement" (p. 137). There the responsibility given to individual teachers implies that "all members of the profession are excellent" (p. 138).

Other countries included in Downing's book likewise seem imbued with high regard for the way reading instruction is approached. The descriptions convey certitude about ways and means and a clearly perceived progression of instructional steps. While there is in no case a single program, within each of these countries there is a consensus about strategies that produce results. In discussing assumptions which underly choice of particular strategies over others, local experts refer fairly regularly to (a) considerations of language variables and (b) children's expected state of maturity at school entrance. It also appears that, by and large, strategies evolved slowly, and changes, when they occurred, were not radical. In a very few instances there is mention that at some time in the past there was a near system-wide shift in choice of basic approach. But even in these cases it seems that once that shift was accomplished there were no further major upheavals.

Fitting in well with this overall atmosphere, is that reports about the state of reading in these countries do not seem overly concerned with problems of reading disabilities. Downing asked all authors to include a section on the treatment of reading disabilities in the country on which they were reporting. Several of the authors complied. However, others wrote only a few short paragraphs or omitted the topic altogether.

Biglmaier's (1973) statement "generally in Germany, reading is not considered a serious problem" (p. 353) mirrors the stance of some of the other contributors.

The feeling that there are countries in which learning to read constitutes less of a problem than in the United States is not confined to present-day scholars or to persons reporting, perhaps overly subjectively, on a reading scene in which they are personally involved.

Rice (1893/1969) decided to include also Toronto, Canada, in his tour of American school systems because he had "heard so much" (p. 228) about the teaching of reading in that city. Evidently Toronto lived up to its reputation. Rice found that by the end of their fourth or fifth month in school, many children were able "to read almost any new word without assistance, and to write from dictation correctly and very rapidly, even words of several syllables. The penmanship of many of these little children is as good as that of the average adult" (p. 228).

Rice felt that these "remarkable" results were due to the fact that the superintendent of schools in that city had given "much attention to phonics" (p. 228). Rice's evidence also seems to show that the emphasis on phonics had not been at the expense of other aspects of children's learning situation. "In Toronto the cheerfulness of the classrooms is almost without parallel" (p. 228).

The fact that Rice singled out an English-speaking school system as a model for instructional practices which he felt were superior to those used in his day in the towns he had visited in the United States seems to show that the English language per se may not necessarily be the villain it has so often been made out to be.

Downing's (1973) study and other recent publications in which the problems faced by beginning readers in diverse languages are analyzed by expert speakers of those languages (i.e., Leong, 1978; Liu, 1978; Kavanagh and Venezky, 1980) call into question many preconceived notions about what is easy and what is difficult in learning to read. Could it be that an overemphasis on the vagaries of English orthography has led to a tendency to disregard other pertinent differences between the ways beginning reading is approached in different countries?

The time may be ripe for a thorough re-examination of currently held beliefs on beginning reading. It would seem that an effort to distinguish more clearly between substantiated research results and what is often no more than fashionable fads could lead to more efficient and better focused instructional strategies. Such a clarification could also point the way to needed areas of fundamental and applied research.

CHAPTER 2

A Parting of Ways: Notes on the History of Reading Methods in the United States and German-Speaking Countries

In 1902 William Winch, at that time a British School inspector, who later became chairman of the committee of the Education Guild of Great Britain and a proponent for an introductory alphabet, undertook a study of German primary schools (Winch, 1904). Winch studied four different school systems. His book includes detailed descriptions of lessons he observed. Here is a partial description of a reading lesson in a first grade classroom in Frankfort.

Fifty-four girls were present on the day Winch visited. The female teacher held up a card with the diphtong (vowel combination) "ei" printed on it in Gothic letters $\boxed{ei}$. Girls were asked to supply the sound and did so. The teacher next held up a card with the consonant "n" $\boxed{n}$. Again children supplied the correct sound. The teacher then placed the two cards next to each other forming the word "ein" $\boxed{ei \mid n}$. ("Ein" is the German indefinite article, equivalent to "a" in English. Before a noun "ein" also means "one".) Children read the word "ein". Subsequently the teacher showed another "n" card, suggesting that it should be placed in front of the two others thus forming the word "nein" $\boxed{n \mid ei \mid n}$ ("no" in German). Children read the new word (Winch, 1904). Now let us compare this protocol to a record of my observations in a kindergarten class in Cambridge, Massachusetts nearly 80 years later.

Seventeen kindergartners were present the day I visited their class in the winter of 1980. Several eighth grade helpers were in the room working with individual children or groups. One group was engaged in printing rubber stamp capital letters on sheets of paper. Letters were printed in alphabetical order, one row for each letter. The two eighth graders working with this group were making sure the letters were printed in correct order and position. Everybody in the room invariably referred to letters by their names. From the talk I had with the teacher, I learned that she had a well worked-out, clear program in mind. Capital letters were learned first, lower-case ones second.

Only when children "know their letters," namely, when they are able to pair in correct sequence all upper- and lower-case characters with their names, are letter-sounds introduced. Teachers in several other kindergarten classes I visited in the Boston area that winter, used the same "three-staged" approach to initial letter introduction.

Although they were not aware of it, these teachers were using an approach reminiscent of the alphabet method of teaching reading used already in ancient Greece and Rome. On the other hand, the teaching approach Winch encountered in Frankfort in 1902 is typical of what at the time was called phonetic teaching and would today probably be labeled eclectic or functional.

How did it happen that teachers in Massachusetts in the 1980s were using elements of a teaching method which—according to contemporaries, like the Roman grammarian Quintilian—seems to have caused problems even in ancient times?

The present chapter attempts to answer this question. In it we shall briefly survey characteristic features of the major traditional methods for teaching beginning reading and try to understand what led to their adoption or rejection.

THE ALPHABET APPROACH

The alphabet method or "spelling method," has been in use longer than any other method and in a wide array of language situations. Throughout, its basic tenets have remained remarkably unchanged. In the alphabet method, the first step in learning to read is to learn the names of the letters in their *correct* order. This accomplishment was considered so important that in ancient Greece teachers seem to have required their charges to recite the alphabet backwards as well as forwards, a practice which was still common in fairly recent times (Mathews, 1966).

Once children were well able to recite the alphabet by heart they had to learn to associate each letter name with corresponding graphic symbols. This task was by no means easy. One difficulty seems to have been that children usually were taught all the letters of the alphabet concurrently. The well-known hornbook is a good example of this practice. Hoole (1660), describing the concurrent introduction of letters in his times, remarked that while some "ripe witted" children did learn this way, others "have been thus learning a whole year together (and though they have been much chid, and beaten too for want of heed) could scarcely tell six of their letters at twelve months' end" (Charles Hoole, 1660, reissued 1912, p. 33, quoted in Mathews, 1966, p. 29).

Another difficulty was that in the days before print, handwritten letters were not uniform in appearance (Cubberly, 1920). Also, in many old alphabets, individual letters resembled each other much more than in modern scripts. Further, in many orthographies, letters are represented by more than one graphic symbol per letter. In the Roman alphabet, for instance, many letters have two forms—capital and lower-case—while in Arabic most consonants have as many as four forms used according to ordinal position in the word.

Also in this second phase of learning, the goal to be achieved was faultless performance. One of the exercises used to achieve this had the pupil who had mastered a letter symbol "pick out every occurrence of it in a specific piece of writing," most often a lengthy religious text (Mathews, 1966, p. 4).

Learning one's letters in this fashion was thus an exceedingly difficult task, requiring many months. In the first century A.D., the Roman grammarian Quintilian found fault with the pedagogical wisdom of teaching letter names and sequence before their shapes. According to him this method interferes with letter recognition, as during the initial stage the students "do not fix their attention on the form of the letters" (Watson, 1875–76, quoted in Mathews, 1966, p. 11).

Once a child was able to associate all the characters of the alphabet with their names, and knew their ordinal position, the third phase in learning to read was reached. Combinations of consonants with vowels, or vowels with consonants were now drilled by way of sing-song recitation of nonsense syllables such as "ba, be, bi, bo, bu; ab, eb, ib, ob, ub; bab, beb, bib, bob, bub," and so on. In addition to being both time-consuming as well as extremely boring, this kind of rote drill sometimes included letter combinations that did not occur in the particular language a child was learning to read.

Syllable drill was often followed by a stage in which rules about reading were taught in abstract fashion. "When two vowels go walking the first one does the talking" is a familiar example. Only when children had memorized these rules, and were able to recite them with great facility, were they at long last introduced to words. However, even this brought little relief from the tedium associated with learning to read. For a long time to come, single words would be sounded out laboriously, with no attention whatsoever paid to their meanings. In colonial times for instance *The New England Primer* presented children at this stage with the task of mastering "eighty-four 1-syllable words, from *age* to *would;* forty-eight 2-syllable words, from *ab-sent* to *mu-sic;* twenty-four 3-syllable words, from *a-bu-sing* to *ho-li-ness;* eighteen 4-syllable words, from *a-bi-li-ty* to *gra-ci-ous-ly;* fourteen 5-syllable words, from *a-bo-mi-na-ble* to *ge-ne-ro-si-ty;* and twelve 6-syllable words, from *a-bo-mi-na-ti-on* to *qua-li-fi-ca-ti-on*" (Hodges, 1977). Yet this seems relatively light fare compared with usages in some other societies. Among Kurdish Jews who lived in the remote mountainous region of what today is northern Iraq, a boy at this stage was made to read the entire first five books of the Old Testament solely as a decoding exercise, not understanding a single word of the Old-Testament-Hebrew, a language which at that time was no longer used in daily life by his people. The process usually took several years (Brauer, 1947).

In retrospect the classic alphabet method seems extremely laborious, yet educators in the 18th and 19th centuries complicated it even more. In ancient Greece the lengthy syllable drill at least provided a direct stepping stone to reading proper. Dionysius of Halicarnassus's description of about 20 B.C. is apt:

> When we are taught to read, first we learn off the names of the letters, and their forms and their values, then in due course syllables and their modifications, and finally words and their properties, viz., lengthenings and shortenings, accents and the like. After acquiring the knowledge of these things, we begin to write and read, syllable by syllable and slowly at first. And when the lapse of a considerable time has implanted the forms of words firmly in our minds, then we deal with them without the least difficulty, and whenever any book is placed in our hands we go through it without stumbling and with incredible facility and speed. (Roberts, 1910, p. 269, cited in Mathews, 1966, p. 6).

By contrast in the not-too-distant past pupils in many countries were made to continue to "spell" syllables and words, that is, to say all the letter names one by one *before* pronouncing a syllable or word as entity (Reeder, 1900; Huey, 1908/1968). According to Huey (1908/1968) and others who criticized this approach, it was an outcome of the great concern with correct spelling that was prevalent in some societies till fairly recently. It is this specific practice, namely the spelling out aloud of a string of letter names before pronouncing a word and the lack of concern for meaning that are most often associated with the "spelling method" by critics of this method.

Learning to read by the alphabet method was thus a lengthy and difficult task, requiring in many cases years rather than months. Paulsen (1920) called German reading instruction "a torture protracted through years" (Cubberly, 1920, p. 454), while Diesterweg (1846) writing on the same subject, maintained that "many did not learn in four years." It may be that during the relatively long periods in history when education was considered the rightful province of only the few (Goody & Watt, 1972). this characteristic of the alphabet method was considered an advantage rather than a shortcoming.

For learning children the significant characteristics of the alphabet method were these: First, learners are taught to recite letter names in alphabetic order. Secondly, they are trained to associate letter names automatically with the characters which represent them. Later there will come a stage when they will have to unlearn most of what was acquired with such difficulty in these initial stages. Third, there is a long preparatory stage during which learners are taught facts related to reading before the actual task of reading is approached functionally. And finally, reading is initially acquired as a mechanical skill with little or no regard for the content of the texts read. Even at more advanced stages of learning, content was arrived at largely by laborious processes of translation and/or grammatical dissection, rather than by direct spontaneous reaction to the text and its content.

Because educational reformers were well aware of the disadvantages of the alphabet method, most reform proposals were addressed to one or a combination of several of these specific issues. Over the years a great number of alternative approaches came into being, often spreading much beyond the confines of the language and country in which they had originated. For our present purpose, we shall reduce a bewildering profusion to two main categories—phonemic approaches and word methods.

THE MANY FACES OF PHONEMIC TEACHING

The basic tenets of the alphabet method were essentially the same in different locations and over long periods of time. On the other hand phonemic teaching assumed many different forms and even names. Initially, and in continental Europe till fairly recently, phonemic teaching was most often referred to as "the phonetic method." In English-speaking countries the term "phonics" is used both in regard to phonemic teaching in general, as well as in regard to that specific kind of phonemic teaching, which became most widely used in them. The terms—phonetic, phonic, and phonemic—have thus come to mean many different things. Moreover, varying interpretations of these terms were associated with particular geographic locations, or specific points in time. In trying to focus only on main issues this presentation will of necessity be overly simplistic. We shall use the terms phonetic, phonic, and phonemic the way they were usually used in the times and localities described.

Phonetic teaching was conceived as a way of dealing with the most persistent problem inherent in the alphabet method. This difficulty occurred when the beginner had to progress from associating letters with their names to pronouncing syllables or words. After having been drilled to respond automatically to the sight of a letter by saying its name, the learner now had to suppress that automatic response. Instead, he or she had to abstract a sound value from the name of the letter which, when combined with other sound values derived from further letter names, would hopefully enable him or her to pronounce the required syllable or word.

Reading even a relatively simple regular word like "wing," for instance, meant in fact that the associations "double yoo," "ie," "en," and "soft gee," which would float automatically and uncalled for into the beginner's mind on seeing the word, had to be first of all transformed into a string of sounds which bore no real resemblance to them, namely "w", "i", "n" and "g". If a beginner was indeed able to effect these transformations, no mean task in itself, he/she still had to draw them together into one ejaculation: "wing." Further, unless the learner realized while laboring on these tasks, that the word being deciphered was old familiar "wing," his/her efforts would most probably remain useless, as no amount of "blending" artificially derived isolated sounds would result in a recognizable typical British or American "wing."

The lengthy process just described required well developed ability to abstract. It would have been quite difficult for the average school beginner, even when the target word was familiar. When reading matter was classic texts, where the words being deciphered were unfamiliar and sometimes in a foreign tongue, the task may often have been beyond reach.

The core of the difficulty lay in the need of the learner to suppress a strongly bonded association, which had been established at great cost, and to relearn to respond to a by now familiar cue in a new way. Modern learning theory has coined a special term "negative transfer" (Gage & Berliner, 1984, p. 356) to describe this difficulty.

Negative transfer occurs when a new response to a familiar stimulus is substituted for one that was already established. When this happens the original response interferes with the bonding of the new association.

German educators were the first to become aware of the difficulty of trying to infer speech sounds from letter names. In 1527 Ickelsamer prepared a primer predicated on his idea of basing the learning of letter symbols on the speech-sounds for which they stood. Ickelsamer maintained that it should be possible to teach reading by his method in a matter of days and even claimed to have done so successfully in a few instances (Mathews, 1966, following Vogel, 1894, and Kehr, 1888). Apparently, however, Ickelsamer became so intrigued with the analysis of words into their sounds that he tended to overdo work on sounds, once again creating a lengthy introductory stage before reading proper was started. In time his followers simplified matters, allowing pupils to begin to read before they had mastered all the sounds and letters (Mathews, 1966, p. 33). By the time phonetic approaches to teaching beginning reading became widely accepted in German-speaking countries, they were firmly rooted in a number of basic principles. Winch's description of the first grade class he observed in 1902 in Frankfort provides a good example of these shared basic principles. First and foremost, and in striking contrast to the alphabet method, in phonetic teaching children learned to associate *sounds* with the symbol or symbols representing them. In present-day linguistic terminology one would say that what was learned were phoneme-grapheme relationships. Further characteristics were: one, that functional reading of words was most often begun fairly early and certainly much before all possible sound-symbol relationships had been studied, and two, that the sequence in which symbols were introduced depended on functional considerations, namely on the usefulness of a given symbol for word construction at any one particular stage of learning, rather than on ordinal place in the alphabet. A third common practice widely used in phonetic teaching was the construction of words and sentences out of letter, or letter-combination cards in the way described by Winch. Children thus had the actual experience of combining words out of their parts, and taking them apart again. The use of letter cards in this manner illustrates another basic principle of phonetic teaching, namely that letter combinations which represent unique sound values were taught in addition to the single letters from which they are composed. This means that a German child taught by the phonetic method would learn in addition to the 26 letters of the alphabet also blends like "st" and "sp," digraphs like "ch", and "ck"; diphthongs like "ei", "ai", "au", and "eu"; Umlaute like "ä," "ü" and "ö," and combinations of vowels with silent "h" or "e."—altogether more than 40 symbol-sound correspondences.

The most characteristic difference between the alphabet and the phonetic methods is reflected in their original German names. The alphabet method was called "Buchstabieren,"—literally, *saying letter names*—while the phonetic method was called "Lautieren"—*sounding*. Unfortunately the English term for the alphabet method "spelling" tends to confuse, as it implies a relationship to spelling ability. There is no trace of this in the German term.

While phonetic approaches prospered in continental Europe, their fate was far less benign in the United States. Farnham (1887), the originator of the sentence method, reports: "In 1858 the phonetic system was introduced into the schools of Syracuse, N.Y., and for a time it was thought that the true method of teaching children to read had been discovered . . . pupils learned to read by this method in much less time than usual, and attained a high state of excellence in articulation . . . " (p. 3). However, according to Farnham this method was superseded "after a trial of five years" in favor of "the word method" (p. 4).

Reeder (1900), who had a broader perspective, bears out this assertion when he describes in a very short passage that the "phonic" method developed from no particular center, "but was tried as an experiment in different parts of the country in the (eighteen hundred, D.F.) fifties and sixties. It was short-lived wherever introduced" (p. 80).

Reeder may have slightly overstated the case. A few mainly phonetic approaches, that is, the "snythetic method" developed by Pollard, the "Beacon Readers," and the "Ward Rational Method in Reading" seem to have enjoyed considerable popularity over somewhat longer stretches of time (Smith, 1965). Also the very widely used *McGuffey's Eclectic Readers* shared many of the characteristics of functional phonetic teaching. In fact, according to the authors, the *First McGuffey Eclectic Reader* edition 1874, could be used in conjunction with any of the methods of the day, "but it is especially adapted to the Phonic Method, the Word Method, or a combination of the two" (p. 11).

There can be little doubt that the rising eminence of word and sentence methods were at least partly responsible for the abrupt termination of phonetic teaching in some areas in the United States, and a slower phasing out in others. According to Fries, by 1842 the word method was not only in active use but was also "grasped clearly in theory" (Fries, 1962, p. 15).

One result of the fact that phonetic instruction was by and large superseded in the United States before empirical research on reading got underway is that few modern American researchers or school practitioners ever had an opportunity to observe this approach at first hand. Consequently, the functional aspects of the phonetic approach seem to have gone largely unrecognized. Instead, "phonetic teaching" has often come to be associated with protracted and tedious exercises in letter sounding. Such exercises were indeed incorporated in some better known phonetic sets of materials, used in the United States, such as Pollard's (1889) popular synthetic method. However, they were not thought necessary in continental Europe, where variations of phonetic approaches continue to be used very widely in some countries, for instance France (Ruthman, 1973) and Finland (Kyöstiö, 1973, 1980). A further cause for confusion in America about what is meant by "phonetic approach" is that the term "phonetic" came to be used in conjunction with recurrent proposals to reform English orthography (Balmuth, 1982).

A good example of this use of the term phonetic is Leigh's (1864) system which was adopted by the St. Louis schools, and used there and in other cities for more than 20 years (Reeder, 1900; Huey, 1908; Smith, 1965; Mathews, 1966; Balmuth, 1982). Like many other spelling reformers, Leigh developed not only a transitory alphabet but also an instructional approach to go with it, including a primer and readers.

To sum up. "Phonetic teaching" in the sense in which it was used in the past, and continues to be used in some European countries refers to an instructional approach. The outstanding characteristic of that approach is that from the outset, beginning readers are taught to relate graphic symbols to sounds. Letter names are introduced only at a later stage, frequently not before the second or third year of learning, when the erstwhile beginner is supposedly already well able to read.

Because of a variety of historic reasons contemporary American scholars tend to understand the term "phonetic method" differently. They associate "phonetic method" with either great insistence on articulation, and tedious prereading exercises to improve articulation or a reading method based on a modified or augmented alphabet such as the Initial Teaching Alphabet (i.t.a.) devised by Sir James Pitman (Harris & Hodges, 1981).

In the United States phonetic teaching was short-lived, despite the fact that wherever it was tried it was judged to be most successful (Mathews, 1966). The early demise of phonetic approaches seems to have been an outcome of the rise of global ways of teaching reading, that is "the word" or "sentence" method, or popularly "look-and-say."

THE WORD METHOD'S ORIGINS

The first American reader based on the word method was published in 1840 (Anderson & Dearborn, 1952). About 15 years later John Russell Webb (1855) published his *Normal Readers* which did much to propagate this approach to teaching beginning reading. By 1870 the word method was being used by progressive teachers in many parts of the country (Smith, 1965).

Since then the word method in one form or another has remained dominant in the United States. Anderson and Dearborn's (1952) statement of the mid-1950s remains applicable "in combination with other methods, it [the word method, D.F.] remains fairly universal today. In one way or another, every teacher of reading uses the 'look-and-say' method, even if it is only to supply a word which has caused the pupil to hesitate" (p. 212).

In order to appreciate fully the initial impact and overwhelming acceptance of the "word method" it must be remembered that its great appeal lay in the deliverance it promised from the drudgery of the alphabet that is, spelling method. Indeed, it first appeared in European enlightenment as a reaction against the artificiality, dry scholasticism, and learning by rote of the day. Just as in the wake of Rousseau, children were supposed to study natural "wholes" in their environment, in learning to read the child was likewise to start from "natural wholes," namely books. Sentences, words, and only in the last resort their constituent parts were to follow later and in that order (Mathews, 1966). Farnham (1881, 1887) can probably be considered a fairly representative proponent of these ideas on the American scene.

The core of Farnham's (1887) argument is that "things are recognized as wholes" (p. 16)[1] and that it is only through knowing the "whole" that one will eventually learn about its constituent parts. As reading is the extraction of thought from written language, the unit analogous to thought is a sentence. Thus it is sentences a child should learn to recognize first, proceeding eventually from these to words. At no stage should attention be diverted from the "forms of the words" to the names of the letters, as translation of written words into spoken words via letters would interpose a "barrier" between the mind of the child and the thoughts in the text. Therefore, "phonic analysis of words should have no place in the primary schools" (Farnham, 1887, p. 43). It is symptomatic of the disciplined bent of mind of the day that this advocate of a "natural" way of teaching in fact devoted the main part of his treatise to a detailed step-by-step plan, complete with time approximations, of a very systematic approach to teaching by the "sentence method," even asserting explicitly in one place that "the introduction of new words is placed entirely within the control of the teacher" (p. 33).

The word method first became popular because American educational opinion leaders had been impressed by what they saw on visits abroad. Its popularity was enhanced when it was advocated by Dewey and other key figures in the progressive movement. It gained further credibility when it turned out that it was in accord with some tenets in newly developed scientific psychology. A consequence of this has been a tendency to link look-and-say retrospectively to a variety of psychologi-

---

[1] Like Mathews (1966) I was unable to obtain a copy of the first edition of Farnham's book which was initially published in 1881. References and page citations are, therefore, to the second edition.

cal theories. In some cases these links were not justified, and have led to confusion about the psychological foundations of the word method.

A RE-EXAMINATION OF LINKS OF THE WORD METHOD TO PSYCHOLOGICAL THEORIES

Gestalt Psychology

It is frequently believed that the scientific origins of look-and-say are empiric findings in Gestalt psychology. These experiments purportedly showed that whole words are learned more easily than single letters, and that letters which stick out above or below the line in lower-case writing (so-called ascenders and descenders) contribute especially to characteristic word configurations, and thus ease acquisition. Long words with many ascenders and descenders like "shotgun," "steamroller," or "alligator" are therefore supposedly easier for beginning learners than words like "were," "come," "was," "in," or "on," as the former have distinct visual patterns of their own, in other words, "Gestalt" which the latter lack (Schonell, 1966).

In fact in the Gestalt literature "of the Wertheimer, Köhler and Koffka school" (Blumenthal, 1970, p. 169) there is no mention of beginning reading, because leading Gestalt psychologists were mainly interested in high level mental processes (Diack, 1960; Blumenthal, 1970). Moreover Brown (1958) showed that believing that look-and-say is an application of Gestalt theory, because what the child learns are "meaningful wholes," namely, words, is a misconstruing of Gestalt theory. Meaningful learning in Gestalt literature is learning based on insights about systematic relations and underlying principles. Brown (1958) feels that "in learning to read there seems to be more insight provided by phonetic rules than by the look-and-say method" (p. 72). Therefore, according to him, "Gestalt theory . . . would seem to favor the insightful phonetic method" (p. 72).

Studies on Perception

A series of studies on perception in the late nineteenth century and the beginning of the twentieth exemplify the best in scientific endeavor. Within a relatively short period of time, scholars in Europe and in the United States, who were moreover in intensive contact with each other's work produced experimental results which were to influence the reading scene to the present. Previously reading had been believed to be a continuous phenomenon, during which the reader processes letter symbols one by one. This notion was seriously challenged when the French scholar Javal (1878–1879a, 1879b) and his associates discovered in studies of eye movements of competent adult readers, that reading proceeds in a series of jerks interspersed with fixations. This discovery was followed in short order by Cattell's (1885) findings that when words were exposed momentarily, they were processed nearly as quickly as single letters. Numerous and varied experiments in which single letters, meaningless groups of letters, words and sentences were exposed for short durations followed. In these, Cattell (1886a, 1886b, 1890), Erdman & Doge (1898), Huey (1898, 1900, 1901), Messmer (1904) and Dearborn (1906) confirmed and reconfirmed each other's findings, showing that experienced adult readers recognize familiar words faster than it would take them to read off the same number of unconnected letters, and that when connected by content even several words are recognized in a single exposure. Erdman & Doge (1898) went on to argue that in words, like in physical objects, it is not single constituent parts that make the perceived object recognizable, but rather a familiar overall arrangement. According to them, just as we recognize a house, wall, tree, or even a whole landscape for what it is without recourse to its constituent parts, so it is with words.

The belief in overall "word-shape" as a main cue in word recognition led to a preoccupation with efforts to discover what specific characteristics of word shapes contribute most to speedy and accurate recognition. In this context Huey (1898) found that the first half of a familiar word is of considerably greater importance for recognition than its second part, and that the upper part of a word printed in Roman characters is more helpful than its lower part.

To today's reader the statements of these early researchers seem amazingly precise and careful. For instance, Huey pointed out that in studies on the recognition of familiar words and sentences by competent readers, one will have to distinguish "between what is actually seen during a reading pause and what is mentally filled in" by the reader (Huey, 1908, p. 63). However, succeeding generations of scholars tended to pass on these early findings with little of the exactitude of their originators. Even respected authors like Schonell (1966) and Gray (1956) sometimes made sweeping statements which went far beyond the factual evidence on which they were supposedly based.

This tendency to overgeneralize was probably a result of the authors' referring to each other rather than going back to the original studies. A reason for this may have been that the original studies were often not easily available and were sometimes in a foreign language. Had, for instance, Messmer's (1904) study in German been better known, reading theory and practice in the past 70 years might well have taken a different course.

In his study Messmer documented in painstaking detail how the reading of children differs qualitatively from that of experienced adults. Messmer's results show that reading develops in stages from that of "beginners" (in fact, second graders who had already some decoding experience), through the intermediate stages of his fourth and sixth graders. Messmer found unequivocally that the bases for a person learning to read are optic perceptions[2] divided into letters and acoustic-motoric perceptions divided into sounds. Thus, the model for the reading process at the initial stage is letter by letter decoding linked to sound by sound pronunciation according to the following scheme:

Mutter

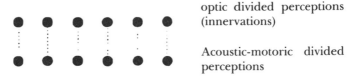

optic divided perceptions (innervations)

Acoustic-motoric divided perceptions

(Messmer, 1904, p. 25). Moreover, these two modes of processing do not proceed at an equal speed, and it is the optic mode which is the faster.

Messmer's most important observations are in regard to the transition from letter-by-letter, sound-by-sound perception to holistic perception typical of experienced readers. According to his findings, whenever a combination has become sufficiently familiar it will be apprehended holistically, while other less familiar combinations will continue to be processed unit by unit. Thus, when clusters of two or more letter-sound combinations or short words are already perceived holistically, other parts of a long word may still be processed in segments.

Messmer's findings were supported in the single short passage Dearborn devoted to children's reading in his oft-cited study on eye movements (Dearborn, 1906). From this passage it is clear that Dearborn also

---

[2] There does not seem to be an agreed-upon translation for the German term "innervation" in the sense used by Messmer. In his own writings, Dearborn simply used the German term as an English word. In present-day English dictionaries innervation is interpreted as "the sending out of nerve impulses" (Webster, 1983, p. 945). However, the 1914 edition of Webster, which more closely corresponds to the time when Messmer wrote, has the following entry: "Consciousness of a characteristic sort held by some psychologists to accompany the excitation of motor nerves." Consequently, the closest modern English terms would probably be "perception," "apprehension," or maybe "processing," and these have been used interchangeably here.

believed that "unitary word perception" (his term) develops only with time. Having studied three children aged nine, 10, and 11 respectively, he takes care to point out that the greater frequency of fixation-pauses of his nine-year-old subject prove that at this stage word processing (innervation) is still very fragmented. The eye movements of the two older children Dearborn studied resembled those of adults more closely. Dearborn saw this part of his study as only a very preliminary effort, soon to be followed by a much more substantive undertaking (Dearborn, 1906, p. 96). However, barely two years later, by way of being partially misquoted by Huey, Dearborn's findings became part of reading research lore, albeit in a badly garbled form. As this is a particularly interesting instance of the way results of rigorous research are sometimes distorted during the process of being handed on supposedly intact, from researcher to researcher, it may be worthwhile to pursue it in detail.

Huey (1908, p. 48) opens his discussion of Dearborn's study of children's eye movements by stating: "Children of from nine to eleven years, the only ages tested, were found" . . . and so on, thus implying in a way that the findings he was about to relate were obtained in a study of a representative population, whereas Dearborn throughout insists on the preliminary nature of his findings, and on the fact that only three individuals were studied. Furthermore and more importantly, while Dearborn clearly feels that there is a developmental process, and that "progress takes place as the child learns to read" (Dearborn, 1906, p. 96), Huey mainly quotes verbatim Dearborn's passages relating to the eye movement records of his 10-year-old subject, and more particularly those statements which stress similarities to adult reading behavior (Huey, 1908, p. 48). Thus, the overall effect of the passage in Huey's book is that children's eye movements are indeed rather similar to those of adults, while in Dearborn's study the eye movement records of his 10-year-old subject are described mainly in the context of the difference between them and those of the nine-year-old.

Early Behavioristic Theory

Studies on perception in the early years of the century had provided much data on the nature of reading processes of adult facile readers. In the years that followed,with the mounting ascendence of behaviorism in American psychology, it was tempting to believe that it should be possible to train beginning readers from the outset towards competent adult performance. A short, authoritative tract prepared by Gates (1953) as the first in a series—"What research says to the teacher"—issued by the prestigious American Educational Research Association is a good example of this position: "The principles described above clearly suggest that research over the years has shown the merits of teaching in such a way that pupils really read quite realistically and naturally from the early stages as adults do, that is, they begin by learning the "whole" typical activity and not by learning pieces or details of the reading performance." Such a view was probably attractive during a period in which there was a great belief in the need for speed and efficiency. When motion studies were in vogue, and the overall feeling was that modern man would have to learn to deal effectively with an ever-increasing input of information. In the opening pages of his booklet Gates refers explicitly to this consideration when he states that modern conditions "demand that both children and adults learn to read better today than in days gone by" (p. 4), and when he concludes that, "The school today must set up as one of its objectives the development of more rapid, more versatile, and more varied reading techniques than were considered necessary a generation ago" (Gates, 1953, p. 5).

The emphasis on the immediate instilling of "correct" reading habits led to a tendency to diagnose cases of poor readers via records of their eye movements (Judd, 1918). Treatment of such disorders was thus perceived in terms of correcting faulty habits of "inefficient" readers (Buswell, 1937; Gray, 1949). In line with this tradition was the great attention given to increasing speed and therefore silent reading, while behavior which was apt to impede speedy reading, such as lip reading or pointing, were to be discouraged (Klapper, 1926).

Proponents of efficient reading behavior for beginners did not seem aware of what Blumenthal (1970) calls the "logical error" (p. 167) of basing pedagogical techniques on psychologists' discussions. Blumenthal (1970) warns: "A description of the skills of efficient, mature readers" are "not a description of how the skills were attained" (p. 167). The tendency of many experts to overlook this distinction, and to imply that research results which pertained exclusively to adult facile readers may have practical implications for teaching beginners, is at the root of much of the confusion which characterizes the reading scene in recent years.

Researchers on perception who had used adult facile readers as subjects were most explicit about the fact that their results pertained to the recognition of familiar words and phrases. However, latter-day reading experts who referred to these findings in relation to beginning readers applied them, without further thought, to situations in which the decoder was actually *not acquainted* with the visual shape of the word he/she was trying to decode. For in the initial stages of learning, it is not a case of recognizing something familiar, but rather one of trying to make sense out of a combination of letters one *has not* met before.

Motivational Aspects

Research on motivation has also been used to bolster the arguments for look-and-say. In look-and-say, so this argument goes, learners experience immediate gratification because from the initial stages they are "reading." This gratification, so it is believed, will provide powerful motivation for further efforts and will spur the child on to greater feats of learning. By contrast, a long introductory stage, like in the outmoded alphabet method, is apt to present reading as an extremely difficult task with no intrinsic reward of its own and may therefore lead to negative attitudes to reading.

It was this line of thought and the opportunity to use children's personal interests as sole criterion for the selection of reading texts which made look-and-say especially attractive to progressive educators.

The supposed motivational superiority of look-and-say over other methods continues to be frequently mentioned in comparisons of the relative merits of different beginning reading approaches.

WORD METHODS IN THE UNITED STATES DIFFER FROM THE GERMAN MODEL

Reading theory and research in the United States were initially strongly influenced by German scholars and German educational practices. However, once these practices were transplanted to America they tended to assume a course all their own.

The word method spread in the United States much more rapidly than it did in Europe. But the way the word method came to be widely practiced in the United States differed radically from the German Normal-Words-Method which had in the first instance aroused the enthusiasm of American educators like Horace Mann and Colonel Parker, who were subsequently instrumental in establishing it in America (Mathews, 1966).

Mathews (1966) calls the German Normal-Words-Method a "words-to-letters method" (p. 63). An example from the ninth edition of a primer purporting to use the "Normal Wörter Methode" (Erika Fibel, 1899) will help us understand what Mathews means by that label. The first three pages of the primer introduce each of the vowels "o," "e," "i," "u," and the diphthong "ei" separately, by way of illustrations of objects whose names start with these letters. On page 4 there is the first word "seil" (rope), accompanied by a drawing of a rope. Underneath, the two consonants "s" and "l" are printed in isolation. There follow 15 new words, both long and short, structured from the previously learned vowels in combination with the new consonants—that is, "so," "eile," "elise." The page closes with two short sentences "sei leise" (be quiet) and "luise eile" (Luise hurry). Only lower-case letters are used. This leads in fact to spelling mistakes, when nouns which in German should invariably start with a capital letter are presented here with a lower-case initial, such as seil, and luise for Seil and Luise.

On the next page, page 5, there is a drawing of a nose, and its appropriate title "nase." Subsequently two new letters, "n" and "a" are isolated. Twelve additional words are formed from combinations of the letters learned so far. By page 31 four-line poems begin to appear. In the early part of the book words are printed segmented into syllables, that is, "na se" (p. 5) or "men schen" (people, p. 31). Capital letters are introduced from page 36 onwards. The whole primer has only 82 pages, and is both in size as well as contents, fairly representative of several other dusty specimens I was able to locate in American libraries.

By contrast the word method as it became eventually established in the United States was, according to Mathews (1966), a "words to reading" (p. 63) method. Here children were taught to recognize between 100 to 200 words by sight before beginning to learn about sounds and single letters (e.g., Arnold, 1899, p. 70). The most typical characteristic of this approach was that words were initially introduced as entities, and that word analysis, if practiced at all, was started only after a very considerable number of words had already been acquired.

In the German "Normal-Words Method" on the other hand, words served only as a short-term stepping stone to single letters. Overall instructional strategies remained much as they had been in the superseded phonetic method. The main difference was that, in the Normal-Words-Method, sounds of single letters were derived from a word in which the letter appeared, while in the phonetic method letters were learned in isolation and learners were introduced to the "correct" sound of letters by way of elaborate explanations and exercises in breathing and positioning of one's speech organs.

The remarkable difference between American and German educational traditions is at the root of many of the issues we shall discuss in the following chapters. Therefore, it seems that even at the danger of further confusing the reader, we cannot avoid adding another pertinent episode to what is at best already a confusing story. During its migration to the New World the German Normal-Words-Method underwent a transitory stage before it turned into Look-and-Say, for it is Look-and-Say which Mathews (1966) labeled a "words to reading method."

In the early days of adapting the German Normal-Words-Method for use in the United States, American educators too perceived starting off with words mainly as an effective device for learning one's letters and not as an overall new approach. However, the special propensity of American educators for spelling caused them to substitute letter names for what in German had been letter sounds. Those on the scene at the time seemed well aware of this crucial distinction. Mathews (1966) quotes the superintendant of the Cincinnati Public Schools who, in his Annual Report for 1857, wrote: "The process of teaching the first lessons of reading, generally adopted in the schools of this city, during the last year or two, differs from that which is pursued in the Prussian Schools in this regard, that, after the word is learned, the names of the letters are taught, and then their sounds, instead of the sounds first" (Rickoff, 1857, p. 47, quoted in Mathews, 1966, p. 99).

Dr. Rice's (1893; reissued, 1969) descriptions of American reading instruction at the turn of the century document how the Normal-Words-Method imported from Germany was, in fact, taught by the familiar spelling way, so that, despite the new name, it was nearly undistinguishable from the supposedly superseded Alphabet approach.

For the sake of clarity it may thus be helpful to add a third sub-category to the two proposed by Mathews in his attempt to keep apart what in fact were very different instructional approaches. Instead of distinguishing only between a "word to letter" and a "word to reading" approach, as Mathews did, it would perhaps be best to have three categories of word method:

1. "Word to letter-sound," as in the original German Normal-Words-Method.
2. "Word to letter-name," as in the United States in the nineteenth century.
3. "Word to reading," namely Look-and-Say mainly in this century.

Proponents of the "words to reading method" and the great number of teachers using it, believed implicitly that research had proved the superiority of this approach over all others. While there is evidence that during the early years of the present century educators were intimately acquainted with latest findings in reading research (i.e. Laing, 1911), in later years it became acceptable to quote "research results" without having, in fact, consulted research reports firsthand. In time, there developed what perhaps may be best described as "research lore," linking prevalent teaching practices to a long list of supposed findings and most prominently to the oft-repeated claim that experienced readers and beginners alike apprehend words as entities.

Historically these were the years during which expertise in reading emerged as a discipline in its own right, with a great proliferation of reading clinics, reading specialists or coordinators, and reading programs for all grade levels including high school and college. Professional organizations, journals dealing with reading, and college and university reading programs were all part of this trend. It was also during this period that the hegemony in matters concerning reading, especially research on reading, passed to the United States. Henceforth, leading trends in reading would emanate predominantly from there.

THE ASCENDANCE OF PHONICS IN THE UNITED STATES

At a time when interest in reading continued to flourish as perhaps never before, the cause of holistic reading instruction experienced a resounding setback. Starting with the publication of Flesch's controversial bestseller in 1955, but also as a result of research in Britain (Morris, 1959), the work of linguists such as Bloomfield (1942) and Fries (1962) and most especially Chall's (1967) epoch-making study, long established beliefs were suddenly viewed with misgivings and became open to serious questioning. Chall's painstaking investigation left little doubt that, contrary to widespread opinion, research over the years had demonstrated time and again that initial instruction programs which emphasized decoding skills consistently yielded better results than those which were mainly meaning oriented. Meaning oriented in Chall's terminology was a synonym for Look-and-Say, or Mathew's "words to reading approach."

Chall's findings came at a time of grave concern over the poor school performance of large groups of students in the American school system, and a commitment to rectify this situation by way of concentrated efforts. Unprecedented sums of money were made available for this purpose, and numerous extensive projects were initiated. A considerable proportion of ensuing endeavors were directly in the area of reading. Many others were aimed at developing preschool and kindergarten programs which would more adequately prepare young children for the tasks they would face upon entering school. In fact also they dealt in large part with reading. Set against this background, the impact of Chall's findings was of an immediacy and scope probably seldom rivaled in the annals of educational research. In a very short time the textbook market was inundated by an avalanche of so-called phonics materials guaranteed to train decoding skills. An analysis of basal readers, conducted eight years after the publication of Chall's study, showed corre-

sponding change. Popp (1975) found that compared to readers published in the 1950s and 1960s, code emphasis had become measurably
stronger by the 1970s.

The term "phonics" as it is generally used in America refers broadly
to any teaching materials or activities which direct a learner's attention to
sound-symbol relationships (Harris & Hodges, 1981). We shall use
"phonics" in a more restricted sense, as a convenient label for modern
decoding-oriented instructional strategies typically used in American
schools in conjunction with other reading activities.

We have already witnessed the recurring pattern that, irrespective of
place and time, teachers tend to return to familiar practices, even when,
on the surface, these are called by a new name. Much the same happened in the United States in the wake of the call for more emphasis on
proficiency in decoding. By and large, Look-and-Say remained the preferred approach to beginning reading. However phonics were now introduced much earlier than before, and most often taught separately
from connected reading.

Phonetic teaching in the German sense, namely, as a coordinated
sequenced program based on letter-sounds, had, as we have seen, never
really caught on in the United States. The alphabet method had always
remained much more familiar. Therefore now that educators felt
pressed to start "phonics" early, they tended to reach back to it. The
early intensive learning of the alphabet which we witnessed in Cambridge kindergarten classes is a good example of these overall trends.

In contemporary usage "intensive phonics oriented instruction" or a
"decoding emphasis approach" is therefore usually taken to mean that
children will engage in large quantities of drill exercises. Often these
exercises will have little relationship to functional reading. Sometimes
their value for learning to read is in question.

The apprehensions of opponents of overly structured teaching approaches may thus seem well justified. Small wonder that once again
reaction is in the air. Proponents of taking the teaching of reading out of
the hands of professionals are getting a hearing. Only now, those who
proposed to phase out teachers because supposedly teachers were not
single-minded enough about the teaching of reading are joined by those
who would do the same, but for the opposite reason. According to them,
the best way of learning to read is informally at home. There, reading
could be learned incidentally and naturally, in the same fashion children
acquire language. In Chapter Three we shall examine several aspects of
this position.

CHAPTER 3

Is Learning to Read "Natural"?

The artificiality of the formal school situation is to blame for much that is problematic in learning to read. If only children were allowed to acquire reading naturally through their own efforts, the way they master language, many of the difficulties often associated with learning to read would cease to exist. Or, so we are told.

Proponents of this view hold that some children come to school already well able to read. They acquired reading at home, in the same way they first acquired speech, by participating in everyday functional language experiences. In modern societies children are bombarded with print and have many opportunities to use written language. They look for favorite merchandise in supermarkets, receive letters from relatives, are read to by their parents, and are left notes by them. They also watch television and orient themselves with the help of street signs. In time, children will become able to categorize their experiences with written language and to abstract printed word symbols from contextual settings (Ylisto, 1977). In literate societies, reading is thus no more than a further extension of natural language learning, and should be learned by all children through functional use. On the other hand, deliberate teaching is apt to fragmentize reading experiences and to create in the learner an awareness of what it is one does when reading. Formal reading instruction had therefore best be avoided, because through it reading might be set apart from natural use of language.

These sentiments are not new. One hundred years ago Farnham (1881, 1887) suggested that the preferred model for learning to read was to be the acquisition of "speech and understanding what is said, both come to the child by a process so simple and natural that he is conscious of no effort to acquire them" (p. 14).[3] Farnham (1887) proposed that

---

[3] Page citations are from the 1887 edition of Farnham's book as I was unable to obtain the original 1881 edition.

written language should be learned in the same way, namely, "indirectly, while attention is directed to the thought expressed" (p. 20).

Huey (1908/1968) was another early proponent of an informal approach to reading instruction. Believing that children should learn to read at home rather than at school, he too pointed to parallels between the acquisition of language and reading. Huey felt that "we have a valuable suggestion as to the right method [of acquiring reading, D.F.] given us by those children to be found now and then who learn to read for themselves, no one knows how or when. They grow into it as they learned to talk, with no special instruction or purposed method. . . the natural method of learning to read is just the same as that of learning to talk" (p. 330). According to Huey (1908/1968), it is these readers who "are the best . . . readers of all" (p. 330).

Learning to read may not be quite that simple. A recent study by Goodman and Altwerger (1981) shows that some children may find it far from easy to extrapolate from everyday experiences with written language to reading competencies. In a "print awareness task," preschoolers were shown familiar labels of household goods, the same labels stripped of accompanying pictures, and only the words of the label copied in manuscript letters. Children's appropriate responses dropped from 37.4% for the familiar label to 19.7% for the label without support of pictures, and to only 1.5% for the written message itself. Recognizing labels did not mean that children had acquired reading skills.

It is with the feeling that the "natural model" of reading acquisition may be misleading on several counts that we shall now turn to a few of its underlying assumptions.

First there is the assertion that planned reading instruction would make learning to read artificial, and hence more frustrating and less intrinsically rewarding, than learning modeled on natural language acquisition. This position is based on the implied assumption that in human societies learning to speak is easy.

But is language learning easy? Even the most optimistic students of language agree that it takes about three years till a child can communicate more or less freely via language. Throughout the first three years of a child's life, communication often breaks down. A healthy one-year-old may resort to shrieking at the top of his/her voice, because he/she has failed to make a want understood, while a distraught caretaker tries one tried and true remedy after another.

Humans appear to possess biological predispositions to language (Liberman, 1977). However, unfolding of language ability is influenced by many factors and proceeds step by step. Menyuk (1971) has demonstrated the very gradual way in which young children learn to differentiate and reproduce phonemes. But even when they have mastered this skill as long as children are not yet able to articulate correctly, they may have great difficulty in making themselves understood. Snow (1984) describes how despite her 31-month-old only son's considerable language and cognitive competence, his inability to pronounce the word "supermarket" so that it would be understood by her, short-circuited a family conversation in which he was trying to take part. As a result her son's "opportunity to receive confirmation of his prediction that the family would be visiting the supermarket, any further information about the proposed visit, a model for improving his pronunciation of the word 'supermarket,' or a model for a more complex or correct utterance about visiting the supermarket was lost" (p. 26). Snow adds that this "communicative frustration" was experienced "frequently" by her son during his third year and that the experience her son had in the described instance "represents a breakdown of precisely the kind of semantic contingency between child speech and adult speech which is generally recognized to be crucial to normal language acquisition" (p. 27).

Besides being slow, and emotionally stressful, speech acquisition, according to Snow is thus heavily dependent on what surrounding adults do at crucial moments.

CAN ALL CHILDREN LEARN TO READ AT HOME?

Holding the view that reading should best be acquired at home could result in home variables becoming a major factor in determining children's level of reading competency and eventual school attainments.

Studies have documented repeatedly that only a small percentage of children come to school already reading (Clark, 1976; Durkin, 1959, 1961, 1984; Mason, 1980). It seems likely that these children may have had highly sophisticated direct help at home. Skilled parents are frequently unaware that the way in which they are attuned to their children's needs and able to expand and scaffold their learning experiences is in any way exceptional. Statements by such parents that they did not actively engage in teaching their child may reflect what they believe to be true without being completely accurate.

In her in-depth study of young readers in Scotland, Clark (1976) found that in addition to direct access to books, much reading at home, warm and supportive parents, a great deal of interaction with the child and willingness to participate in the child's play activities, the variable which was the most important differentiating factor between early readers and their siblings was an adult who, because of special circumstances, devoted a great amount of time to that child when he or she was young.

It may have been a grandmother or aunt who was living temporarily with the family.

Childhood experiences with written language which proponents of a "natural" approach deem important often tend to be typically middle class. Children who lack such experiences will most probably not learn to read at home. When this is the case, the "natural" approach must be interpreted to mean that children will, in fact, learn to read in school, but that schools should try to model reading instruction on the way language is learned in the home.

Let us see to what extent it is feasible to hope that schools can duplicate the conditions of language acquisition in the home. Typically a young infant is surrounded by parents, grandparents, relatives, and acquaintances, as well as paid caretakers and siblings, all of whom address themselves to the child and shower that child with repetitious snatches of speech. Nelson (1973) found that the number of adults other than parents the children she studied saw regularly during the week correlated positively with the rate of early language acquisition. Conversely, studies of twins have consistently documented relatively poorly developed language skills in comparison to same-aged single children (Davis, 1937; Mittler, 1973; Howlin, 1980). While twins' delayed language production has often been attributed to the ways of communicating with each other that they develop on their own, Goshen-Gottstein's (1981) recent study indicates that a further contributing factor may be that in multiple birth families the double load of caretaking may interfere with time available for adult-child language and language preparatory interplay.

Language is typically acquired by a single child surrounded by several doting "teachers." This numeric relationship is reversed in the school setting. Here it is one teacher who has to instruct 25 and sometimes many more students. It is in part on account of the numerical disparity that Cazden (1972) feels that one cannot really generalize from learning to talk to learning to read. At home the child is exposed to "a rich set of pairings of meanings and sounds—for that is what language in the context of ongoing experience is" (p. 141). Rich sets of pairings of oral and written language are, on the other hand, "much less available" in school (Cazden, 1972, p. 141).

Time is also a factor. The three years or more required for language acquisition occur when the infant is in need of intensive physical care, which means that caretakers are in close proximity to the child. Their verbal exchanges can be frequent and do not interfere with other activities.

None of this applies to learning to read in school, where there are fewer opportunities to match writing with relevant sound (Cazden, 1972), and much less time is available.

Learning to read also needs to be accomplished quickly, for it is an important prerequisite for other types of school learning.

In the intimate give and take during which much of language learning occurs, a child's caretakers make use of their close acquaintance with its preferences, interests, and range of experiences. By comparison, teachers are less knowledgeable, and less able to adapt teaching encounters to a child's personal characteristics.

Finally, the small size, softeness, and manifest helplessness of a young human being and its utter dependence on others, seem to arouse loving attention and readiness for protracted service unrivaled at later stages of development. A great deal of patience, and a willingness for endless repetitions of verbal routines are part of this situation. This is demonstrated by the fact that a household repeatedly will undertake the bringing up of a baby. On the other hand, in cases of severely retarded adults, verbal interaction and personal responsibility, which do not develop beyond early stages, tend to become an unbearable burden. Thus it seems that the special characteristics of infanthood and evidence of growth and progress are essential for mustering the continuous engagement and energy needed in order to provide the kind of inputs necessary for cognitive growth and language acquisition.

It hardly seems realistic to assume that the emotional involvement typically accompanying first language learning situations could be replicated in public school classroom settings. From the viewpoint of mental hygiene, it probably would not even be deemed desirable.

This does not mean that the question of whether it would be possible to adapt beginning reading instruction more closely to individual development and interests, even in schools, ought not to be reexamined. We shall return to it in Chapter Nine.

ON LEARNING ARBITRARY CODES

The faculty for language is biological. Except under extraordinary circumstances nonimpaired human beings growing up in a society acquire the speech patterns of their society. Written language, on the other hand, is a cultural artifact, an invention of sorts (Liberman, 1977). Writing is only one of many abstract graphic representational systems developed by humans such as musical notation, chemical formulas, numerical systems, technical blueprints, topographical maps, diagrams, charts, and so forth. All these representational systems are in essence arbitrary codes, and not in every case especially efficient ones.

Considering writing within the framework of other representational systems invented by humans is useful in that it highlights the improbability that a naturalistic model which relies mainly on exposure and immersion can adequately represent the complexity involved in acquiring such systems to the point of facile use. Would one, one wonders, expect even well-versed users of a particular symbolic representational system to be able to pick up different ones entirely on their own? Would a mathematician be able to make sense of a passage of music, or a chemical formula unless he had been taught the underlying principle of that particular representational code? Even with help, abstract representational systems are not always acquired easily.

At a recent world congress of the International Reading Association one morning was devoted entirely to sessions in which participants learned initial decoding skills in non-European languages. To their surprise many of those assembled reading specialists found that despite the fact that they were being taught in every case by an acknowledged authority on teaching to read the particular language they were learning, they acquired, during a whole morning's intensive work, only a few rudiments.

A similar episode a few years previously should have prepared me for that experience. A British Council expert on teaching English as a foreign language had been sent to Israel to aid in developing modern instructional approaches. Early on in her stay she decided that her work would be more effective if she could converse with local teachers in Hebrew. Unexpectedly, this expert, who was a strong proponent of oral methods of foreign language learning, found that she herself was unable to learn that way. She therefore decided that, as an essential first step, she wanted to be able to read and write Hebrew. I undertook to teach her with the aid of materials which had been designed for slow first graders. Both of us assumed that, given her professional background, it would be enough to just "explain" the system to her. Instead, it turned out that she needed ten longish sessions before she could even decode haltingly.

That it may be exceedingly difficult, if not sometimes impossible, to discover reading, so to speak, on one's own is also brought home by the efforts required from modern-day scientists in order to decipher ancient inscriptions.

Cazden (1972) suggested that children's learning of their native language may not be a useful model for learning to read. Wardhaugh (1971) after a literature search undertaken for the U.S. Office of Education also concluded that "language acquisition and learning to read are quite different tasks" (p. 190), and that therefore, "theories of language acquisition that are available to us today are largely irrelevant in deciding issues in beginning reading instruction or even in devising models of the reading process" (p. 191).

In modern societies, large numbers of children will have to learn to read as quickly, painlessly, and efficiently as possible. Many of them will have to approach this task unaided by effective help from their parents. Hoping that children will "learn to read regardless of teaching method" (Fishbein & Emans, 1972, p. 15) may not be enough. The answer seems to lie in trying to establish what it is that may make some approaches to reading instructions more effective than others.

This is the topic we shall examine from a variety of aspects in the following chapters.

PART II

Curricular Issues

CHAPTER 4

The Learner Vis-A-Vis the Task

An experience a colleague and I had during an intensive tour of British Infant Schools in the spring of 1973 helped us appreciate more fully the potential role of skilled adults in simplifying potentially complex learning situations.

Our visit to schools in Devonshire happened to coincide with the week in which swimming instruction started in that area. Swimming instruction from age five had recently become mandatory and was usually taught during the last six weeks of a school year, in outdoor, unheated pools. Most pools we saw had been erected above ground in a closed-off section of the infant school yard.

In the school we happened to visit on the first day of swimming, the diminutive headmistress, fully clothed for the brisk British spring weather, took all swimming classes herself. A number of mothers stood by in order to help with dressing and undressing. The day before their first lesson, children had been reminded to bring bathing suits, towels, rubber caps for the girls, and a handkerchief each. Swimming was in groups of 12, and only the children about to enter the pool undressed while their classmates watched. Undressing children were told to spread their towels on the ground, arrange clothes in a neat heap nearby, and, finally, stand on the towel, handkerchief in hand. After inspecting that instructions had been followed to a tee, namely that all girls were wearing caps and that each child was indeed equipped with a handkerchief, noses were blown in unison, handkerchiefs put down, and children reassembled in line next to the steps leading up to the pool. Standing on top, the headmistress demonstrated with one child the way they were to walk up the steps facing the pool, turn around on top, and descend the ladder into the pool backside first. Not relinquishing her post, she supervised each child's performance, lending a helpful hand, and bodily turning around those who had difficulty. Once inside the pool, children lined up along two sides, facing each other. Water was only knee high, and children had no difficulty moving around and following directions. Children were directed in quick succession to jump, stomp, and runningly exchange sides, all executed so quickly that before they were aware of it, children were wet all over. Next, sides were exchanged to and fro by crawling, and finally by walking on one's hands, with legs floating backwards or hitting the water up and down. Lining up for getting out, turning on the top step to descend backwards to the grass, wrapping up in the ready towels while mothers commenced to rub, concluded the session. Meanwhile, the next group, all prepared and ready, started on the choral nose-blowing procedure.

All told, children had been in the water less than ten minutes, yet, essential first steps in learning to swim, as well as prescribed conduct for safe and hygenic pool use, had all been introduced and drilled. Even more essential, initial hesitations and fears had been disposed of before they had a chance to take root. As the morning progressed, we watched in growing admiration as group after group went through their paces with not a single child refusing to enter the pool or lie down in the water.

The following day we witnessed first-time pool encounters in another school. This school had a modern plant, and children emerged at poolside properly costumed, after having undressed in rooms designed for that purpose. The actually shallow pool was fully filled, the water reaching to children's chest or shoulders, depending on individual height. At all times, at least one and sometimes two teachers were in the water with the children. According to the youngish headmistress, the aim of initial lessons was to get the children "acquainted" with the water, and no formal instruction was planned. Encouraged by bystanding adults, the children got into the pool. Once inside, they splashed about, a few daring to wet their faces or dive. Adults inside the pool were very appreciative of such endeavors and would suggest to more hesitant souls to follow suit. From time to time teachers organized some kind of joint activity such as forming a circle and dancing. Some children just stood around shivery, not participating in any activity, nor getting wet beyond the point the water reached. Others refused to go in altogether, or ventured only a few steps down the ladder. Much attention and coaxing was lavished on the refusenicks by adults both inside the pool and beside it. Each group was in the water for about twenty minutes, and by the time children and teachers came out, some of them seemed quite cold, with instances of chattery teeth and bluish lips. We did not get a clear notion about the number of children in the pool at any one time.

For us, as feverishly note-taking bystanders, what was so especially fascinating about these two episodes was the way they seemed to exemplify two diametrically different approaches to instructional processes and to the role of the educator. In the first approach, it is clearly the teacher who orchestrates the learning experience. Making judicious use of his or her professional expertise, the instructor segments the learning task into a series of steps through which the learner is subsequently led. The crucial point in this approach is that learning tasks are subdivided in such a way that each step can, according to the professional judgment of the instructor, be undertaken by the prospective learners without undue difficulty. In addition to the subject matter, this approach thus takes into account learners' abilities and prior experiences as well as their anticipated reactions to the planned learning experiences.

The second approach exposes the learner to unadulterated subject matter. Consequently, personal differences are apt to stand out more and become especially apparent in collective learning situations. The swimming lesson we happened to observe was typical in this respect as it is often the more skillful, or perhaps self-assured individuals who attract more than their share of attention and favorable comments in such situations, while other learners become even more aware of their own shortcomings.

It is not an easy decision to plunge into a cool pool in which one has never been before. Even more so when the pool is populated by boisterous and splashing classmates who are egged on to additional feats of daring by one's own teacher. Under such circumstances, how much easier to fall back on opting out altogether. Especially when opting out becomes, in fact, a subtle maneuver for garnering teacher attention in one's own right. Would it be going too far to feel that perhaps an initial experience such as the one described here could harbor the first seeds of what next year's teacher might well call a "problem swimmer" to become in time, in case no effective corrective steps were taken, a full-blown "nonswimmer"?

What was revealing for an observer of the two episodes was the self-assurance which accompanied first confrontations with the new situation in the one school, as opposed to the trepidation, hesitancy, and lack of confidence in the second.

Opinions are divided on whether differences in teaching approaches at the initial stages of learning to read have lasting impact on achievements. Many studies seem to show that early outcomes of particular methods of teaching tend to wash out over time. However, the great importance of the *personal experiences* a child has in the early stages of learning to read are today widely recognized (Bloom, 1976; Stevens & Rosenshine, 1981).

The rest of this chapter examines some of these experiences.

EXPERIENCING PROGRESS

Montessori was one advocate of children's rights who translated lofty sentiments into practical working reality. Realizing that from a child's point of view the simple everyday world of objects resembled Gulliver's experiences in the land of giants, she pioneered the design of small-scale furniture and tools. While this innovative, relatively recent idea is by now generally accepted, the lesson it teaches has yet to be applied in other areas.

Even a cursory look into a typical first grade classroom at the beginning of the school year reveals what many teachers know in their hearts. Only too often classrooms are equipped with a view towards transient adults, such as parents, colleagues, or school administrators rather than being geared to their rightful residents—school beginners.

One may well wonder how the profusion of labels, reading games, and reading-oriented materials mounted on walls which greeted us on first arrival in class would make us feel were we, in the wake of Montessori, to put ourselves in the shoes of a nonreading first grade entrant? Would stunned and overawed be terms too strong to use? Is it not as if somebody had set up a graphic display of the extent of our ignorance?

The design of instructional materials intended for a child's intensive use, namely, primers and workbooks, would also seem to contribute to children's possible feelings of dismay at the enormity of the task before them. One has to remember that in the initial stages of using such books the number of pages one is not yet able to deal with looms much larger than the number of those one has already learned. Thus, day by day, the learning first grader is confronted with tangible evidence of the fact that as yet only a very small portion of all there is to know has been learned.

Would it not be possible, one wonders, to adopt the strategy of the partly filled pool also in regard to the design of learning materials? Primers, for instance, could be conceived as binders in which pages accumulate one by one according to rate of progress. For a first grader, two to three weeks in school, taking home a binder which was initially completely empty and which now contains a few pages, could turn into a joyful exhibition of acquired skill. Moreover, children would be rightfully confident of their ability to read "their book" to whoever showed an inclination to listen.

All other learning materials could be redesigned according to the same principle. When school starts, classroom walls would be nearly bare. Posters, charts, and additional written materials would go up only as children become able to read them. Once again, whenever children glance at a wall, they are confronted with welcome proofs of accomplishments, in addition to having an opportunity to reinforce newly acquired skills. Also in terms of learning theory, the presentation of only those items that have already been explicitly taught, instead of a great mass of undifferentiated information, much of which is still meaningless, seems to make good sense.

Consistency in adopting sequentially designed learning materials does not mean that a classroom would have to be devoid of items which could spur children on to further learning and which could serve the needs of the more able ones among them. A library corner could still be well stocked with trade books, and time could be set aside for daily browsing or actual reading as the case might be. A writing area could provide resources for going beyond what had been learned collectively in class.

The reading programs developed by my coworkers and me in Hebrew and Arabic were designed in the way suggested here. When the materials were first published commercially 25 years ago, there were apprehensions about the logistic difficulties of distributing sequentially staggered materials and the problems teachers would face in storing them. It soon turned out that these problems were surmountable, and other authors followed suit. Today, what was once regarded as problematic has become acceptable and has even generated some unforeseen benefits. The new design was cheaper and easier to manufacture than traditionally bound books. In addition book-covers damaged by use could be exchanged at practically no cost. Even more important was the curiosity children tended to exhibit in regard to every new page they were about to get and their eager anticipation of additional accumulating items. The accumulation of materials which are evidence of progress thus became an additional source of motivation for learning.

SELF-CONFIDENCE AND THE LACK OF IT: THE PROBLEM OF GUESSING

Guessing per se has long been accepted as a useful and legitimate reading strategy. In a classic article "Reading: a psycholinguistic guessing game," Goodman (1967) showed that "efficient reading does not result from precise perception and identification of all elements, but from skill in selecting the fewest, most productive cues necessary to produce guesses which are right the first time. The ability to anticipate that which has not been seen, of course, is vital in reading; just as the ability to anticipate what has not yet been heard is vital in listening" (Goodman, 1967, p. 127).

The fact that in this model Goodman refers to the reading processes of skilled readers is made quite clear in his use of the terms "efficient reading," "skill in selecting . . . cues," "guesses which are right the first time," and "ability to anticipate." All these are results of prior experience in reading. Even in those sections of the paper in which Goodman refers to less experienced readers, he indicated that the children he has in mind have already acquired at least some proficiency.

As we shall see in Chapter Eleven on the post initial stage of learning to read, there comes a time when a beginning reader who has already acquired some decoding ability should not be constantly interrupted by minor corrections. When used by proficient readers, and in the later stages of learning to read, a certain amount of guessing is thus an appropriate reading strategy. It is not this kind of guessing, that is, guessing in the sense used by Goodman, that we shall be discussing now. What will concern us here is guessing as a prime word attack strategy in the *initial* stages of learning to read. Let us first try to understand what it is that may lead beginning readers into becoming habitual guessers. Nowadays, most beginners are introduced to reading via so called "eclectic" approaches and materials that combine sight word vocabularies with a gradual introduction of decoding skills (Harris & Sipay, 1975; Fry, 1977; Aukerman, 1981). Depending on the particular program used—and on the teacher—many children are thus expected to learn to recognize automatically at least a few and sometimes a considerable number of words before they have the skill to decode them.

"Sight words" are high frequency words which are memorized as wholes so that they can be recognized instantaneously without using any word-attack skills (Fry, 1977). A common reason for stressing sight words is that a relatively small number of very frequent words make up a high percentage of all reading material. Introducing children to such words will thus provide a shortcut to many texts.

Another reason for introducing sight words is that these high frequency words occur so frequently that if a child had to use word analysis skills on them, his/her "train of thought would be broken and comprehension would suffer" (Fry, 1977, p. 74). Also, some very common words in English "do not follow the most common phoneme-grapheme correspondences" and will therefore be taught as sight words even in phonemically structured programs (Harris & Sipay, 1975, p. 361).

A variety of strategies for introducing children to sight words are described in teachers' manuals. Here we shall mention only a few.

Many authors believe that words should at all times be introduced in meaningful context (i.e., Karlin, 1975). First, learners are exposed to a meaningful text based on their own experiences or crafted by the authors of a primer. Only when children are quite familiar with this text, and it has been repeatedly read in class, are specific words singled out.

Another way to introduce words is via teachers' oral stories, spoken sentences, or through pictures. "The child looks at the picture and is told the word or guesses what the word must be" (Harris & Sipay, 1975, p. 354). One advantage here is that the pictures can serve as an aid in recalling the word when the child subsequently happens to forget it.

Children may also be encouraged to infer words from the context. "They study the illustration on the page to find out what new character, object or action is portrayed. They read the rest of the sentence and try to decide what the missing word must be" (Harris & Sipay, 1975, p. 355). Other strategies are configuration clues, flash cards, and tracing. Not all authors seem equally enthusiastic about these devices and some hint that their effectiveness has not been proven (Harris & Sipay, 1975). Nor is the way in which beginners do, in fact, learn sight words clearly understood (Aukerman & Aukerman, 1981).

Stauffer's (1970) description of the first time a collective text is read in a first-grade class using a "language experience approach" provides insight into the experiences individual learners may have in these circumstances. The teacher had brought a white mouse to class. After children had watched and discussed it, she wrote down the remarks of six of them about it and read the resulting text to the class. The next day, when rereading the text with groups and individual children the teacher discovered that one boy, Bill, was able to read back nearly the whole text. Thereupon the teacher interrupted the others at their work and gathered the whole class. Bill, the center of attention, was asked to point out single words in the text, count how often particular words occurred, and finally read out of context words the teacher indicated. The other children in class were not provided with any insights as to how Bill did what he did so well. It was only evident to them that, mysteriously, he was able to do it.

Probably given time and many further experiences of having reading modeled, additional children would get the knack and suddenly realize what reading was all about. For others, however, confusion and uncertainty might grow day by day.

One possible way to defuse such a situation at least partly is to introduce ability grouping. This is indeed what the teacher in Stauffer's (1970) description does, by about the third week of instruction. In Chapter Nine we shall return to the issue of possible advantages and disadvantages of ability grouping in the initial stages of reading instruction. Here, let us examine in greater detail what may happen to children who are expected to read back sight words without having been provided with relevant information to help them accomplish this task successfully? What seems to happen is that, when left to their own devices, children will sometimes adopt behavior strategies which have little intrinsic relation to the task at hand. Many reading specialists are aware of this problem and have described these misguided strategies in some detail. Gates and Boeker (1923) found that young children tend to focus on single details as clues for word recognition. Asked, for example, how they remembered the word "monkey", the children studied by Gates and Boeker mentioned "two wavy things" (presumably the "m" and "n"), the "hole" ("o"), "the funny chair" ("k"), or "the monkey's tail" ("y") (Gates & Boeker, 1923). One consequence of this approach to word recognition is that "youngsters frequently confuse words which have the same letters in them" (Anderson & Dearborn, 1952, p. 215). What is happening in this case is that letters are not recognized as such, but merely as signs representing a particular word in the beginner's mind. Mistakenly focusing on only a part of the word seems, relatively speaking, to lead to less serious problems than some of the other unsatisfactory habits a beginner may develop when initiated to reading via a sight vocabulary. Sometimes the associations relied upon for word recognition are completely extraneous and not related at all to the printed symbols on a page. The anecdote about a child who seemingly read a word on a flashcard, while in fact recognizing it only from a smudge on the card, is especially well known (Durrell, 1940; Samuels, 1979). The story is a good example of the way children sometimes manage to seem to be progressing well when in fact they are utterly confused about what it is they are really supposed to do.

Remedial teachers frequently report that it is even a feat to get children to look at the letters on a page. Seemingly the past experiences of such children did not make them realize that information provided by particular letter sequences was the crucial key. Unfortunately, widely prevalent teaching practices may unwittingly assist children develop ways of coping with classroom reading situations without developing necessary skills. Holland (1979) discusses this problem in some detail, retelling the familiar story of "clever Hans," a performing horse who had demonstrated ability to count, solve arithmetic problems, comprehend complex questions, spell, and even read. It later turned out that the horse was responding to subtle cues from the audience or its trainer without the latter even being aware of having given them (Pfungst, 1911). Holland (1979) shows that teachers may unwittingly prompt correct performance by standing near or turning towards a particular word, or by asking a child to read a text that had already been read aloud by someone else.

Guessing as a way of coping with classroom reading situations in the beginning stage may well be counterproductive on several counts. First, because as long as it enables the child to get by there is little chance that more adequate habits will develop. Secondly, it may prevent the teacher from realizing that there is a problem and so postpone the initiation of corrective action. Thirdly, children themselves frequently realize that they are on unsure ground and become increasingly tense and unsure of themselves. Eventually, such children may start to shirk reading activities altogether.

More than 50 years have gone by since Thorndike (1935) wrote "the almost universal tolerance of imperfect learning in the early treatment of a topic, leaving it to be improved by the gradual elimination of errors in later treatments, is probably unsound, and certainly risky" (p. 147). It would seem that the longer the teaching of isolated nonfunctional bits of information continues before crucial insights about the nature of reading processes occur, the more there is a chance for misconceptions and/or faulty habits to develop. On the other hand, experience shows that once a child has realized in what way the characters on a page represent meaningful language, all else follows relatively easily. A phrase used by British Infant School teachers bears testimony to the fact that they consider the crucial point in learning to read to be a sudden act of discovery on the part of the learning child. When discussing reading instruction, British Infant School teachers often refer explicitly to the fact that at some stage in this process "the coin drops" (Downing, 1978). In other words, the child suddenly realizes what reading is all about.

According to current theory learning to read is a process during which the learner discovers the critical relationships between sounds of words and sounds of letters by extrapolation from his or her prior knowledge of the alphabet and of sight words (Mason, 1980). This view assumes that (a) the child has in fact already acquired a considerable number of words and letters he or she can identify and sound, and (b) that the child is able, by way of innate capability and prior experience in abstract reasoning, to engage successfully in the kind of high level extrapolation required.

What is problematic about this model of initial reading is that many children come to school lacking these prerequisites. Indeed, Mason pointed out that her analysis was based on a study of a selective group of children from intact middle and upper middle-income families, attending a university-operated preschool program. According to Mason, the parents of the children were uniformly very involved in fostering reading-related skills.

Let us now see whether it is possible to structure initial reading experiences in such a way that necessary insights will occur at the very beginning of the learning process with no need for prior skills or knowledge?

A Viennese primer which, with appropriate updatings, had been in use from the late 1920s till the 1970s may be especially well-suited for this purpose. One reason for choosing this primer was that German, like English, makes use of the Roman alphabet. Therefore, the following examples will be more readily accessible to the readers of this book than examples in say Arabic, Hebrew, Tagalog, and Thai, in each of which initial reading materials, based on essentially the same principle as the Viennese ones, are used in some elementary schools. To the best of our knowledge somewhat similar approaches are used in many more languages, for instance, Russian (Vasresensky, 1959), French (Ruthman, 1973) and Finnish (Kyöstiö, 1980).

A VIENNESE APPROACH—"WIR KÖNNEN SCHON LESEN," (1964)

A few words of background information are necessary. One point to remember is that in countries less affluent than the United States, store-bought instructional materials are used much less extensively than in American schools. Pages in a primer are thus a summary, following learning experiences which took place in class. In the Viennese method described here letter symbols are introduced one by one and are identified by sound and not by name. Yet, there are no single letters or nonsense syllables in the primer. Nor is the primer accompanied by a workbook. The essence of the Viennese method is that immediately upon introduction, letters are used functionally in order to create meaningful text. Thus contentful reading is achieved when the learner knows but two letters. Let us describe how this is brought about.

The first few pages of the primer present colorful full-page pictures of everyday scenes such as a visit to the grocery store or apple picking. Following these is a child's first decoding experience, comprising what has been learned more extensively in class. The first two letters a child learns are the vowel A and the consonant M. Each is introduced as representing an unvariant sound "ä" and "m" respectively. During the days these are learned, a large portion of children's class time is spent discussing their daily experiences, especially the home scene. Eventually, a mother's daily round of activities becomes a main theme.

Figure 4.1 presents the first contentful reading page which is introduced when all a child has learned are the symbols and sound values of two letters—A and M.

The edition used here, vintage 1964, presents mother engaged in rather traditional activities: cooking at the range, and watching at the window for her child's return from school. However, with the aid of small drawings[4] many additional contentful sentences could be formed

---

[4] A small picture inserted in primary reading materials in place of a word a child cannot read is usually called rebus. However, recently this term has taken on connotations of particular methods of reading instruction (i.e., Aukerman, 1971, pp. 370–371). To avoid confusion it will therefore not be used.

Figure 4.1.   First reading page of the second edition of a Viennese primer published in 1962.

Reproduced from: *Wir können schon Lesen.* Published by the Viennese Primer Committee. Vienna: Hölder, Pichler Tempsky; Leykam; Österreichischer Bundesverlag; Verlag für Jugend und Volk. pp. 1. (Original in color).

for which the German word AM (at the) would be grammatically correct, such as mother engaged in phoning, watching T.V., or riding a bike. In effect, even at this early stage, children could make up and also put to paper their own sentences, using only the two letters learned so far in conjunction with their own drawings and/or illustrations cut from magazines.

The first reading page of the Viennese primer well illustrates that, contrary to popular opinion, emphasis on decoding need not be at the expense of meaning. Nor need early reading experiences be restricted to inane passages and repetitive word patterns such as *rat sat mat,* or *Nan ran.* By judicious and well thought out sequencing of the very first letters, a child can be made aware of the nature of the reading process right from the start. By choosing two letters which are then combined into two very dissimilar words, one a two-letter single syllable word starting with a vowel "AM," and the other containing four letters, two syllables and starting with a consonant "MAMA," the child also learns to remain flexible and read in the full sense of the word. Consequently, there is little likelihood that reading will deteriorate into rote recital of words sharing the same pattern.

A further consideration, also evident in the choice of the third letter, "I," is that letters introduced in the early phases of learning should be easily pronounceable in isolation and should blend well.

The addition of the third letter, "I," (pronounced invariably "ee") enables the learning child as well as the instructor to create three new words: "MIMI" (a girls name), "IM" (in, inside), and "MAMI" (a term of endearment commonly used for one's mother in Vienna). With the aid of drawings it is now possible to create a practically unlimited array of statements about the whereabouts and, by implication, doings of the two protagonists Mimi and mother. Thus Mimi can be in bed or on a chair, at the window or in a baby carriage, car, playing in the garden, sand, or snow. Mother can sail a boat, bathe in the sea, stand on a balcony, or be in the kitchen, office, shop, or a great variety of additional places. Further, by referring to mother sometimmes as Mama and sometimes as Mami, it is impressed upon the learning child that reading is, in fact, the *accurate* translation of graphemes into meaning.

What is impressive about this Viennese approach is that, from the very first, meaning is associated with reading. At the same time, because of the minimal number of letters learned and the fact that they are introduced gradually, there is nothing obscure about what it is one does. Reading is not a magic art, accessible only to adults or to one's more gifted classmates, but a functional reaction to different sequences of letter symbols, resulting every time in a contentful message.

"T" is the next letter introduced, leading to "MIT" (with) and "TIM" (here used as the name of a dog). Now sentences become longer and still more varied, as it is mother with Mimi or Tim, or Mimi with, alternatively, her dog or mother, who can be in, at, or on a variety of drawable objects or surroundings. (See Figure 4.2 for an example of a primer

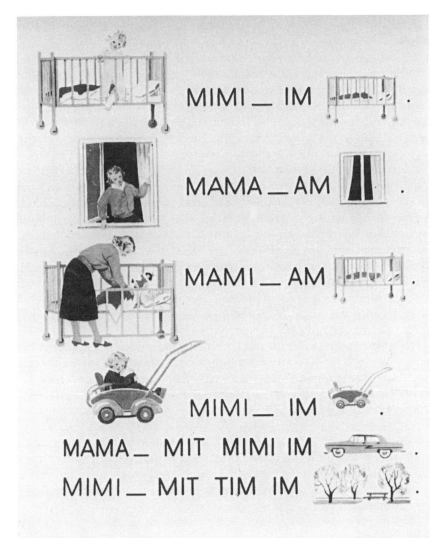

Figure 4.2. Fourth reading page of the second edition of a Viennese primer published in 1962.

Reproduced from: *Wir können schon Lesen.* Published by the Viennese Primer Committee. Vienna: Hölder, Pichler Tempsky; Leykam; Österreichischer Bundesverlag; Verlag für Jugend und Volk. pp. 4. (Original in color).

page at this stage, when all a child knows is two consonants and two vowels).

Two additional German words could be formed from the four letters introduced so far, namely, "matt" and "Amt." That these are not included in the primer at this stage indicates the concern of the authors for an instant fusion of decoding and content. One way of achieving this is by using only words that are so familiar to six-year-olds that their meaning is self-evident and impresses itself on a novice reader even when words are sounded out somewhat slowly.

It is here that it might be well to remember Messmer's (1904) findings as well as realize the attendant teacher's functions in the learning process. According to Messmer's results, different levels of reading behavior co-exist at one and the same time in a beginner's repertoire. While familiar words are already perceived as entities, less familiar ones are still processed segmentally. It is exactly this that is happening during the very early stages of learning described here. Often children will read a text like the one in Figure 4.2 fairly smoothly without resorting to syllable by syllable sounding out. However, in cases of doubt or when a word was misread, sounding out can be used as an auxiliary strategy.

The well-trained teacher's expertise comes into full play at this stage. For it is up to the teacher to help learners progress from segmented to unitary perception and sounding, by training them to read words aloud only after having made them out silently first. On the other hand, if, at this stage, a teacher continues to insist on a syllable-by-syllable sounding strategy, he/she may in fact retard the acquisition of sound reading habits.

A further aspect of reading that skillful teachers may take pains to emphasize at the initial stage of instruction is that reading is not necessarily an oral behavior. To this end teachers will make sure that at least part of daily reading and writing tasks require children to engage in silent reading.

That beginners can very early on conceive of reading as an activity which can be carried out both orally as well as silently, is borne out by the following anecdote. In Israeli infant schools, first graders' progress in reading is runningly monitored by Head Teachers (see Chapters 9 and 11). The usual procedure is that children are asked to read to the head teacher words, sentences, or short passages from cards that she had prepared for the occasion. One of the head teachers reported that recently children in her school considerably altered usual proceedings. On joining her, they would rapidly go through the prepared stack of cards, sorting them in two. Then they would declare that one of the stacks constituted the "ones" that they knew, and settle down expectantly with her in order to work on the second stack, namely, words and phrases that by their own judgement they were not sure about. Thus they showed clearly that they were taking in familiar words by sight without feeling they had to sound them out in order to convince their "examiner" that they indeed knew them well. Whereas for the others, they were ready to engage in a joint process of searching for sound and meaning, clearly aware that this was the way to proceed with a word one failed to recognize immediately.

In order to take in the message conveyed by the Viennese model of beginning instruction let us now examine some of the strategies used to help beginners cope successfully with difficulties inherent in learning to read. The basic policy of the Viennese approach is to simplify to the utmost the very first reading experiences and subsequently to introduce the difficulties inherent in German orthography one by one in well-planned sequence; this, when from the very beginning texts are meaningful, and the beginner engages at all stages in functional reading.

One of the arguments frequently used against sequential teaching based on letter sounds is that most consonants and, more especially, so-called "stops" (i.e., "b," "p," "t") cannot, according to current linguistic theory, be pronounced in isolation. Therefore, it is claimed, a child will introduce a schwa when trying to sound out one of these letters, resulting in a distortion of the word so that it is no longer recognizable. However, when the first letters introduced are vowels and continuants (i.e., "s," "m," "n") this difficulty is postponed till *after* a child has had prior experience with easily blendable letters. Also, when correct letter sounds and blends are always first modeled by the teacher there is little reason to expect difficulties of the kind implied in some of the research literature.

In the first volume of the Viennese Primer (edition 1964) only capital letters are used. By postponing the introduction of lower-case letters, the memory load a child has to cope with in the initial stage is reduced by nearly half. When learners have to recall the sound value of only two and then three or four characters rather than at each step double that number, they can more readily concentrate on the crucial aspects of the task at hand, namely, the sounding-blending process leading to word recognition and understanding of content. The choice of all capitals instead of all lower-case letters which were used in the past in German school readers (see Chapter Two) may have come about in order to eliminate instances of incorrect spelling, which authors in earlier times seem not to have found objectionable. In terms of German spelling rules, MAMA, MIMI, and TIM are correct, but *mama, mimi,* and *tim* are wrong.

Young children are sometimes stymied by the technical vocabulary used in reading instruction (Reid, 1966; Downing, 1970, 1979). The

Austrian approach bypasses this problem, as no technical terminology whatsoever is used in the early stages of instruction. Even letter names are not taught in first grade. This practice seems to go back a long way. In Winch's (1904) description of his visits to German schools, he mentioned explicitly that in their first year at school children learn solely the "powers of the letters" (p. 102). Letter names were taught only in children's second year at school when children needed them for their work on spelling (Winch, 1904).

Thus, a further basic principle of the Viennese method is that in the early stages of learning only those contents and skills which are of immediate functional use are taught. All other information is postponed till later and introduced only gradually when children have already gained some proficency in reading.

CHAPTER 5

The Role of Writing in Beginning Reading

The importance of having children engage in writing activities as an aid for learning to read has by now been widely recognized (Hildreth, 1963; Chomsky, 1979a; Clay, 1980). In this chapter we shall examine in what ways writing can benefit beginning reading.

THE KINESTHETIC ELEMENT OF WRITING

One school of thought holds that the very motor activity involved in tracing and/or copying the outlines of letters or words is an important element in learning to recognize these same letters or words. Maria Montessori and Grace Fernald are the names that come most easily to mind in association with this approach. Montessori's own work incorporated, in this instance, that of others who had preceded her by many years. A common denominator among the pioneers of a "tactile" or "kinesthetic" approach was that they were most often involved in educating severely retarded or otherwise afflicted children. Montessori, who at that stage in her career still worked as a medical doctor, was influenced by the writings of Edouard Seguin (1846, 1866), a leading French authority on the education of the severely retarded half a century earlier (Montessori, 1912; reissued, 1965).

Seguin in turn had been influenced by Pereira, a noted educator of deaf-mutes in the eighteenth century, who had shown how the sense of touch can be developed to further more general learning (Kramer, 1976). Seguin's scheme led in sequential stages from physical movement to the development of the intellect. "His children progressed from drawing lines to copying letters, a method which—contrary to what was done in the schools—led to writing before reading" (Kramer, 1976, p. 61).

In one of her first public addresses, Montessori suggested that the alphabet could be introduced "not in a book, but on a little table on which are raised letters, painted different colors, that can be touched and traced with the fingers" (Montessori, 1898, quoted in Kramer, 1976). Subsequently, sets of sandpaper letters and letter-tracing activities became part of the Montessori equipment and method (Montessori, 1912/1965).

Grace Fernald's insistence that extremely disabled readers should start by tracing words directly with their finger rather than with a stylus pen or pencil was clearly derived from Montessori (Fernald, 1943, p. 29).

Fernald is especially remembered for the kinesthetic elements of her work (Fernald & Keller, 1921; Fernald, 1943), but there were many other elements and stages in the strategies she described. Finger-tracing was used mainly in the early stages of remediation.

Both Fernald (1943) and Terman (1943), who wrote the introduction to her book, believed that even the most severe cases of what they called "word-blindness" of "alexia," were amenable to treatment. Throughout her work Fernald (1943) clearly projects the view that the disabilities she treated successfully were at least partially attributable to the past learning experiences of her patients rather than to underlying physical or emotional problems. Moreover, failure in learning to read frequently leads to a variety of further problems. Fernald (1943) felt that these *by-products* of reading disability have unfortunately frequently been mistaken for the *causes* of the condition.

There are few experimental studies on possible relationships between the physical acts of writing and reading. Gates and Taylor (1923) found that preschool children who had practiced copying letters were better in forming new letters than a comparable group who had practiced tracing letters. Actually, in Fernald's approach tracing per se is only an opening step, analogous to a warming-up exercise. The learner soon proceeds to reproducing the word in writing from memory, and only when the learner is able to perform faultlessly is the word considered acquired. Thus it is the cognitive process in which words are internalized to the point where they can be reproduced at will which is the critical component in Fernald's approach. Gates and Taylor's (1923) results indicate that to this end copying symbols was more productive than tracing. It may be that a combination of copying and tracing would lead to even better results. This could be interpreted to mean that tracing facilitates copying. Experimental research on this issue would be of interest.

WRITING AS DISCOVERY OF SYMBOLIC
REPRESENTATION

Montessori's sandpaper letters as an invitation to letter tracing have a firm niche in educational lore. Other aspects of her use of writing are less well known.

Most of the equipment Montessori developed during her work with the feeble-minded was also used in the institutions she later established for normal but sadly neglected preschool children in the slums of Rome. In her first school, a single room in a large apartment complex, the children surprised their teachers by "discovering" writing on their own. Having been given letter cards and having evidently been told their sound values, the children in this first group of 50 three-to-six year olds, became intensely interested in their letters, often holding them up and parading in the room with them. One day Montessori was surprised to find a little boy "who was walking by himself and repeating: 'to make Sofia you have to have an s, an o, an f, an i and an a,' and with this he repeated the sounds making up the word" (Montessori, 1966, p. 131). According to Montessori, the children's discovery of writing "was the greatest event to take place in the first Children's House. The child who first made the discovery was so astonished that he shouted out loud: 'I've written, I've written.' In fact he had traced words on the floor with a piece of chalk" (p. 131). From then on the children wrote endlessly on every available surface—blackboards, floors, doors, walls and even at home on loaves of bread. An interest in books and an understanding of the nature of reading developed only a few months later, partly as a result of planned intervention by adults. From Montessori's descriptions it seems likely that her pupils discovered writing, not by writing single letters and then words but by the simpler device of putting ready-made letter cards or shapes next to each other. In fact, the underlying principle of both is the same: Letters put together make words.

Montessori's young slum children may have attained this insight so readily because of the language they spoke, Italian—a language in which symbol-sound correspondences happen to be nearly perfect. In such a language setting, transcribing speech would not be fraught with the difficulties likely to beset similar efforts in English.

There also can be little doubt that adults in the Casa Bambini, among them Montessori herself, actively helped children in their efforts. The Montessori method is child-oriented in that it is the child who chooses his/her own activities. However, Montessori's own descriptions show clearly that there was also much adult instruction. Anyone who taught her little charges to blow their noses circumspectly, modeling every step in great detail (Montessori, 1966, p. 126), is not likely to have refrained from giving advice about how to put a word together. Insistence on correct use of implements and perfection in performance of tasks were among the basic tenets of the Montessori Method. Consequently, "even before they read from books and learned to respect them, the children with some help on our part had learned to spell and to write so perfectly that they were compared with children in the third grade in grammar schools" (Montessori, 1966, p. 134). Vygotsky (1978) later was to criticize the fact that children's written work he was shown on his visit to Montessori's school was so clearly adult-inspired.

Summing up her "Method" in a few strong paragraphs, many years after the actual events, Montessori (1966) includes in a list of things children like:

> Writing separated from reading.
> Writing before reading.
> Reading without books (p. 138).

Several contemporary investigators have since reconfirmed Montessori's experience. Studies of children who learned to read early in informal settings seem to indicate that in many cases interest in writing and ability to write preceded reading (Durkin, 1966, 1974a; Chomsky, 1971, 1972b, 1976; Hall, Moretz, & Statom, 1976). Durkin's (1966) two longitudinal studies of children who learned to read at home prior to entering school revealed the interest of such children in learning to print, so that "ability to read seemed almost like a by-product of ability to print and to spell" (p. 137). Similarly, Hall, Moretz and Statom (1976) report that among the 18 early writers, aged 3.4 to 6.1 they investigated by way of parent interviews, interest in writing had preceded interest in reading in all cases but one. Most of the parents were college graduates, and writing materials and books had been very accessible in the children's homes.

Recently a strong case for using writing as an avenue for learning to read has been made by Carol Chomsky (1971, 1972b, 1976, 1979a). Her interest was sparked by the achievements of her son. When he was encouraged rather than corrected in his own highly individual way of using letters to represent words, this 3¼ year old "discovered" writing within a single sitting.

Judging that sounding out words created by an adult is much more difficult for young children than composing words on their own, Chomsky urges that children be encouraged to discover reading by way of learning to write first. Helped by a knowledge of letter sounds and a supply of alphabet cards or blocks children could literally assemble words out of their component parts. The final product—a word—is, in this case, not something alien, imposed by an adult from without, but rather a product of the child's own mind (Chomsky, 1971).

Of course the words children create in this way will bear little resemblance to conventionally spelled words. Chomsky suggests that correcting a child's invented spelling in the initial stages is harmful and might impede the entire process (Chomsky, 1972b). Similarly Read (1971), who studied the invented spelling of 20 preschoolers feels that parents' "tolerance for what appears to be bad spelling" (p. 4) may be a "necessary condition for spontaneous spelling to occur at all" (p. 27).

WRITING AS A BRIDGE TO MEANING

Today reading is frequently discussed within the cognitive tradition of information processing. A voluminous literature deals with the difficulties readers encounter in trying to extract meaning from text (i.e., Pearson & Johnson, 1978; Spiro, Bruce, & Brewer, 1980; Guthrie, 1981; Schank, 1982).

Factors frequently discussed in this context are vocabulary, syntactic structure, discrepancies between oral and written speech, as well as additional difficulties users of nonstandard language may have when confronted with reading materials in an unfamiliar idiom. Beside linguistic factors the reader must also grasp the particular situational context in which a given story occurs, the so-called script (Schank & Abelson, 1977). A prerequisite for this is a store of previously acquired knowledge about the characteristics of everyday occurrences (Anderson and Pearson, 1984). This assumes a common frame of reference about signifying characteristics shared by the neo-reader and the adult who originally composed the text the neo-reader is trying to decode and comprehend.

It is here that we reach an important issue. The literature dealing with reading comprehension most often conceives of the text as a given. The text exists, and researchers try to discover in what way it poses difficulty. In this scheme the beginning reader has to try to reconstruct a message, penned by an adult, about an event which might be unfamiliar, or lack interest. A message that is, moreover, rendered in unaccustomed language, by way of abstract graphic symbols which the reader is still in the process of acquiring. A truly formidable task!

However, once we execute a turnabout and assume that it is the *child* who puts together his or her own message, many of these difficulties cease to exist. When children themselves are the originators of written messages there is no divergence between content and its symbolic rendering. The child knows what he or she wanted to say. In fact, as clearly emerges from Chomsky's and Montessori's descriptions, it is the act of

transferring a *known* message into symbolic form which intrigues learners at this initial stage and motivates them to persist in their efforts.
Chomsky (1979a) found that reading back what they have written, or
having other persons read it, is of much less interest to young writers.
The fact that in the rush of discovery children initially sometimes tend to
transcribe only single words may further simplify the situation. Instead
of facing an extremely complex task, the beginning reader is thus introduced to the meaningfulness of written communication via a succession
of single words, or short phrases, all of which originated in his or her
own mind.

THE LANGUAGE EXPERIENCE APPROACH AS AN
INTRODUCTION TO READING AND WRITING

The Language Experience Approach in beginning reading (LEA for
short) has in recent years gained, or perhaps more correctly regained,
considerable popularity.

Classroom applications of LEA vary considerably. But underlying this
manifest diversity is a core of basic assumptions on which there is
consensus.

The rationale of LEA, as a strategy for teaching beginning reading,
rests on the assumption that reading is but an additional expansion of
language skills in which the child is already well versed (Stauffer, 1970;
Karlin, 1975). Written language is thus conceived as "talk written down,"
and LEA as a natural way to teach young children to read, since the texts
they read relate to their personal experiences (Allen, 1964/1973). LEA is
usually implemented via the following steps:

1. An experience, activity, or drawing of the learner(s) is discussed
   spontaneously.
2. A more permanent record of said event is suggested.
3. The student(s) dictate, or are helped to dictate, their ideas to the
   teacher, and watch while they are written down.
4. The student(s) read(s) what has been dictated.
5. The dictation may be preserved in more permanent form, such as
   typed, or transcribed on a ditto, to be reread and shared with others.
6. Dictated stories may eventually be used in teaching decoding skills,
   but this is not usual in the initial stages (Askov & Lee, 1980).

An attempt to clarify three questions related to characteristic features
of LEA may help us to better appreciate the potential of this approach
and show ways by which its implementations could be further enhanced.

LEA: Collective or Individual?

There can be little doubt that the original exponents of Language Experience had in mind a highly individualized process. In describing the initial stages of Language Experience, Allen (1964/1973) refers to children exclusively in the singular form. It is only "*after* reading his own language in written form" (p. 162) that the child moves to reading the written language of other children and adults. Sylvia Ashton-Warner, the well-known author who sparked much interest in LEA, describes in detail how the intensely personal reading vocabulary she created for *each* of her pupils was intimately linked to that particular pupil's life experiences (Ashton-Warner, 1963). In the British Infant School tradition in which she worked, the individual child's writing serves as a stepping stone to reading. In a typical British beginner's class a teacher spends time with each child, discussing first the sentence the child might want to write on that day. Next the teacher writes down the sentence in the child's own book, or assists the child in assembling it from word cards. The child then copies the sentence in his/her book, either underneath the teacher's writing or directly from the assembled word cards (Goddard, 1974; Mackay, Thompson, & Schaub, 1979).

However, in other countries the language experience approach is often conceived as a collective act. The whole class—or a group of children—discusses a joint experience which they all shared. They then take turns in formulating sentences which the teacher commits to the blackboard or a chart. In some places children are made to copy the collective text. In others, it is used only for reading practice (Harris & Sipay, 1975; Karlin, 1975).

Individual language experiences uses the very real personal involvement of the learner to arouse interest in the text and as motivating factor. Translated to a group situation, there is the well-known danger that the more able and/or motivated students will participate most actively in formulating the text and watching the teacher write it down.

As long as children's writing emanates from each individual's own efforts, there is likely to be no great difference in levels of children's absorption in their self-chosen tasks. Children's early written efforts can not be deciphered easily by their peers, and perceptive teachers tend to preserve them as exclusive possessions of their authors. Consequently children have little opportunity to compare their work with that of others, nor do they seem to feel the need to do so (Chomsky, 1972b). However, when the situation becomes a collective effort, individual differences in ability come to the fore, and the more able, self-assured, and outgoing children will contribute most actively to the communal text, or at least greater amounts of their contributions will prove acceptable.

Consequently, they will probably also monitor the actual transcribing by the teacher more carefully and with better understanding. Shy and less able children may not only tend to leave the initiative in group situations to others, but may also derive less benefit from watching the teacher write as they may be less clear about what it is the teacher actually does. Especially as most often the teacher is not transcribing their personal contributions.

Personal Effort or Teacher-Mediated?

Montessori's (1966) description of her pupil's discovery of writing is permeated with the intense feeling of joy the children exhibited. Most of us are probably familiar with similar reactions whenever a young child attains mastery of a new skill, be it the ability to pull himself up to a standing position, to crawl, walk, or climb stairs. Who has not been deeply impressed by an infant's complete absorption in such new conquests, an absorption which often leads to prolonged bouts of performing the new skill over and over and over again?

The importance of feelings of successful mastery and hence competence in encouraging further endeavors has been widely discussed in the literature on intrinsic motivation (i.e. White, 1959; Deci, 1975; Stipek & Weisz, 1981). In turn, it is interesting to note that pleasure in mastering a task is greatest when the learner feels personally responsible for his or her success (Harter, 1974, 1978).

When successful performance is achieved only via the teacher, these important attributes of self-generated writing may be lost.

When, instead of children writing by themselves they are made to dictate to adults, the message emitted is that writing is so difficult that only the all-knowing teacher can do it successfully.

Ability to write letters depends on the development of manual skills like eye-hand coordination, fine motor control, and use of writing implements. Over the years, educators seem to have tried to enable young children to engage in symbolic representation of speech without being impeded by lack of manual dexterity. In his description of the American public school system of his day, Rice (1893) writes in regard to reading instruction in Indianapolis: "The child is permitted to alternate between the use of letter-cards and the pencil in forming his words, so that he may be relieved of the physical strain consequent upon writing" (p. 107). In his book there are several examples of texts created by assembling letter cards, proving that this technique was used even when texts were fairly long and complicated (see Figure 5.1). The texts in Rice's book show that an essential prerequisite of this approach was that several

Figure 5.1.   The use of letter cards in children's writing in Indianapolis circa 1893.

Reproduced from Rice, J. M. 1893. *The public school system of the United States.* New York: Century. pp. 107.

copies of each letter were available to the composing child. Montessori (1912/1965) stipulates four copies of each alphabet card in the early stages of writing, increasing this to 20 later on.

Chaos would most certainly ensue from equipping each child with several copies of all letters of the alphabet unless there was a way to keep them neatly sorted and ready at hand. In Montessori's schools letter-cards were kept in a "storage box modelled on a printer's type-case" (Mayer, 1965, p. 35).

A variety of storage and assembly devices, some of them extremely well designed and very compact, were also found in schools the present author visited in Britain and Vienna. In both places assembling letter or word cards to form words or sentences is a frequent activity of beginning readers.

Does Speech Necessarily Precede Writing?

According to Allen (1964), two of the basic tenets of language experience are: "What I can think about, I can talk about. What I can say, I can write—or someone can write for me" (p. 59). Viewed this way writing is inevitably preceded by oral communication.

However, this assumption seems unwarranted on several counts (Johnson, 1977; Klein, 1980; Dyson, 1982, 1983). Johnson (1977) and Klein (1980) imply that psychologists sometimes have an exaggerated opinion of the link between the level of dialogue of school beginners and meaningful written texts. Young children's utterances in a face-to-face discourse situation are, at best "sentence fragments" (Klein, 1980, p. 40).

The common practice of having an adult serve as recorder of children's contributions in LEA may actually imply tacit acknowledgement of the fact that the level of speech of school beginners, does not generate language which can serve unaltered as meaningful written text.

However, when one conceives of children's writing as direct expression in a new medium, without assuming mediating conversation or monologue (Johnson, 1977), this source of difficulty ceases to exist. When children cut out pictures of simple objects from magazines or old books and label them, the path is a direct one from the child's stored knowledge of object names to transmitting these names to paper, with no intervening stage of oral discussion with another person. An experience the present author had in a Circassian village school in Israel can serve as proof of the immediacy with which school beginners attain written labels, and the fact that in such activity there need not necessarily be an intermediary oral stage. Circassians are a small minority group of Russian origin and Moslem faith, inhabiting two villages in Israel. As there are no textbooks or curriculum in the Circassian language, the language of instruction in the government-maintained village school formerly was Arabic. In the particular village the author visited, the village council had suddenly decided on a switch to Hebrew after nearly 30 years in which the school had functioned in Arabic. Consequently first graders that year were learning to read in a language which for all practical purposes was an unknown, foreign tongue to them. Instruction in Hebrew had started only at the beginning of the term, concurrently with initial reading. Leafing through children's written work a few weeks later, the author discovered that, when labeling pictures cut from magazines, children had sometimes used Circassian words, but had written them in Hebrew characters. As in truly multilingual situations where constant code switching is a way of life, these first graders were probably not even aware of what they had done. Kolers (1966) describes how, when preparing linguistically mixed texts for experimental purposes, he and his co-workers "would lose the ability to identify to which language a given word belonged. The meaning of the words was always present, but whether they were French or English rapidly became a difficult decision to make" (p. 375). When this happens to adult scientists, native speakers of one language, while they are engaged in experiments with two languages, how natural that first graders, in the early stages of mastering writing would write the label which came most *spontaneously* to their mind on seeing a picture. The important point to notice is the direct link between the concept in the child's mind and the act of transferring that concept to paper, without mediation by spoken word. Had speech intervened the child would have groped for the Hebrew label, or would have asked a teacher to provide it, given the special circumstances of that school at that particular point in time.

One, assuming a necessary initial oral stage, introduces an intermediary process which may be unnecessary and perhaps counterproductive. Montessori (1966), Chomsky (1971, 1972b) and others who witnessed the spontaneous advent of writing in young children have described how the children, realizing that letters represent sounds, suddenly discovered that by combining several letters they could represent a word. Their aim was to master the symbolic system by which they could commit concepts in their mind to paper. Discovering writing meant for them finding a way to represent thought on paper, much like what they had been doing up till then when drawing.

Vygotsky, the Russian psychologist, whose writings from the early 1930s have become available to the English reading public only recently (1978), seems to have been the first to stress the crucial role of writing in children's development. He talks of "the enormous role" that writing plays in children's "cultural development" (p. 105). According to him the mastery of written language "heralds a critical turning point in the entire cultural development of the child." "A feature of this system is that it is second-order symbolism, which gradually becomes direct symbolism. This means that written language consists of a system of signs that designate the sounds and words of spoken language, which, in turn are signs for real entities and relations. Gradually this intermediate link, spoken language, disappears, and written language is converted into a system of signs that directly symbolizes the entities and relations between them" (p. 106).

According to Vygotsky, "make believe play, drawing and writing can be viewed as different moments in an essentially unified process of development of written language" (p. 115). While speech is the basis for all three, Vygotsky also specifies a direct link between drawing and writing, as he feels that the written language of children develops by shifting from drawings of things to drawings of words (Vygotsky, 1978, p. 115). The most essential feature of Vygotsky's theory is that "developmental processes do not coincide with learning processes. Rather, the developmental process lags behind the learning process" (p. 90). The fact that in the schools of his day writing was taught as a "motor skill" instead of "a complex cultural activity" precluded the observations and research Vygotsky felt were necessary in order to examine in greater detail just how the transition from drawing to writing had best take place. Contemporary American preschools provide the opportunity Vygotsky lacked. Dyson's (1982, 1983) studies of writing behaviors of kindergartners who were "preconventional writers" (Dyson, 1982, p. 364) supports Vygotsky's (1978) theoretical position. For Dyson's five-year-olds writing did "not begin as speech written down" (p. 379). Instead they tended to intermingle or combine writing and drawing as alternative forms of graphic representation, viewing print as "direct graphic symbolism, rather than as a representation of speech, which in turn stands for referents" (p. 379).

Once we accept the notion that developing written language essentially means that the child develops access to a symbolic system which represents thought, many of the difficulties often postulated by linguists in regard to decoding disappear. This is especially so of the arguments that the teaching of symbol-sound correspondences in the early stages will inevitably lead to efforts at "sounding out" words, and that letter sounds added to one another do not recreate language. On the contrary, knowledge of sound-symbol correspondences enables the learner to structure a contentful message according to his/her understanding of the symbolic system at that particular stage of personal development. As it was the child who was the originator of the message, he/she can repeat the message in normal everyday speech whenever he/she should feel called upon to do so. Experience, in fact, shows that the child's main gratification at this early stage is in encoding the message, *not* in reading it (Chomsky, 1979a). What difficulty there is will be mainly on the part of the grown-up, that is, the teacher, when trying to understand what it is the child has written. Here we come to the issue of spelling in children's self-generated writing.

THE PROBLEM OF SPELLING IN BEGINNERS' WRITING

In Fernald's kinesthetic method mastering the correct spelling of words is synonomous with learning to read. Describing her method for curing "word-blindness," or "total reading disability," Fernald (1943) writes "the essentials of our technique consist in 1) the discovery of some means by which the child can learn to write words *correctly* [my emphasis, D.F.] 2) the motivating of such writing 3) the reading by the child of the printed copy of what he has written 4) extensive reading of materials other than own compositions." (p. 33).

Learning to write words "correctly" meant in this context finger-tracing while saying each part of a word many times over, till the learner is able to write it correctly from memory. By Fernald's account most words learned this way were still written correctly weeks after the initial learning experience. Eventually finger-tracing is discontinued, but the principle that each word has to be practiced to the point of automatic correct spelling before it may be used in children's writing remains throughout all stages of learning. Fernald felt that usual classroom practice in which words are written only once or twice, lead to what she called "bad habits" or "lack of habits" and should therefore be prevented. It must be remembered that Fernald's techniques were developed in the context of treating extremely severe reading and spelling disabilities of children who were well past the beginning stage. The secret of her success lay in developing ways which were both failproof, and at the same time radically different from earlier unsuccessful experiences her patients might have had, either in school or during previous attempts at remediation.

While few practitioners today would care to interfere with a beginner's experiments with spontaneous written expression in order to drill every word used, there is a fairly widespread feeling that "knowing" a word leads automatically to the ability to spell it correctly.

Theoretical discussions of models of reading processes sometimes seem to imply that decoding and spelling skills go hand in hand. For instance Ehri (1980) speaks of an "orthographic image" which is stored in memory and becomes a "visual symbol" for the word (p. 156). It is easy to see how this terminology might lead from the notion that learning to read means assembling an ever-growing store of visual word-images to the assumption that this results automatically in the ability to reproduce these words correctly in writing.

The British scholar Uta Frith (1979, 1980a, 1980b; Frith & Frith, 1980) has in recent years been especially concerned with clarifying the relationship between reading ability and spelling. Frith's research shows that reading and writing are not merely the same process in reverse. Cerebral accidents sometimes lead to the loss of one of these abilities without impairment of the other. Even in unimpaired individuals there is often marked divergence between levels of achievements in the two areas. Frith analyzed the basic processes involved, which according to her "are not biological functions for which the brain may be uniquely equipped, but highly artificial processes which depend on specific learning and instruction" (Frith, 1980b, p. 220). Reading requires input analyzing strategies. Frith assumes that input conditions tend to vary tremendously and that, in order to cope with this diversity, reading strategies have to be flexible. On the other hand, writing, which is an output process. needs to be rigidly controlled. Frith's research seems to show that good spellers rely on specific programs learned by rote. Thus, while skilled reading is characterized by flexibility, skilled spelling is characterized by rigidity (Frith & Frith, 1980). The ability to write words correctly is therefore no prerequisite of learning to decode them. Both Ehri and Frith refer to the fact that sometimes especially able readers are atrocious spellers. Among the better-known poor spellers were Robert Louis Stevenson, Ernest Hemingway, and Agatha Christie. Frith's conclusion raises the question whether insistence on correct spelling in the early stages of reading acquisition may not even be counterproductive. Chomsky (1972b) and Read (1971) clearly think that this is the case.

So far research on spelling has not addressed the widespread assumption that allowing children to engage in writing before they know how to spell may lead to the perpetuation of spelling mistakes. Though the assumption, seems to make good sense, the few studies available point in the opposite direction. The invented spellings of the preschoolers studied by Read (1971) did not become habitual, but changed according to children's increasing level of competency. Chomsky (1975) reports that standardized spelling tests taken by a group of children who had spelled inventively all through first grade showed grade-level scores in second grade and above grade-level scores in third grade. Similarly a follow-up study of a representative sample of first graders from 11 experimental infant schools throughout Israel (Strauss, Harrison, Gross, & Kedem, 1976) indicated that there was no significant difference between their spelling ability and that of children in control classes. Children in experimental infant schools engaged in spontaneous writing and their work was not corrected. Children's writing in control classes was restricted to copying and to work in workbooks.

The arguments presented here should not be misunderstood to mean that attention to spelling can or should be relegated entirely to later school years. Many learning activities concerned with broadening children's mastery of language contribute to their propensity to write correctly. Read (1971) found that the speed with which the early writers he studied converted from their invented spelling to standard spelling, was dependent in great part on their later school environment.

Teachers in the Israeli Infant Schools reported that soon after the initial stages of self-generated writing had become established, some children tended to enquire about the correct spelling of words they wanted to use. Typically these children did not ask for help in creating the whole word, but rather pinpointed their query specifically to particular spelling options, such as which of two t's or two k's they were to use. (In Hebrew there is a redundancy of symbols over sounds. Therefore in a number of instances a phoneme can be represented by two graphemes).

Further research is clearly called for. However, even the relatively scant evidence already available seriously challenges the wisdom of the tendency to curtail children's self-generated writing in the initial stages of learning, because of concern for possible harmful effects on spelling ability. Virtually everyone of the scholars who have concerned themselves with the question has found that encoding seems to be an easier process than decoding. Moreover, especially self-attained encoding seems to open up an understanding of the basic nature of written language in a flash of insight. As we have seen, this understanding encompasses from the very first the fact that written language is contentful. Approaching reading via children's own writing could thus, in effect, completely bypass the oft-mentioned supposed dichotomy between attention to decoding processes and attention to meaning. The fact that investigators reported that in the initial stages children enjoyed writing more than reading, and engaged in writing very readily, would seem a further reason for allotting a major role in initial reading programs to writing.

At this stage a perceptive reader may well ask whether there is not a paradox between the views expounded in this chapter and the apparent advocacy of sequentially structured reading programs in preceding ones. It would seem that almost by definition structured instruction is a predetermined, teacher-controlled, stage-by-stage process. How, then, can such an approach to instruction go hand in hand with unconstrained free writing which originates solely in the child?

Are not preplanned sequential reading instruction and children's self expression in writing almost by definition incompatible? In the following chapters, and especially in Chapter Nine, we shall examine ways in which structured reading instruction and child-initiated individual writing can be integrated so that in terms of the learner they become a unified learning experience.

CHAPTER 6

Are Decoding-Oriented and Meaning-Focused Instruction Incompatible?

Extreme positions on initial reading are today a thing of the past. Most look-and-say approaches have strong phonics components and, conversely, phonics' first programs lead sooner or later to words and contentful passages (Gibson & Levin, 1975). Despite this overall reapproachment and earnest efforts to arrive at a viable synthesis of both elements, the underlying assumptions of many researchers continue to lean heavily in one direction or the other.

On the one end is the insistence that children will develop into readers by being exposed to meaningful naturalistic written language. Through this exposure, the child will eventually infer crucial insights about the way written symbols represent underlying meaning. Proponents of this line of argument are often rather vague about specific procedures teachers could and should adopt in order to facilitate this process. Smith's (1973) statement can serve as example: "There are no rules of reading, at least none that can be specified with sufficient precision to teach a child. All proficient readers have acquired an implicit knowledge of how to read, but this knowledge has been developed through the practice of reading, not through anything that is taught at school" (p. 184). Or Kenneth Goodman (1964): "The basic units of speech are phonemes, but they have no existence outside of morphemes, the molecules of the language. Morphemes are the minimum units of language that can carry meaning, but they have no existence outside syntactical structures. Syntactical structures, such as sentences, have reality only in the stream of language" (p. 360). Goodman goes on to declare that "words taken out of language context cannot be defined, pronounced, or categorized" (Goodman, 1964, p. 360).

The passages by Goodman and Smith were penned as ammunition in their struggle against certain teaching practices, about which they had serious, and probably justified reservations, such as in Goodman's case the use of word lists in teaching reading.

The problem lies in both authors' great gifts as writers. Their formulations are often so apt and memorable that they tend to become catch phrases in their own right and consequently to be quoted out of context. Taken literally they seem to imply positions which may well be more extreme than their erstwhile originators actually had in mind. In fact, Smith seemingly contradicts himself when he declares in the same chapter that it would be "instructive to examine how children learned to read in the bad old days of the past" (Smith, 1973, p. 194) or "my interest is in fact that for so long, with so many children, teachers have been doing things that are obviously right" (p. 196). Thus, far from saying that schools are superfluous in the acquisition of reading, he, seems to feel that sometime in the dim past schools were effective in the way they approached reading instruction, only that he himself is not too sure what it was that teachers did. What he does criticize, however, are certain kinds of prepackaged reading instruction materials used today in many schools.

However, in their attack against specific materials and practices to which they object, Goodman, Smith, and many of those who share their views seem to imply that all attempts at sequencing instruction are to be condemned. Thus vocabulary control practiced in practically all Look-and-Say approaches would presumably be considered as objectionable as instruction focused on spelling patterns a la Fries, or, sin of sins, the teaching of sound-symbol correspondences. According to this school of thought, meaning and natural language are of prime importance and should never be tampered with in the name of other considerations. In making a case for their beliefs, adherents of these opinions tend to rely both on learned argument as well as on delightful lampoons of classroom learning situations.

However, many of them avoid the question of what exactly it is that teachers should be doing in the initial stages of children's learning. Most of the learning experiences they describe and criticize are of children who have already acquired the rudiments of reading. Typically the situation depicted is that of a child already able to derive at least some meaning from the printed page, whose progress is now impeded as a result of teaching practices overemphasizing attention to phonics.

As we shall see further on and especially in Chapter Eleven, the contributions of Smith, Goodman, and other scholars who are in accord with their opinions are of great value when applied to that stage of learning to read in which they are clearly most interested, namely, the transition to independent reading. It is when these theories are extended to include also the beginning stage that their applicability is questioned.

The initial stage of reading acquisition seems to have the community of reading researchers most confused (Gough, Juel & Roper/Schneider, 1983). Gibson and Levin (1975) put it aptly—"Despite all the current emphasis on literacy, the wealth of programs commercially available, the 'learning specialists' who have set up in shopping centers, and the arguments over phonics or whole-word methods, it is the beginning phase of learning to read that we seem to know least about" (p. 264). A tempting way out of this difficulty is to imply that when reading instruction is allowed to happen "naturally," children will develop initial reading skills on their own. In contrast, proponents of phonics-oriented instruction are concerned most especially with the early stages of reading. Their ultimate goal also is meaningful reading; however they feel that the effectiveness of comprehension depends in part on facility in identifying words correctly and automatically. The less effort readers have to expand on decoding per se, the more will they be able to concentrate on extracting meaning (Lesgold & Perfetti, 1981; Liberman, 1982; Perfetti, 1985; Stanovich, 1986). Unfortunately, when trying to translate theory into practice. authors of so-called phonic or linguistic reading approaches tend sometimes to commit the very sins with which they are charged by their opponents. In many of the available sequentially structured schemes, children are made to learn a considerable number of isolated letters, or even all of them, before they are ever shown how these can be combined into meaningful words. Other common problems are the propensity of letter-pattern controlled programs to rely unduly on workbook exercises, and to limit themselves—especially in the early stages—to very few sound patterns that are repeated over and over again in "man ran" "cat sat" type of sentences.

These practices have been taken to task so often that there seems little point in repeating familiar criticism. It may be more profitable to proceed on a different track. Let us assume that the critics are right and many of the practices presently associated with phonics-oriented beginning reading instruction are indeed as counterproductive as the critics say. Is it not possible that the goals of phonics-based reading instruction could be attained also by different strategies and materials?

In that case the practices which were so heavily criticized would not be an intrinsic, unavoidable component of code emphasis reading programs, but rather incidental techniques which had developed as a result of particular traditions and conditions.

This is, in fact, exactly the argument we would like to advance here. What we shall try to show with the help of examples from different countries is that the specific practices which have often become most strongly associated with sequentially structured, phonics-oriented reading instruction are not the only possible ones. Code-emphasis instruction can avoid the characteristics that have drawn negative comment. In using examples from other countries, we shall at this stage focus on main issues and momentarily overlook problems arising from language differences. Chapter Seven will be devoted entirely to specific problems associated with beginning reading in English. It is there that adjustments of general principles to the particular circumstances of the English language will be discussed.

BASING DECODING-ORIENTED INSTRUCTION ON CONTENTFUL TEXTS

Most examples in the following sections will be of instructional strategies which were perfected outside the United States. This is not because practices described here are not to be found also on the American educational scene. Quite the contrary, it is precisely the great number and diversity of offerings on the American market and the rate at which new materials become available that make one feel that it may be preferable to abstain from singling out any particular approach lest, unwittingly, other equally deserving ones might be slighted.

We shall start by examining a recently published Austrian primer. The examples in Chapter Four were from the 1964 edition of a Viennese primer which had been developed from earlier editions all the way back to the 1920s. More recently, a different primer has been very widely adopted (Kunschak, Rinner, Schraffl, & Vavra, 1978). The new primer is based on the same basic approach to beginning reading instruction employed in the older version. However, in content the new book is more contemporary and more in tune with present concerns.

For example, in the early pages it is no longer the housebound mother and her young child in their orderly home who command center stage. Now the central figure is a paper puppet named Mimi. Mimi, in full color, with movable arms and legs and twice the size of the book actually comes with it. Children thus possess a Mimi of their very own and can play with her and act out her doings and whereabouts before reading instruction proper starts. The word Mimi which they will soon construct from the first two letters they learned, the consonant "M" and the vowel "I", is thus not an abstract concept, but a concrete joyfully recognized presence, their very own puppet. Thus play episodes that actually took place can be described in writing. Mimi sleeps in a doll's pram or bed, sits in a toy lorry, or performs in a puppet theatre (see

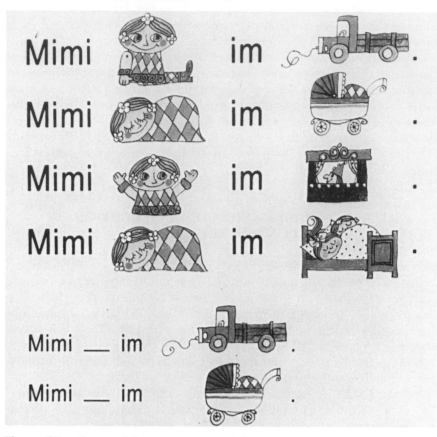

Figure 6.1.   Contentful text constructed from the first two letters children learn in a modern Austrian primer.

Reproduced from Kunschak, E., H. Rinner, H. Schraffl and W. Vavra. 1978. *Frohes Lernen.* Vienna: Österreichischer Bundesverlag für Unterricht, Wissenschaft und Kunst. pp. 7. (Original in color).

Figure 6.1). With the addition of one further vowel "A" three new protagonists enter the scene: "Mama"—the mother; "Mia"—the house cat; and "Ami"—the dog. Content now becomes more diversified. Mama reads in the garden. Mia sleeps in her basket or climbs a tree. And Ami walks in the garden or barks at the front door. (see Figure 6.2). On the next page the heroine leaves for school with Mimi in her satchel while mother stands at the window, Ami barks his farewells, and Mia watches from her basket on the windowsill (see Figure 6.3). On this page mother is referred to as "Mami," so that besides content, accuracy in decoding is impressed on the beginner. Concern for accuracy is kept up throughout.

Figure 6.2. Contentful text constructed from the first three letters children learn in a modern Austrian primer.

Reproduced from Kunschak, E., H. Rinner, H. Schraffl and W. Vavra. 1978. *Frohes Lernen*. Vienna: Österreichischer Bundesverlag für Unterricht, Wissenschaft und Kunst. pp. 9. (Original in color).

Page 30 (Kunschack, Rinner, Schraffl, & Vavra, 1987) is a good example. Here Aunt Erna is invited to have tea. The difference in number of cups of tea drunk by Aunt Erna and grandmother and in kind of pastry taken by Susi and her baby sister Irmi provide opportunities to discriminate on one and the same page between "nimm" and "nimmt," "Tasse" and "Tassen," "nur" and "nun," as well as among "Tante," "Tanten," "Nasen," "Tassen," and "Rasen" and "rote" and "rosa" (see Figure 6.4).

Figure 6.3. Contentful passage leading to accurate decoding, constructed from the first three letters children learn in a modern Austrian primer.

Reproduced from Kunschak, E., H. Rinner, H. Schraffl and W. Vavra. 1978. *Frohes Lernen*. Vienna: Österreichischer Bundesverlag für Unterricht, Wissenschaft und Kunst. pp. 10. (Original in color).

There would be little point in describing once again salient features of a particular Austrian program were it not for the fact that it is fairly representative of programs in several other languages we had a chance to examine, that is, Finnish, Tagalog, Malay, Russian, Arabic, and Hebrew.

In all these approaches meaningful words and contentful phrases are

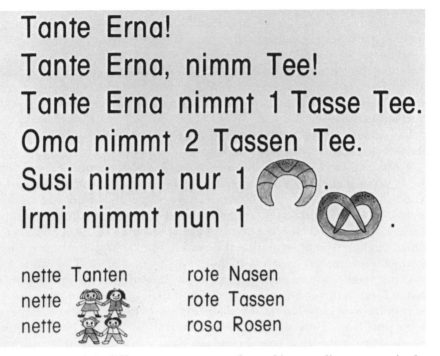

Figure 6.4. Subtle differences among words used in a reading passage in the initial part of a modern Austrian primer.

Reproduced from Kunschak, E., H. Rinner, H. Schraffl and W. Vavra. 1978. *Frohes Lernen.* Vienna: Österreichischer Bundesverlag für Unterricht, Wissenschaft und Kunst. pp. 30. (Original in color).

formed when only very few letters, sometimes no more than two, have been learned. Further, right from the beginning, contentful statements are not merely descriptive but they tell action-stories. Thus every page has a theme and a central happening even when as, for instance, in a very early page of an Arabic primer, this consists only of Bad'r beating up his sister Rabab; a familiar event among siblings the world over, conveyed in this case by three consonants and one vowel.

The reasons for elaborating once again on a Viennese approach instead of describing any of the other ones were: first, that in terms of language and alphabet this example is more accessible to the English-speaking reader than examples in some of the other languages; secondly, that the two Viennese approaches are a good example of how basic principles can be implemented in different ways. Thus, consensus about underlying processes and effective learning strategies does not necessarily mean lack of choice among different programs. Actually, both Viennese programs begin with the same three letters. Yet their opening passages are entirely different.

So far we have dealt with the issue of meaningful content in sequentially structured reading programs. It was shown that contrary to often voiced assertions, it is possible to combine consideration of letter-pattern control with contentful action-type stories even in the very early stages of reading instruction.

Let us now proceed to a second aspect of meaning in relation to phonics-oriented reading instruction.

Today, in contrast to the heyday of Look-and-Say, most experts on the reading scene feel that early on in the learning process beginning readers will have to be introduced to the way speech sounds are represented by letters and letter combinations (Chall, 1983a). A frequently discussed problem in this context is that the teaching of letter sounds to school beginners may mean that they will have to struggle with learning abstract meaningless symbols (Gibson & Levin, 1975). The value of teaching symbol-sound relationships is also questioned on the grounds that in English these are not consistent, and that some consonants cannot be pronounced in isolation. We shall return to these issues in Chapters Seven and Nine. Here we shall focus on whether learning letter sounds entails unavoidably that young children have to contend with acquiring abstract, meaningless, unrelated bits of information.

DO LETTER SOUNDS HAVE TO LACK MEANING?

An especially popular way of teaching letter sound correspondences is to associate letter sounds with initial letters of object names. Familiar examples of this approach are the letter friezes and charts that decorate many kindergarten and first grade classrooms. Typically, each letter of the alphabet is accompanied by illustrations showing familiar objects whose names start with the sound the particular letter represents, such as "pig" and "pram" for "P" or "cup" and "car" for "C". Exercises in many popular phonics workbooks are based on the same principle. Page after page, children are made to circle or otherwise single out small drawings of objects whose names start with the target letter of that particular lesson, in contrast to further drawings of objects the names of which have other initial letters.

It is exactly in connection with such humdrum everyday exercises that one suddenly realizes how the very familiarity of given tasks seemingly exempts them from serious consideration and from a re-examination of their advantages and disadvantages in the light of their purported aims. However, once opportunity arises to compare long familiar practices with entirely different strategies, initial steps towards a better under-standing of learning processes become possible.

Like their American counterparts, British infant-school teachers whose classrooms the author had occasion to observe also introduced letter sounds via initial letters of object names. However, the way they went about this was different on certain pertinent details. A child would be given his/her personal "sound book" only when the teacher consid-ered that he/she was ready for that particular kind of work. The first sound in each child's book—actually a simple notebook usually on the smallish side—was the initial letter of the child's name. The teacher wrote the letter in both capital and lower case form on the first page, and the child added drawings of objects whose names start with the same initial letter. From now on new sounds were introduced intermittently with the child producing appropriate drawings each time according to his/her choice. Like all other work in British infant-classes, the child's products were closely monitored and discussed at length. The introduc-tion of each new letter was by way of a tete-a-tete session between teacher and child in which the new sound and suitable illustrations were dis-cussed while the teacher carefully wrote the appropriate symbols in the child's book. Letter combinations such as "sh" or "ck" were learned in their own right. As far as I could tell, letters were not introduced in any preordained sequence, but rather according to the needs of the moment in connection with individual children's written work or reading. In terestingly enough, while the "sound book" was a common feature in all classes visited, there was no mention of it in the teacher's manual (Mack-ay, Thompson, & Schaub, 1979) of the currently favored reading ap-proach used in most of these classes.

The Tagalog primer mentioned earlier approaches sound-symbol re-lationships somewhat differently. Here the child is first made aware of a *meaningful* sound, for instance, a long drawn out hummed *m m m* to represent the sound of an airplane in flight. Only after a meaningful sound has become "very familiar" (Nooraihan & Urbano, 1967, p. 2) is the child introduced to the corresponding letter in lower case form (See Figure 6.5). The second sound in the primer is "s." "It is the sound mother makes as she makes the baby do his morning chore sssssssss" (Nooraihan & Urbano, 1967, p. 5). Once again the learner masters the sound and its letter-symbol by many and varied activities: stories in which the sound occurs, flash cards, matching activities, tracing on sand or in the air, forming the letter from molding clay, bits of string or wire, and writing it on the blackboard or on paper. The third sound is "a." Now children combine the three letters they know into meaningful words and contentful episodes.

Let us see in what way the three approaches just described differ from

m   *m*   *m*   *m*   *m*

m   *m*   *m*

m   *m*

m

m

1

Figure 6.5.   Introducing a "meaningful" sound on the first page of a Philippine primer.

Reproduced from Nooraihan, A. and J. O. Urbano. 1967. *Bumasa Tayo at Sumulat.* Los Santos, Philippines: De Los Santos Community School. pp. 1.

each other. For short let's call them "American," "British," and "Philippine," though it has to be clearly understood that this does not imply that any one of them is the only approach used in a particular country.

The success of the American approach depends in large measure on the new learner entering school already well equipped with certain prerequisite skills. In this approach the child has to be able to infer initial sounds of words from accompanying illustrations. This means that the child has first of all to be familiar with the depicted object and secondly to be able to identify the object in the particular illustration used. Thirdly, the child has to instantaneously recall the name of the object. Fourth, the child has to be able to segment the initial sound from the oral impression which represents the name of that object in his/her mind. And, fifth, he/she has to be able to compare the sound arrived at in this fashion with the sound which is represented by the target letter just being learned in order to infer whether the picture should indeed be circled or otherwise marked.

Our analysis shows that some of the prerequisite skills for successful performance of the task rest on acquired factual knowledge. Others require high level inferential ability. Children who lack experience with objects which the text authors assumed were familiar, or who were not sufficiently exposed to illustrations, may either not know the pictured object or may, while knowing the object, not recognize its picture (Sigel, 1970). Also, when the language of instruction is not the child's native language or when the child speaks a dialect, the object-name which comes to the child's mind may not be the one the program designers intended. In such cases the initial sound of the name will not necessarily correspond to the letter the child is meant to learn.

Many of these difficulties will not arise in the British approach where it is the child itself who supplies the drawing, so that the problem of familiarity with the object, ability to recognize pictures, and lack of match of the initial sound of the object-name with the letter learned do not exist. However, the need to infer from object-name to letter-sound, a string of abstract manipulations, is common to both the American and British approaches. Liberman and her colleagues (Liberman, 1973; Liberman, Shankweiler, Fischer, & Carter, 1974; Liberman, Shankweiler, Liberman, Fowler, & Fischer, 1977) found that even the simpler subskill of segmenting spoken words into phonemes causes difficulty. Pursuing in addition a many-staged inferential operation at an age when inferential ability is often not yet fully developed (Kuenne, 1946) may prove extremely difficult for many five-to-six-year-olds. Furthermore, the final product is an abstract entity, namely, an isolated letter sound. It is this fact which gives some scholars special reason for concern because, according to them, isolated letter sounds do not exist in speech (i.e., Goodman, 1964; Gibson & Levin, 1975).

The Philippine primer approaches these extremely complicated issues in an entirely different way. Here letter sounds are not abstract entities laboriously derived by way of inference from existing words. Instead a meaningful sound closely connected to a child's interests and daily experiences comes first. Only when that sound has been savored in different guises and used with zest in a variety of situations (Nooraihan and Urbano, 1967) is it translated into a symbol. A letter or letter combination thus directly represents a familiar meaningful sound. Moreover, experience has shown that the more closely the meaning of a particular sound is associated with areas of interest to school beginners, the better are the letter symbols representing that sound retained.

When working on these problems in the late 1950s the present author and her colleagues were surprised by a dramatic drop in difficulty children were experiencing in learning the Hebrew letter "p" when the sound association was changed from a cork popping out of a bottle to a disgruntled truck driver blowing his horn. This, despite the fact that bottles had been made to pop right in class, while the driver blowing his horn was shown only as picture.

Previously the special difficulty in learning "p" had been attributed to intrinsic difficulties connected with this letter. Hebrew P changes form when it is the final letter in a word (from פ to ף). In addition the symbol for "p" also serves as "f" on deletion of a single dot (p = פּ f = פ). This experience should not be erroneously misinterpreted to mean that the idiosyncrasies of the Hebrew "p" do not pose very real problems for beginning readers. All it is meant to show is that by finding an association with special appeal to typical six-year-olds an objective difficulty was considerably reduced. This takes us back to one of the basic premises of this book, namely, that the task faced by a beginning reader should not be conceived as a naturalistic situation in which he/she flounders unaided. It is the responsibility of the educator, and it should most certainly be within the educator's capacity to restructure the situation in such a way as to make it more easily manageable.

Examples of meaningful letter-sound associations can be found closer to home than in a Philippine primer or old Israeli educational experiment. On browsing through the absolutely breathtaking array of offerings educational publishers exhibited at a recent Annual Convention of the International Reading Association, the author came face to face with a display of "wall sound cards" of the Open Court Publishing Company. There on the panel were colorful action pictures representing sound associations of the English language. Underneath each was a list of all the main graphemes or grapheme-combinations by which that particular phoneme of the English language could be represented. Nor were the associations any less ingenious than the foreign ones. Here *m m m* was not the hum of an airplane, but the appreciative humming of a little girl licking an ice cream cone while *sss* was associated with air escaping from a flat tire rather than with "a little morning chore." The captions under the picture of an angrily roaring lion were: r, wr, er, ir, ur. Nor was the interest of young children in airplanes overlooked only, in this case, the noise of the engine was associated with the letter v. We shall return to the question of whether it is possible to map sound-symbol relationships adequately in English in Chapter Seven.

What is at issue here was that particular approaches to introducing sound-symbol relationships seem to be influenced more by local educational traditions than by rational decisions based on awareness of all possible alternatives. That this would be so even in regard to so basic and universal an issue as the one discussed here seems rather surprising.

Moreover, the divergencies in traditions we have come up against seem to go back a long way. An early example of introducing letters via meaningful sounds is a recently published facsimile edition of a 1741 primer dedicated to Maria Theresa's first-born son who, in time, became Emperor Joseph II (Antesperg, 1741, 1980). The slim volume was originally published in Vienna. Dedicating it to the little prince and future sovereign who, at that time, was only three years old, was one way of ensuring its widespread use. In fact its contents show clearly that the book was intended mainly for the general public (Mraz, 1980).

The book opens with colored picture plates introducing the letters of the alphabet each with appropriate verse and illustration. Also here associations are *meaningful sound* associations. For instance "When the boy sings he crieth a, a, a."[5] Or a picture of a mother holding out an apple to two of her offspring—"When mother asks who wants the apple the children say i, i, i."

Contemporary approaches in English-speaking countries also seem rooted in old traditions. A recent collection of early eighteenth century English nursery rhymes (Opie & Opie, 1980) includes several alphabets. In each of them letters are related to object names rather than to sounds.

Let us now sum up. The two issues discussed in this chapter showed that the often repeated assertion that phonics-focused beginning reading instruction necessarily mitigates against attention to meaning is without factual foundation. There is no contradiction between letter-pattern controlled sequential instruction and narrative action-type stories. Nor need the acquisition of sound-symbol relationships be an exercise in abstraction, or deal with meaningless units.

---

[5] Freely translated from German.

CHAPTER 7

The Special Case of English

English is frequently cited as an example of a language in which the apparent inconsistencies of translating speech to writing and vice versa create much hardship for a beginning reader. Consequently, there is a tendency to assume that learning to decode English is fraught with more difficulty than learning to decode most other languages. The present chapter examines the validity of this claim.

BEGINNING READERS VERSUS THE IDIOSYNCRASIES OF THEIR MOTHER TONGUE—PERTINENT CASES

It is relatively easy to achieve literacy in languages in which translation from writing to speech is predictable (Hildreth, 1965, 1966, 1968; Downing, 1973; Venezky, 1973; Malmquist & Grundin, 1980); German, Russian, Armenian, Hebrew, Arabic, and especially Finnish are among the alphabetic languages which are mentioned in support of this assertion. It may therefore come as a surprise to learn that reading in Finnish is not all clear sailing, especially in terms of the beginner.

The often lauded, nearly one-to-one, correspondence between phonemes and graphemes in Finnish (Malmquist & Grundin, 1980) developed only in the nineteenth century (Kyöstiö, 1973). In the sixteenth century, when the earliest books were printed, Finnish writing was still highly irregular. The sound /K/, for example, was written in eight different ways (Kyöstiö, 1980). Moreover, even present day "regular" Finnish writing may well pose problems for beginning readers that scholars in other countries are not aware of. Not only are there more diphthongs in Finnish than in any other European language, but the duration of long vowels and geminated consonants—of which there are a great many—is very important. Kyöstiö (1980) illustrates this with the following examples in which each word has a *different* meaning—*tule, tulee,* and *tullee* (all derived from the verb "come"—*tulla*) and *tuule, tuulee,* and *tuullee* (derived from the verb "blow"—*tuulla*). Also, Finnish words generally consist of a relatively large number of syllables. In fact, according to Kyöstiö (1980) there are only about 50 monosyllabic words in Finnish. This is a consequence of the fact that Finnish is a highly inflected language, in which semantic information is conveyed by adding suffixes to a core. Thus the average Finnish word contains considerably more semantic information than the average English one. For instance, three English words "in my house," become, in Finnish *talossani* (*talo* means "house") (Björnsson, 1983). It would seem that the particular characteristics of Finnish orthography impose a need for absolute accuracy already at the initial stages of learning to decode, as mere approximations could pervert the meaning of even relatively simple passages.

Rewriting an English paragraph in Finnish requires about one-quarter more space (Kyöstiö, 1980). In purely quantitative terms (assuming for a moment all else was equal), a Finnish beginning reader would thus have to put in a quarter more effort than an English one in order to arrive at the same message. Furthermore, in Finnish all elements of the word convey essential information. The additional quantity is thus not a matter of increased redundancy, and consequently cannot be considered to aid reading as redundancy per se supposedly does (Gibson & Levin, 1975; Adams, 1981).

Before we turn to the example of a further language—German—a word of warning may be in order. It is well known that it is exceedingly tricky to try to compare various aspects of different languages with each other. Thus any statement purporting to claim that the orthography of one language is more (or less) "transparent" than that of another, or that grammatical structures in one language are more "complex" than in the next would need substantiation much beyond the scope of the present discussion. Nothing of the kind is implied here. We are not discussing languages per se, but viewing them solely through the eyes of school beginners. This, in order to alert readers who are familiar mainly with English to the fact that from the point of view of six-year-olds trying to access their first written language, different languages pose a variety of obstacles native speakers of English may not be aware of.

Returning to German, from the examples of the Viennese approaches in Chapters Four and Six it might seem that in German there is a perfect one-to-one correspondence between sounds and symbols. Actually matters are a bit more complicated. German phonemes are represented relatively frequently by letter combinations rather than by single letters. This means that certain letters are sounded in more than one way. The consonant "s" is a case in point.

Like in English double "s" indicates a sharper sibilant than a single "s". When "ch" is appended to "s", the combination—"sch"—is sounded like the English "sh". However, "st" and "sp" are pronounced "scht" and "schp" without the "ch" being added. As if all this were not enough, "ch" is also a digraph in its own right, representing a German speech sound entirely different from "sch" (as well as from its English counterpart). Even the vowel "a", introduced as second or third letter in the two programs described in Chapters Four and Six, is not as unambiguous as it might appear from the examples there. Besides its simple sound value (ä) used in those sequences (i.e. MAMA, AM), "a" can be sounded in several other ways. When "a" is followed by "u" it becomes the diphthong "au", as in *Auto, Aufgabe* or *baut*. When it is followed by "i" it is pronounced "ei", a phoneme which can also be written another way: "ei". Followed by "h", "a" sometimes turns into a long vowel sound in which the "h" is silent, as in *Hahn,* or *Ahne*. However, at other times an "h" which follows an "a" is sounded, as in *Ahorn* (the name of a tree) or *Aha* (an exclamation). With the addition of two dots above it "a" becomes the "Umlaut ä as in the plurals of *Wand* (wall)—*Wände;* or *Mann* (man)— *Männer*.

The last example illustrates that also in terms of language usages, German can be far from simple. For example instead of denoting plural by merely adding "s" as in most English nouns, plural in German assumes a variety of forms. The addition of an "n" to *Tasche* (pocket)— *Taschen;* an "e" to *Tisch* (table)—*Tische;* an "er" to *Mann* (man)—*Männer;* and an "en" to *Frau* (woman)—*Frauen,* illustrate this. At times the change to plural also affects the vowel *Baum* (tree)—*Bäume* or only the vowel *Garten* (garden)—*Gärten*. At other times the vowel remains intact, as in some of the previous examples. Sometimes nouns do not change at all, and what does change is only the article preceding the noun, that is, *das Mädchen* (singular)—*die Mädchen* (plural). More confusing still is that in German the change to plural can change the gender denoting definite article—"der Mann"—"die Männer." Altogether there are three gender-bound, definite articles—"der", "die", "das"—instead of the simple all-encompassing English "the." There are also masculine and feminine/indefinite articles—"ein" and "eine"—for the English "a." Besides three genders, four cases which affect word endings are another cause for difficulty in accurately deriving meaning from context at an age when faultless use of the language is normally not yet fully developed. For instance, instead of the simple personal pronoun "you" a speaker of German has to steer an accurate course, employing three forms of one pronoun: *du; dir; dich*. The consequence of all this is that written German sentences may well be phonemically much less predictable for German six-year-olds than comparable sentences for English-speaking ones.

Presumably, therefore, German-speaking school beginners may have to rely more on their ability to decode accurately in order to arrive at meaning. On the other hand, semantic predictability could aid an English child to access phonemic form. As in Finnish, the idiosyncrasies of German grammar also require attention to detail and accuracy in decoding, as gender and case often cause words to differ by only a single letter. A further difficulty for German school beginners is that German syntax is very convoluted. By English standards German sentences tend to be inordinately long, in addition to often not opening with a subject. In addition, German words are longer than English ones (Björnsson, 1983). For instance, bookings for the Seventh World Congress on Reading which met in Hamburg were handled by the 23-letter "Fremdenverkehrszentrale." It could be argued that this example is not particularly pertinent. After all, first graders do not normally attend scholarly conferences on reading. But most everyone would agree that "Tiergarten" would seem more of a puzzler to a child than "zoo," especially when one notes that the first "e" is silent while the second is not and that the letter "t" appears in both upper and lower case. The above list is by no means a full inventory of potential difficulties a beginning reader faces when learning to decode German. It is intended only as an example of a few of the problems a beginner will have to cope with when learning to read.

Let us turn now to the example of Hebrew, a non-European language noted for especially consistent symbol-sound relationships. Based on this criterion alone Hebrew far outstrips German, and is close to Finnish. In fact only two Hebrew consonants and two Hebrew vowels correspond to more than one sound, and each of these can be read in only two ways. However, considering only symbol-sound relationships creates a deceptively simple and wholly unrealistic picture of the tasks faced by a beginning reader in Hebrew. Contrary to Finnish, symbol-sound and sound-symbol relationships in Hebrew are not symmetric. Though most graphemes correspond to only one phoneme the reverse is not true, and in many cases a phoneme can be represented in more than one way. For example, there are two symbols for the sound "t", two for "s", and two for "k." Also, there are five consonants that change form when they are the final letter of a word, meaning again that in each case a phoneme is represented by at least two symbols. To compound matters, there is some overlap between these two categories. Thus, one of the two "k" letters is also among those which change at the end of a word. There are four consonant symbols that have two sounds each with only a single dot indicating which of the two is meant (פ = p; פ = f; ב = b; ב = v; כ = k; כ = ch; שׁ = sh; שׂ = s). To further complicate matters, two of these consonant symbols (פ and כ) are again among the five which change form when used at the end of a word, while the sound of two others is represented also by another symbol (s by ס and v by ו). However, ו also changes into two different vowels depending on whether or not a dot is added above or beside (וֹ = o; וּ = oo). Again, each of these vowel sounds is also represented by another symbol.

Except for readers well conversant with Hebrew, all others are probably utterly confused by now. Yet the ground covered so far has been only a very superficial account of a few of the intricate symbol-sound relationships in Hebrew which, while evidently quite complicated, are still highly consistent and therefore presumably predictable. Predictable to the initiated, one should hasten to add, hardly to a beginner.

Primers can sequence instruction in such a way that consistencies stand out. Left to themselves, beginning readers in Hebrew could well feel that sound-symbol relationships are highly spurious. It has been my experience that student-teachers are frequently quite surprised when first told that symbol-sound correspondences in Hebrew are considered exceptionally consistent. Often they tend to debate the matter, because when they studied Hebrew grammar in the course of their own education they tended to feel on unsure ground and confused. Actually, one reason teachers tend to omit vowels when writing on the blackboard (see further on) is that they are afraid that they might make a mistake. Transposed to English, this would be like saying that the system is so ambiguous that, except for specialists, hardly anyone feels that he/she is able to spell correctly.

A further source of considerable difficulty for beginning readers is that contrary to the Roman alphabet, vowels in Hebrew are infrequently placed beside consonants. Instead they are sometimes above and most often below them. Also, vowels are usually much smaller than consonants, and are mainly combinations of dots. Thus three dots below a consonant can be either "e" or "oo" depending on configuration (ֶ versus ֻ). Two horizontal dots below a consonant are also "ë" while two vertical dots are sometimes "ë" and sometimes silent (*shwa* is one of the two vowels which correspond to two sounds). According to its location a single dot can have eight different vocal connotations, serving among other things as two vowels ("ee" when below a consonant, and "o" when above and to the left of one).

Vowels are usually omitted in everyday writing and in printed matter intended for facile readers of Hebrew. Consequently, prereaders are not automatically exposed to vowels every time they encounter print. This in turn might lead to a predisposition to disregard vowels. However, vowels are of crucial importance in the early stages of reading acquisition. Altogether, it is hardly surprising, that vowel errors are the most common type of miscues among first graders (Cohen, 1975).

We have already seen that in both Finnish and German, relative ease or difficulty of access to written language seems to depend not only on symbol-sound correspondences but also on additional factors. The same is true of Hebrew. Like Finnish and Latin and unlike English, Hebrew is an inflected language in which information about tense, gender, mode, possession, relations, and so on is indicated by prefixes, suffixes, and vowel changes. Most often a so-called root combination of three letters provides part of the semantic information, while the rest is indicated by auxiliary letters before, after, or sometimes interspersed with the root letters. Thus three discreet words in English—boy, girl, children—are in Hebrew variations of the verb to bear children—יֶלֶד, יַלְדָּה, יְלָדִים (yeled, yaldah, yeladim). The adjective "childish," nouns like "childhood" and "midwife," as well as declinations of the verb "to bear" indicating past, present, or future performance by the person who bore the child, by the child born, or even by the male progenitor of said child, are all derived from the same verb, and contain the three identical "root" letters. In such circumstances deriving meaning necessitates not only complete accuracy in decoding but also sophisticated language knowledge.

Short auxiliary words like "and", "to", "from", "in", and "the" are also denoted by single-letter prefixes. Once again. we have a situation in which a single word contains much more semantic information than in English, though, with vowels seldomly taking up space of their own, words are also more condensed, and a Hebrew text is approximately a third shorter than its English translation. What effect this has on reading processes has not yet been studied. Clearly, even voweled Hebrew lacks redundancy, while redundancy is believed to facilitate reading in English (Adams, 1981). It should be remembered that our description so far pertains exclusively to beginning readers. Printed matter intended for facile readers consists entirely of consonant strings, and so not only lacks redundancy but even withholds essential information, as one and the same consonant sequence can represent different words, that is shmsh (שמש) could be shemesh—sun, shamash—attendant, and many forms of the verb "to use."

Without having fully covered the idiosyncrasies of Hebrew ortography, let us now touch briefly on one other language—Arabic. Arabic is a further language which has been mentioned by researchers in relation to the assumption that its regularity would make for ease in learning to read (Hildreth, 1965). Yet native speakers of Arabic point to a very long list of potential difficulties which, in their opinion, make learning to read in Arabic exceedingly difficult.

Arabic, like Hebrew, is a Semitic language, and both share many common features, the first and foremost being that they are not written in Roman characters. This, at least, is one area in which comparative data is already available, and it is generally assumed that "because of their simplicity and the ease with which they can be written and read, Latin characters are used more widely than any others" (Gray, 1956, p. 39). German is a good example for the seemingly universal tendency to adopt the Latin alphabet. During the first third of this century, German was still widely written in Gothic characters.

There are many additional complexities in Arabic. In Hebrew only five consonants change form when they are the last letter of a word. In Arabic most consonants have four different forms, depending on whether they are written by themselves or occur in the initial, medial, or final position in a word. Also, in Arabic writing letters are joined to each other even in print, reminding one of cursive English. Over the years, many Arabic letters have become so similar that today they are distinguished mainly by diacritical markings. For instance, there are five consonants which in the initial position share the same character and are told apart only by dots above or below this identical symbol (b = ﹾ ; n = ﻨ ; y = ﻲ ; t = ﻨﺗ; th = ﺜ). The same is true for additional groups of consonants. Short vowels in Arabic are written above and below consonants along with the diacritical marks which distinguish consonants from each other. Thus, Arabic writing resembles at first glance a series of intricately interwoven lines with a host of tiny satellites above and below. Moreover, because in Arabic, like in Hebrew, the vowels are eventually omitted, exposure to everyday reading matter does not automatically familiarize preschoolers with the medium they will acquire in school. A further major obstacle for beginning readers in Arabic is that literate Arabic differs greatly from local colloquial speech. Not only are there variations in the way letters are pronounced, but many words are entirely different. Even a simple everyday expression like the imperative "go!" is "rooch" (RŪḤ) in conversational Arabic, but "ith'hab" (IDHAB) in literary language.

It seems that the oft reiterated belief that, compared to other languages, learning to read English is especially difficult is in need of reexamination. While it is true that symbol-sound relationships in English are more complex than in some other orthographies, idiosyncrasies of other languages may create difficulties for beginners that scholars not intimately acquainted with them may be ignorant of. So far, comparative research in this area has been mainly descriptive, and studies which truly compare the relative ease or difficulty of pertinent variables at the very initial stages of learning to read are lacking. In this respect, superficial observations by outsiders who sometimes do not even speak the language may prove misleading. Gibson and Levin (1975) comment critically on a series of articles in which Hildreth (1965; 1966; 1968) blithely described reading instruction in Arabic, Armenian, and Russian, based, in each case, on visits to a single school where she did not understand the language of instruction.

Let us now proceed to the second topic of this chapter—the question of whether or not learning to decode in English is indeed as difficult as is often implied.

THE BEGINNING DECODER AND ENGLISH ORTHOGRAPHY

The assertion that the "irregular" character of English orthography causes hardship is far from new. As early as 1551, John Hart suggested that changes were necessary (Gillooly, 1971). In this, Hart was but one in a long list of would-be reformers, who proposed more or less wide sweeping changes of English writing. Some of the other well-known names associated with proposals for spelling reforms are William Thornton, Edwin Leigh, Alexander John Ellis, Bernard Shaw, Sir Isaac Pitman, and his grandson Sir James Pitman, and Mont Follick. The purported aim of many of these crusaders for spelling reform was to rectify what they saw as the deficiencies of the English writing system which they tended to catalogue in great detail.

One by-product of the agitation for spelling reform has been that the many ways in which English spelling deviates from easily predictable symbol-sound relationships has today become a matter of general knowledge and concern. Especially ludicrous examples are often cited in popular as well as professional literature. Take, for instance, Shaw's tongue-in-cheek assertion that the transliteration "ghoti" represents the sounds of the word "fish" (Tauber, 1965), or a remark on page 86 of the highly serious Bullock Report (Bullock, 1975) which states that, according to spelling conventions that "are common enough in English orthography," the word "chemist" could be rendered "calmbost." Wijk (1977) calls these and similar examples "grotesque" (p. 13), maintaining that they are in no way typical of the "traditional orthographical system" (p. 13) but were obtained by joining together exceptional spellings for various speech sounds. Nor can they serve as faithful illustrations of the difficulties which confront children who are learning to read" (p. 13). Substituting an "o" for a short "i" in "chemist," for instance, is based solely on the word "women" and can in no conceivable way be called a "common enough spelling convention" in English orthography (Wijk, 1977, p. 13). Nor is it, one would assume, an association which would readily come to the mind of a five- or six-year-old. Some of the examples used by present-day psycholinguists seem similarly far-fetched in connection with school beginners. Goodman's (1969) use of verb-noun pairs, like produce/prodúce, cóntract/contráct, récord/recórd to illustrate his contention about the lack of correspondence between words and morphemes is such an example.

The question which ought to be asked instead is how difficult is English orthography, actually, in terms of school beginners who are fluent speakers of the language? Unfortunately, there is no objective, cut-and-dried answer to this question. Furthermore, the problem has seldom been examined dispassionately in its own right. Usually, highflowing rhetoric with emotional overtones and preconceived notions seems to have prevented a thorough discussion of available evidence. Also, there has been a tendency to confuse matters further by including issues which have no direct bearing on the main point. Let us not forget that, in the present context, the question is not how adequate or inadequate a representation of spoken language English orthography is. Nor are we concerned with the problem of teaching children to spell correctly.

The following discussion will be mainly inferential, as empirical research isolating and comparing the relative difficulty of subvariables in different orthographies is still in a very early stage. Even so, the discussion in the first section of this chapter established that at least in the areas of visual, syntactic, and semantic clues a beginning reader in English might well have to contend with fewer difficulties than a beginner in, say, Finnish, German, Hebrew, or Arabic. The special difficulty ascribed to beginning reading in English is related to one area and one area only, so-called "phonemic irregularities" of English orthography. It is this area of English orthography which will concern us in the remainder of this chapter.

Over the years there have been recurrent attempts to introduce order and system into the array of sound-symbol relationships a beginning reader has to master in English. It is possible to roughly group these attempts under three general headings: (a) transitional mediums; (b) the use of diacritical marking systems; and (c) sequencing instruction so that for the most part only regular spelling patterns will be encountered in the early stages.

Some of the proposed approaches have included elements from two or all three of these options. To fully cover the history and details of attempts to systematize beginning reading instruction in English would require a volume of its own. Here a brief and, alas, superficial discussion will have to suffice.

Transitional Mediums

Language and spelling reforms have taken place from time to time in many countries. The introduction of the Latin alphabet in Turkey and simplifications of Russian spelling and of Chinese characters are among this century's better-known cases. In other instances changes were more gradual and less extreme, like, for instance, emerging differences between English and American spelling. Permanent reforms of this kind are not our concern here as, by and large, there seems to be a consensus that for mature readers the advantages of English writing outweigh purported disadvantages (Chomsky & Halle, 1968; Gillooly, 1971; Gibson & Levin, 1975; Barnitz, 1978; Balmuth, 1982).

In the present context, "transitional mediums" mean only proposals for the temporary use of modified orthographies in order to aid reading acquisition during the initial stages of learning. Unfortunately, this distinction is sometimes overlooked, and in the resulting confusion, the discussion turns to the question of whether present-day English spelling is adequate in its own right and to a listing of its purported advantages or disadvantages, instead of focusing on the main issue, namely, whether transitional scripts help beginning readers master the intricacies of English orthography and whether the use of these scripts has negative side effects? Worse still, despite the huge sums of money and relentless effort which have been devoted to reading research in English-speaking countries, detailed proposals for temporary learning mediums seem to have been based mainly on intuitive guessing instead of on well-planned investigations.

The "initial teaching alphabet" (i.t.a.), developed by Sir James Pitman, is at present the most widely known proposal for a transitional alphabet and can therefore serve as a pertinent example. The research connected with i.t.a. in both Great Britain (i.e., Downing, 1965; Warburton & Southgate, 1969) and the United States (i.e., Kirkland, 1968; Tanyzer, Alpert, & Sandel, 1968; Mazurkiewicz, 1968) dealt exclusively with efforts to evaluate the achievements of pupils taught by this new medium. The medium itself, however, was designed solely according to linguistic calligraphic, typographic, and financial considerations (Pitman, 1968). Thus, decisions on the shapes of the 20 new characters (the so-called "augmentations") and all further details were purely theoretical. No effort was invested in trying to establish whether the proposed letter shapes and correspondences were the best possible solutions in terms of the learning capabilities of typical five- to six-year-olds.

The simplicity and low cost of experiments which could supply information on issues like these make one wonder why tremendously expensive projects such as the development and field testing of i.t.a. were not preceded by fact-finding explorations. We shall return to this issue later in this chapter. At present the thing to note is that the designers of i.t.a. felt that by adding only 20 symbols they could reduce the vagrancies of English orthography to the extent of transforming it to one of regularized symbol-sound relationships. Interestingly enough, other attempts to modify English writing by maximizing letter sound correspondence also rely on adding relatively few new symbols. UNIFON, for instance, makes do with a total of 40 letters (Malone, 1962; Malone, 1965), the "fonetik alfabet," devised by Davis (1963; 1965), with 31, and the alphabet proposed by the non-profit Fonetic English Spelling Association (1418 Lake Street, Evanston, Illinois 60204) with only 29 (Aukerman, 1971, p. 374).

A slightly different approach to simplifying the task faced by beginning readers in English by modifying orthography during the initial learning period is the one proposed by Wijk (1959; 1977). Wijk does not suggest adding letters to the existing alphabet, but simply that irregular spellings be regularized during the period in which children are learning to read.[6] According to Wijk, this would "make it possible for them to concentrate on mastering the regular phonic units of the spelling system before attempting to learn the numerous exceptions to it" (Wijk, 1977, p. 18). Wijk feels that some of the proposals for spelling reforms are far too radical, and therefore, have not succeeded in arousing interest. Instead, the modifications he proposes would make it possible to retain present spelling in over 90 percent of the vocabulary. For example: *"Regularized Inglish* iz a spelling system for Inglish in which aull the irregular spellings in traditional orthografy hav been temporarily eliminated and replaced by regular wuns in order to make it easier for children to lern to read" (Wijk, 1977, p. 41). In order to prove the practical value of his proposal Wijk developed outlines for an instructional scheme in which "phonic units" are introduced in orderly sequence. From the very beginning "phonic units" are combined to form meaningful words which are followed soon by phrases, simple sentences, and connected texts (Wijk, 1972, 1974; Wijk, Cross, Oakensen, Reed, & Tudor-Hart, undated). Wijk's proposals were not tried out during his lifetime. Consequently, their feasibility remains unknown. This situation illustrates a major obstacle to meaningful research in the area of transitional alphabets designed to aid beginning reading. The fiscal burden of developing and publishing reading materials in a new medium is usually far beyond the means at the disposal of run-of-the-mill investigators.

---

[6] A similar approach was used by Frank C. Laubach when in the later part of his career he turned his attention also to reading instruction in English. Laubach, who is best known for the slogan "each one teach one" is credited with having developed teaching devices in 312 different languages and bringing literacy to millions (Aukerman, 1971). In the initial stage of his English scheme Laubach uses a strictly phonemic spelling system which he labeled "Thu new Ingglish Fonetic Alfubet" (Aukerman, 1971, p. 354). Superficially it seems that Laubach's spelling system deviates more from traditional English spelling than Wijk's.

Therefore, it is only in truly exceptional circumstances, such as those accompanying the birth of i.t.a., that the applicability of such proposals can be tested. Consequently, it is not necessarily the best possible proposals which will get the chance of a test-run.

Wijk (1977) tried to anticipate some of the objections that proposals for transitional orthographies seem to arouse. A critique often leveled at modified alphabets is that the transition to traditional orthography will be difficult for the learner. This contention is not based on research evidence. Follow-up studies of children who were initially taught by i.t.a. report that the transition to traditional orthography did not cause a setback (i.e. Hayes & Wuest, 1968; Kirkland, 1968).

Another possible way to increase the predictability of English writing is to add diacritical marks which are later phased out.

Diacritical Marking Systems

Diacritical marking systems and auxiliary typographical devices were widely used before the advent of "modern" primers and readers. It is of interest that diacritical marks and other supposedly helpful devices, for instance, syllabification, were also popular in languages with consistent symbol-sound correspondences. Moreover, contemporary beginners' materials obtained from Finland and Vienna indicate that in both places such devices are still in vogue. Kyöstyiö (1980) reports that "a typical feature of Finnish pre-primers is that they are printed in capital letters and the words are divided into syllables with a hyphen" (p. 39). In part one of *Frohes Lernen* (Kunschak et al., 1978), at present a widely used beginner's text in Vienna, small inverted arcs below diphtongs and digraphs indicate that they should be pronounced as one speech sound and not as single letters following upon each other (see Figures 7.1 and 7.2). Once a letter combination has been introduced in this way the arc is dropped. Another device is the printing of silent letters in grey to indicate that they should not be sounded (see Figure 7.3). Apparently this practice seems particularly useful to Viennese reading specialists, as it is used in most beginners' texts this author has come across, all the way back to the 1920s.

The Finnish and Viennese practices described here are of special interest in that they indicate that educators in both countries feel that in the initial learning stage orthography should be absolutely unambiguous and predictable.

Judging from recently issued facsimile editions of American texts for beginners, which in their day sold many millions of copies, diacritical marks seem to have been a familiar device also in the United States.

Figure 7.1. Inverted arcs below occurences of "ei" in text in which this diphtong is first introduced.

Reproduced from Kunschak, E., H. Rinner, H. Schraffl and W. Vavra. 1978. *Frohes Lernen*. Vienna: Österreichischer Bundesverlag für Unterricht, Wissenschaft und Kunst. pp. 34. (Original in color).

Diacritical marks were a feature of Webster's Blue-backed Speller and its many reissues. In the revised edition, of 1866 (the one facsimiled), repetitions of orthoëpical marks, as they were then called, were omitted when they seemed superfluous (Webster, 1866). Only the first occurrence of syllables and words which share the same spelling pattern are marked (see Figure 7.4). Most sections of segmented and marked words, demon-

„Kinder, ich bin bis abend nicht da.
Ich möchte Vati ein Buch kaufen.
Ich möchte Oma ein Tuch kaufen."

Susi und Martin bleiben allein.

Bald ist es dunkel.
Susi macht Licht.

Bum – bum – bum, hört man am Tor.
Soll Susi aufmachen?
Soll Martin aufmachen?

„Martin, Susi!
Macht auf!
Ich bin doch der Vati,
ich möchte hinein!"

„Du darfst herein!"

Milch
Kuchen
kochen
suchen
machen
nicht
auch

ich

. ich

. ich

. ich

m d s

ch

57

Figure 7.2.   Inverted arcs below occurences of "ch" in text in which this digraph is first introduced.

Reproduced from Kunschak, E., H. Rinner, H. Schraffl and W. Vavra. 1978. Frohes Lernen. Vienna: Österreichischer Bundesverlag für Unterricht, Wissenschaft und Kunst. pp. 57. (Original in color).

strating a particular sound pattern, are followed by a paragraph of regularly printed sentences or connected text. This indicates that the markings were meant as a short-term pedagogic device, and were discarded as soon as the new pattern was acquired.

The same rationale seems to underlie the use of diacritical marks in the 1879 edition of McGuffey's *Eclectic Readers*. Here, each lesson is preceded

Ohren	Seht den alten Mann,
Ohre	den alten Mann mit seinem Hund.
Ohr	
Oh	Der Mann ist fast blind,
O	seine Ohren sind rot,
Oh	ihm ist kalt.
Ohr	Da rennt sein Hund fort.
Ohre	Er rennt mitten auf der Fahrbahn.
Ohren	
	„Lumpi", ruft der alte Mann,
Ohr	aber Lumpi rennt und rennt.
Uhr	Autos fahren, Mopeds fahren.
mehr	Keiner hilft dem alten Mann.
sehr	Susi und Martin helfen ihm.
	Der Mann ist froh,
h	und Susi und Martin
	sind froh.

56

Figure 7.3. Silent "h" is printed consistently in grey on page on which it is introduced.

Reproduced from Kunschak, E., H. Rinner, H. Schraffl and W. Vavra. 1978. *Frohes Lernen*. Vienna: Österreichischer Bundesverlag für Unterricht, Wissenschaft und Kunst. pp. 56. (Original in color).

by a list of new graphemes and words, "marked with diacriticals" (p. 2). Multisyllabic words are segmented and the accent is indicated. The text itself which follows is printed regularly (see Figure 7.5). In each reader there is a phonic chart which illustrates the sounds of the marked letters, grouping them under appropriate headings. There are six headings and a total of only 72 items on these charts (see Figure 7.6). The combined

SPELLING BOOK.   25

MOVE, SON, WOLF, FOOT, MOON, OR; RULE, PULL; EXIST; ∈=K; ∂=J; ẹ=Z; ÇH=SH.

No. 26.—XXVI.

WORDS OF TWO SYLLABLES, ACCENTED ON THE FIRST.

bā' ker	trō ver	sō lar	wō ful	pā pal
sha dy	elo ver	po lar	po em	eō pal
la dy	do nor	lū nar	fo rum	vī al
tī dy	vā por	sō ber	Sā tan	pē nal
hō ly	fa vor	pā çer	fū el	ve nal
lī my	fla vor	ra çer	du el	fī nal
sli my	sa vor	grō çer	eru el	ō ral
bō ny	ha lo	çī der	gru el	ho ral
po ny	sō lo	spi der	pū pil	mū ral
po ker	hē ro	wā fer	lā bel	nā ṣal
tī ler	ne gro	ea per	lī bel	fa tal
eā per	tȳ ro	tī ḡer	lō eal	na tal
pa per	out go	mā ker	fo eal	ru ral
ta per	sā go	ta ker	vo eal	vī tal
vī per	tū lip	ra ker	lē gal	tō tal
bi ter	çē dar	sē ton	re gal	o val
fē ver	brī er	ru in	dī al	plī ant
ō ver	fri ar	hȳ men	tri al	ġi ant

Bakers bake bread and cakes.
I like to play in the shady grove.
Some fishes are very bony.
I love the young lady that shows me how to read.
A pony is a very little horse.
We poke the fire with the poker.
The best paper is made of linen rags.
Vipers are bad snakes, and they bite men.
An ox loves to eat clover.
The tulip is very pretty, growing in the garden.
A dial shows the hour of the day.
Cedar trees grow in the woods.
The blackberry grows on a brier.

Figure 7.4. Syllabification and diacritical marks in revised 1866 edition of Webster's Blue-backed Speller.

Reproduced from undated facsimiled edition. New York: American Book Company. pp. 25.

LESSON XII.

Kĭt′tў

nīçe

swēet

sĭng

jŭst

hăng

eāġe

thĕn

sŏng   pĕt   pụt   nŏt

k   ġ   ç   ā   ў   ng   ụ

Kitty has a nice pet. It can
sing a sweet song.
She has just fed it.
She will now put it in the
cage, and hang the cage up.
Then the cat can not catch it.

Figure 7.5.   Reading text preceded by list of new words and sounds marked with diacriticals in early part of revised 1879 edition of McGuffey's First Eclectic Reader.

Reproduced from undated facsimiled edition. New York: American Book Company. pp. 18.

PHONIC CHART.

LONG VOCALS.

ā,	as in	āte.		ẽ,	as in	ẽrr.
â,	"	eâre.		ī,	"	īçe.
ä,	"	ärm.		ō,	"	ōde.
a̖,	"	làst.		ū,	"	ūse.
a̤,	"	all.		û,	"	bûrn.
ē,	"	ēve.		o͞o,	"	fo͞ol.

SHORT VOCALS.

ă,	as in	ăm.		ŏ,	as in	ŏdd.
ĕ,	"	ĕnd.		ŭ,	"	ŭp.
ĭ,	"	ĭn.		o͝o,	"	lo͝ok.

DIPHTHONGS.

oi, oy, as in oil, boy. | ou, ow, as in out, now,

ASPIRATES.

f,	as in	fīfe.		t,	as in	tăt.
h,	"	hĭm.		sh,	"	shē
k,	"	kīte.		ch,	"	chăt.
p,	"	pīpe.		th,	"	thĭck.
s,	"	sāme.		wh,	"	whȳ.

Figure 7.6. (a and b) Phonic Chart from revised 1879 edition of McGuffey's First Eclectic Reader.

Reproduced from undated facsimiled edition. New York: American Book Company. pp. 95–96.

SUBVOCALS.

b,	as in	bĭb.		v,	as in	vălve.
d,	"	dĭd.		th,	"	thĭs.
g̃,	"	g̃ĭg̃.		z,	"	zīn̲e.
j,	"	jŭg̃.		z,	"	ăzure.
n,	"	nīne.		r,	"	râre.
m,	"	māim.		w,	"	wē.
ng,	"	hăng.		y,	"	yĕt.

l, as in lŭll.

SUBSTITUTES.

a̤,	for	ŏ,	as in	whạt.		y̆,	for ĭ, as in	my̆th.
ê,	"	â,	"	thêre.		e,	" k, "	ean.
e̱,	"	ā,	"	fe̱int.		ç,	" s, "	çīte.
ï,	"	ē,	"	polïçe.		çh,	" sh, "	çhāis̲e.
ī,	"	ē̃,	"	sīr.		eh,	" k, "	ehāos.
ȯ,	"	ŭ,	"	sȯn.		ġ,	" j, "	ġĕm.
o̱,	"	ōō,	"	to̱.		n̲,	" ng, "	īn̲k.
o̤,	"	ŏŏ,	"	wo̤lf.		s̲,	" z, "	ăs̲.
ô,	"	a̤,	"	fôrk.		s,	" sh, "	su̱re.
õ,	"	û,	"	wõrk.		x̲,	" g̃z, "	ex̲ăet.
u̱,	"	ŏŏ,	"	fu̱ll.		gh,	" f, "	läugh.
ṳ,	"	ōō,	"	rṳde.		ph,	" f, "	phlŏx.
ȳ,	"	ī,	"	flȳ.		qu,	" k, "	pïque.

qu, for kw, as in quĭt.

Figure 7.6b

expertise of the "many . . . eminent teachers and scholars" (p. 3) to whom the 1879 revision of the McGuffey Readers is attributed had apparently concluded that 72 symbol-sound relationships were all that was needed to adequately chart English orthography.

Current interest in diacritic marking is not great. Relatively many of the modern scholars who wrote on Webster's *American Spelling Book* and the *McGuffey Readers* do not refer to their use of diacritical marks (i.e. Huey, 1908/1968; Smith, 1934/1965; Fries, 1962; Mathews, 1966; Gibson & Levin, 1975). Among these authors Huey (1908/1968) alone brings up the issue of auxiliary markings in its own right. Possibly, because in his day they were still in use.

Presently the topic of diacritical markings is associated mainly with a proposal by Fry (1964) and the *Distar* (Direct Systems for Teaching Arithmetic and Reading) Program (Engelman & Bruner, 1974).

The objective of the Diacritical Marking System proposed by Fry (1964) is to regularize orthography for beginning reading instruction while at the same time preserving the "basic word form" (p. 527) in order to facilitate later transition to the traditional alphabet. Fry feels that the actual marks used should be very simple so that children could recognize and write them easily. As reading materials are often prepared by teachers themselves, he chose marks which can be made on any standard typewriter. Briefly, they are: a slash mark for silent letters (i.e., writé), a horizontal bar over long vowels, a horizontal bar under *both* letters of digraphs, asterisks to indicate exceptions, no mark for regular consonants and short vowels, and a few other symbols (see Figure 7.7).

Fry's proposal is based on the assumption that the marks would facilitate incidental phoneme-grapheme learning. Therefore, whole texts would be printed with marks which would be "vanished" gradually "as the reading habit is established" (Fry, 1964, p. 527). Also, in Distar the auxiliary system is used in printing *whole* texts. The marks used are different from Fry's and essentially more accentuated so that word form is, in fact, partly changed (see Figure 7.8). For instance, silent letters are indicated by reduced letter size, and bars above long vowels are large an strongly marked.

In contrast to Distar and Fry's system, auxiliary markings in the Viennese Program seem hardly noticeable. Also, once a spelling pattern has been initially introduced, it is printed without marks when it comes up

DMS Specimen

The Littlé Red Hen

Once upon a timé Littlé Red Hen livéd in a barn with hér fivé chiçks. A pig, a cat, and a duçk madé theír homé in the samé barn. Eách day the littlé red hen led hér chiçks out to look for food. But the pig, the cat, and the duçk woúld not look for food.

Figure 7.7.   Text in diacritical marking system proposed by Fry.

Reproduced from Fry, E. B. 1964. A diacritical marking system to aid beginning reading instruction. *Elementary English* 41:526–529; 537.

rēₐd the Ītems

1. when the tēₐcher says "do it," touch your fēēt.
2. when the tēₐcher stands up, hōld up your hands.

jill and her sister

this is the story of a girl nāmₑd jill and her sister. jill trĪₑd to do thiñgs, but her sister did not trȳ.

jill said, "I can not rĪdₑ a bĪkₑ, but I will trȳ."

what did jill sāy?

her sister said, "I can not rĪdₑ, but I do not lĪkₑ to trȳ."

Figure 7.8.   Diacritical markings in typical text page in second edition of Distar Reading II Storybook 1.

Reproduced from Engelmann, S. and E. C. Bruner. 1975. Distar Reading II Storybook 1. Story 19. pp. 36.

again. It would seem that Viennese graphic techniques are more in keeping with the avowed aims of diacritical marking systems, namely, the addition of phonemic information with the least possible distortion of traditional script.

It should not be too difficult to experiment with several alternatives of diacritical marking systems so that future proposals could be based on hard data rather than on a priori decisions. For instance, the three options for indicating silent letters we have come across so far—using grey instead of black, putting a slash mark through the letter, and reducing letter size—could be compared in otherwise unchanged learning situations. Experimental investigations of this kind would indicate clearly which of the three options leads to the best results.

Sequenced Instruction Emphasizing Regularities

Another way to deal with the problem posed by the inconsistency of symbol-sound relationships in English orthography is to limit initial texts to a consistent use of spelling patterns. Bloomfield (1942) and Fries (1962) are probably the best known proponents of this approach. The opinions of Bloomfield and Fries, both noted linguists in their day, are very different from those of many present-day psycholinguists. We shall therefore refrain from using the term "linguistic" in reference to reading theories or programs, and, instead, identify them by their originators. In his exposition on the specific virtues and problems of English writing, Fries (1962) shows that in contrast to artificial alphabets, "practical alphabets for the general reading of languages cannot hope to be 'phonetic'" (p. 160). That is, they cannot aspire to a one-to-one match between letters and sounds in the sense that there is only one letter symbol for each phoneme and only one phoneme for each letter symbol. When judging written languages only by this criterion, some are "well spelled," while others are "less well" or even "rather poorly" spelled (p. 161). Fries feels that Finnish tops the list of the well spelled languages. English, on the other hand, "is very distinctly less well spelled than most of the languages using the Greco-Roman alphabet" (Fries, 1962, p. 161). Fries insists, though, that inconsistencies in English are not so severe that they would make one forego the advantages of an alphabetic system. What one must recognize as far as English is concerned, is that single letters do not match single sound features, but that "word-patterns", that is, sequences of phonemes, are represented by "spelling patterns"— sequences of letters (p. 169). According to Fries two major sets of spelling patterns cover "a large part of the active practices of English spelling" (p. 180). The reader has to learn to recognize these at high speed.

Other spelling patterns have much more limited application. Fries thus distinguishes clearly between the range of spelling patterns a mature reader must know, and those sufficient in the early stages. It may well be that the lack of such a distinction is at the root of some of the prevalent confusions and conflicting opinions about the degree of predictability of English orthography. Major scholarly undertakings, like Venezky's (1970) computer-aided mapping of the eventualities of English writing, which resulted in 79 pages of rules, were in the first place never conceived as proposed curricula for beginners. Approaches which emphasize regularities in beginning reading instruction are often based on a surprisingly small array of basic facts. Yet these cover a wide range of the combinations a beginning reader is likely to encounter in the early stages of instruction. The *New Primary Grades Reading System* developed by Beck and Mitroff (1972), relies, on a sequence of 61 symbols or symbol combinations which children acquire at a fairly rapid rate in individualized classroom settings. *Language in Action* (Morris, 1974) acquaints beginners with the "44 speech sounds" of British English (Morris, 1984, p. 16).

The *abc-dabr* a program (Oliver, Nicholson, Jantzi, & Tanner, 1981) assumes that by the end of the first grade "many of the children will be reading fairly fluently" by way of a primarily synthetic phonemic approach based on 42 sounds (Oliver et al., 1981, p. 5). The *Super Sounder System* (Craig, 1977) introduces children to the 15 vowel sounds heard in Midwestern speech by way of a fanciful story about fairies, elves, and "vowel city," where vowels and diphthongs reside in 15 houses strategically placed along four streets. Street names remind children of vowel characteristics, that is, Long Street and Short Street. In the *Headway Program* of the Open Court Publishing Company, children learn 95 spellings "for the 42 main sounds of English," progressing before long from there to "authentic literature" (Open Court Educator, 1980, p. 8). Children in the *Lippincott Basic Reading* (1975) program are introduced to 103 sound symbols and exposed to over 2,000 regularly spelled words during their first year at school (Osborn, 1977).

It is important to realize that when native speakers learn to read their own language, they will automatically arrive at the accepted pronunciation of familiar words once foundations for reading habits are laid (Chomsky, 1979b). The well-known tendency of young children to "regularize" the pronunciation of unfamiliar words they come across is an example of this ability. Exemplifying this tendency is the fact that mature readers of Hebrew often tend to mispronounce transcribed, foreign, proper names according to Hebrew grammatical usage. It ought to be remembered that due to the omission of vowels and other markings, the pronunciation of Hebrew writing is so ambiguous that proposals for a reform of Hebrew spelling and even the possible adoption of Roman letters have been continuously debated since the last century when the everyday use of Hebrew was revived (Rabin, 1977; Avinor, 1980). In fact, one of the early proponents of a switch to the Latin alphabet was Itamar Ben-Avi, the first-born of Eliezer Ben-Jehuda, the reviver of Hebrew. Ben-Avi was known throughout his life as the first child in modern times to be raised entirely in Hebrew. Yet it was he who pointed out that Hebrew writing was inadequate for contemporary needs (Fellman, 1979).

This author has special reason to be aware of the fact that generally readers tend to apply automatically phonological rules with which they are familiar. English-speaking acquaintances, even of many years standing, invariably tend to misspell and/or mispronounce my name according to English usage, that is Fietelson instead of Feitelson. On the other hand, Israeli students will often call me Peitelson, as, in its initial position, the symbol which stands for both F and P in Hebrew is invariably pronounced P. This example is meant to convey that, contrary to the case of foreigners, children learning to decode their native tongue will successfully arrive at the pronunciation with which they are familiar, once they recognize a word. Holding the view that it is possible in the early stages of written language acquisition to depend on a not excessively large repertoire of fairly regular spelling patterns takes this capacity into account. In fact Fries (1962) specifically points out that

> The process of learning to read in one's native language is the process of transfer from the auditory signs for language signals, which the child has already learned, to the new visual signs for the same signals. This process of transfer is not the learning of the language code, or of a new language code; it is not the learning of a new or different set of language signals. It is not the learning of new "words" or of new grammatical structures, or of new meanings. These are all matters of the language signals which he has on the whole already learned so well that he is not conscious of their use. The child will continue, as he grows in experience, to develop his language capacity, especially in the variety and number of the lexical signals he can control. But this continued growth in meaning and in language signals must not take attention and effort away from the main business of the "transfer stage" of learning to read. During the "transfer stage" that is, during the period necessary to learn to respond rapidly to the patterns of graphic shapes and the correlating portions of the language signals they represent, the language materials available for use should be only those already well-controlled by the pupil. The "transfer stage" is not the time to push the development of additional language mastery. The "transfer stage" will have much less confusion for the pupil if the body of language

meanings and language signals used is limited very strictly to those already within his linguistic experience (p. 120).

Thus, according to Fries, in the initial stages of learning to decode, texts will be limited not only to the most common regular spelling patterns, but also to those language forms with which the child is already quite familiar.

It is unfortunate that the linguistic expertise and intuitive insights of Bloomfield and Fries were not matched by their pedagogical know-how. The reading materials with which their names are associated are partly to blame for the widely held misconception that spelling pattern controlled instruction is synonymous with "dan can pat the fat cat" type sentences and tedious word lists.

Later authors who followed in the footsteps of Bloomfield and Fries were likewise unable to come up with reading schemes which would be attractive and interesting in their own right, in addition to being controlled for phonemic regularities. This gave rise to the widely held opinion that suspenseful, action-oriented content and structured phonics are incompatible. Aukerman's (1981) statement in regard to a structured phonics-based series is a good example of this position "when one opts for such a beginning program, one must be willing to sacrifice quality of literary content for intensity of phonics drill and boring, nonsensical story lines. The end justifies the means" (p. 40). This is one of the basic misunderstandings on the contemporary reading scene. The undoubted insipidness of many pattern-controlled programs is not an inevitable result of language constraints.

Designing a reading program according to spelling patterns does not mean that a single vowel pattern has to be repeated ad nauseam. Over-repetition may even be counterproductive, as young children could become fixated on one pattern, and find it difficult to progress to others. Examples in earlier chapters showed that Austrian educators start off with several vowels in their phonemically-structured reading schemes. It may be profitable to briefly digress here and mention a noted American author of spelling-patterned reading materials, Ted Geisel, better known as Dr. Seuss. An examination of texts written by Seuss for beginning readers such as *Green Eggs and Ham* or *The Cat in the Hat* shows that in spite of their infectious humor, and vivid and fast-moving content, they are based on a small number of regular spelling patterns and very few irregularly spelled words.

It is not the *principle* of control by spelling patterns, but rather the *way* this principle has been implemented which is to be blamed for the lack of content, the tedious repetitions, and the unnatural syntax of many reading programs. Actually, there is little reason to assume that academics, trained all their lives to analyze facts impassionately and objectively, should simultaneously be possessed with the qualities of creative writers. To overcome this problem, developers of instructional materials may find it necessary to cooperate with gifted writers for children. This is, in fact, exactly what in some cases they have been doing all along. The appeal of some of the most popular reading programs, both past and present, is undoubtedly due to their high literary quality. Ironically, so far there seem to have been relatively few attempts to involve creative writers in the production of American spelling-pattern controlled readers. The way this problem was dealt with in Israel may serve as proof that a cooperation between creative writers and program constructors committed to phonemic regularities is possible.

In Israel there are presently more than 30 beginners' programs in Hebrew alone. Most of them are phonemically sequenced. Let us quickly describe the middle stages of designing such a program.

This description assumes that all major decisions about educational strategies have already been taken. Thus it is known, for instance, if instruction will be analytic, synthetic, or a combination of both, what script will be used, and if symbols which are similar or partly identical will be introduced concurrently, sequentially, or interspersed with neutral symbols (Feitelson, 1980). What remains to be done is the preparation of the actual materials. Let us say that the program is at a stage where children have already learned two or three spelling patterns and about eight or nine letters so that they can decode any word conforming to these parameters. We are now faced with a choice among, let us say, three letters, all of which would fit the given contingencies of the present stage. The decision process starts off with a dictionary search intended to elicit *all* additional words one could use in case each of the three letters under consideration became the chosen one. Eventually the search yields three lists of words. At this stage the professional insights of the program constructors, among whom there are always practicing first grade teachers, will be elicited. The lists of words suggest several possible story themes. The team will have to decide which of the possible themes would be best suited to children's interests, curriculum constraints, and contents of previous stories. Sometimes two or three different topics may appear suitable. It is the anticipated appeal of possible story themes, suggested by word lists, which will decide which of the three letters will be chosen. Usually, a professional children's writer who works with the team participates in the discussions and decision. Now the writer takes over. With the help of the word lists the writer comes up with several stories in which he/she tries to incorporate the new words. Experience has shown that creative writers cannot adhere to predetermined spelling patterns or to rigidly controlled story lengths. However, once stories exist, program designers can modify them to fit specifications. On the other hand, program designers, with spelling pattern specifications always uppermost in their minds, turned out to be poor at conceiving stories which would appeal to flesh and blood children. Incidentally, asking children to choose between proposed stories was a useful strategy. It is common knowledge that McGuffey used to test the appeal of new texts he was preparing by reading them aloud to the neighborhood children in his backyard.

At this point, let us sum up. In this section we have tried to deal with the question of whether or not English orthography actually makes learning to decode as difficult as is often implied. Instead of citing, once again, the long list of difficulties a beginning reader faces in English, we chose to examine some of the more popular strategies suggested for reducing these difficulties. In doing so we found that, irrespective of the particular strategy suggested, one common denominator among them was the assumption that each could be achieved by relatively simple means. Thus proponents of transitional alphabets seemed to feel that an addition of at most 20 symbols was sufficient in order to satisfactorily chart English writing. Similarly, only a rather small number of diacritical markings were needed according to the proponents of that solution. Finally, the controlled spelling pattern camp also seemed to feel that learning regular patterns in well-planned sequential stages was not only feasible, but could in fact be accomplished in a rather short time span namely within a child's first or at most second year at school. What is especially intriguing about all these approaches is that each, in its own way, transfers the problem from qualitative terms to practical quantitative ones. Accordingly, inherent difficulties are not only recognized and described but are also translated into an inventory of facts a beginning reader will have to acquire. An inventory which, moreover, was not excessively large in any of the cases.

Before we proceed to the question of whether any one of the three options examined has qualities which would make it preferable to the other two, let us speculate on possible advantages and wider applications of the "inventory of reading facts" concept just mentioned. We have seen that cross-language research in the area of beginning reading is still in a very early stage. The difficulty of adequately accounting for the relative influence of the many factors involved in acquiring initial literacy in different languages bears a large share of the blame. On the other hand, certain contingencies in any one language often exist also in others. In such cases, instructional insights which were achieved in the first could be applicable also to them.

It should be possible to develop comprehensive reading fact inventories, indexing the facts beginning decoders will have to master in the initial stage of learning to read their language. This chapter showed that if such inventories were divided into sections according to areas of competence, languages would differ in the number of facts in any one area. In some languages the number of facts in the area of spelling-pattern sound relationships would be finite and much smaller than in English, while facts in other areas, that is, visual characteristics of letter characters, or knowledge of word declinations might be considerably more numerous.

In this context the contribution of the three approaches discussed here towards simplifying the problem of spelling-pattern sound relationships in English would be that each, in its own way, could markedly reduce the number of facts a beginning reader has to learn. Whether such a reduction is at all necessary is a question which at this stage had best be left open. A recent frequency count of the syllables of the 5,000 most common words on the American Heritage word list showed that a weighted list (by frequency of word occurrence) of only 290 syllables accounted for 72% of the 5,890,868 syllable tokens in these most used English words (Sakiey, Fry, Goss, & Loigman, 1980). This seems to indicate that even without modifications the amount of information required in the earlier stages of reading is not as excessive as has often been assumed.

Now, to return to the question of whether there is one option of the three we have been considering which is preferable to the other two? Controlled research which exposed learners to identical texts printed in different mediums, but capitalizing in turn on the advantages of each of the mediums, is still in the future. Theoretically it would seem that combining several strategies may be preferable to using only a single one. For instance the addition of some diacritical marks to a spelling pattern controlled approach could markedly reduce the constraints of the latter. Further considerations such as ease of transition to traditional orthography, or a wish to include children's writing activities from the outset, would also influence the range of alternatives.

In view of the great number of English-speaking school beginners the world over, it would seem that intensive, well-coordinated research efforts are an urgent priority. Hopefully such efforts would include a re-examination of practices which proved useful in the past.

CHAPTER EIGHT

From Theory to Practice

The pastime we have been engaging in up until now, namely re-examining beginning reading lore in an effort to separate fact from fad, is, in essence, part of scientific effort in any field of knowledge. For what is science if not a searching re-examination of accepted truths leading to either a reconfirmation of what is held as known or alternatively to a striking out in new directions? Despite setbacks, disagreements, and heated disputes which have sometimes turned into prolonged feuds, there is in reading, as in other areas of scientific endeavor, an overall sense of common frame of reference and consensus on many specifics. Nor are the number and severity of clashes of opinion cause for serious concern, for in academic inquiry the areas of dispute rather than of consensus tend to pave the way for further progress.

What sets beginning reading apart from some other areas of science is an emphasis on applicability. Specialists on beginning reading processes may have fruitful dialogue and see eye to eye on many points. It is the next stage, when agreed-upon insights have to be translated into viable instructional strategies, that seems fraught with the most discord.

One of the aims of Chall's (1979; 1983c) proposed scheme of developmental reading stages was to show a way out of this difficulty by providing a conceptual framework for discussing reading research and instruction. The main assumptions of the scheme Chall worked out are that attaining literacy is a prolonged process, and that reading behavior undergoes qualitative changes throughout a person's lifetime. Research findings support this view.

Biemiller (1970) studied reading errors in the early learning stages. By obtaining individual records of first graders' nonresponses and reading errors over several months' time, he discovered that qualitatively different response patterns tended to follow each other in identical order across children. In the first phase children typically made contextually acceptable substitution errors. They then underwent a period of not responding. However, among response errors which did occur during this period there was a significant increase in graphic substitution errors. Biemiller (1970) believes that this reflects a change in strategy on the part of the child, towards increased use of graphic information in word identification. In the next phase there emerged increased ability to use, simultaneously, both contextual as well as graphic information. Perfetti and Roth (1981), who studied reading processes of third and fourth graders, found further evidence of finely delineated, qualitatively different phases in reading development, which follow closely upon each other, or overlap slightly. Biemiller identified no less than three such phases in the first year of instruction.

The implications of more clearly understood and defined reading stages for research could be far-reaching. It could well be that developmental differentiations employed in past studies will turn out to have been too crude. Results of investigations which studied children in a particular phase of reading development may not be applicable to readers at other stages. Studies on beginning reading which used subjects who were already in their second or third years of reading instruction may thus be in need of thorough re-examination before their results can be accepted as relevant to actual beginners.

A stage theory of reading development may have even wider implications in regard to educational practice. When reading development is conceived as an accumulation of skills which are acquired in predictable sequence, it would seem that *different* kinds of competencies need to be emphasized at successive stages of learning. Like reading failure, also success in learning to read could thus be viewed as a cumulative process.

Chall (1977; 1983c) emphasized the importance of environmental factors in ensuring children's progress from stage to stage. Equalizing educational opportunity is increasingly interpreted to mean that schools have to make up for developmentally important experiences children might be missing in their homes. Vygotsky (1978) pointed to the distance between many children's independent developmental level of problem-solving ability and their potential developmental level when guided by adults or working in collaboration with more capable peers. If we do not want to short-change children whose homes do not provide reading-conducive stimulation, we have to make sure that formal educational agencies see to it that at no point in reading development children do miss experiences which are deemed important for the stage they are at. Nor, hopefully, would they ever be exposed to learning situations which are thought to be counterproductive. Reading developmental stages could thus be translated into reading instruction stages—in other words, a stage-oriented reading curriculum.

In the next three chapters we shall attempt to identify and describe many of the competencies needed by beginning readers. We shall also try to make a case for what we feel is an optimal sequence for their introduction.

A good point at which to begin is that moment in children's lives when, according to the conventions of their society, they are expected to start to learn to read in a formal setting.

PART III

From Theory to Practice—A Stage-Based Curriculum

CHAPTER 9

Stage 1—The Onset of Formal Reading Instruction

There's many a slip twixt the cup and the lip. (English proverb)

In many countries the onset of formal reading instruction coincides with school entry, and both occur when children are approximately six or seven years old. Let us examine some of the implications of having onset of formal reading instruction occur concurrently with school entry.

SCHOOL ENTRY AS A CRITICAL EVENT IN AN INDIVIDUAL'S LIFE

The present century witnessed the emergence of public school systems as major socializing agencies. Consequently school entry has increasingly assumed the characteristics of an important rite-de-passage. The centrality of school in today's societies is well illustrated by semantic conventions. In recent years the term "preschooler" is a widely accepted designation for young children. Similarly, educational frameworks which cater to young children have come to be called "preschools" instead of "nursery school" or "kindergarten" as they used to be, implying unfolding and growth from within. These semantic changes are also mirrored in other languages, for instance, "Vorschulalter" and "Vorschulerziehung" in German, the original cradle of the term "kindergarten."

The fact that present-day reading research tends to regard beginning reading within a framework of long-term cognitive and linguistic developmental processes may have deflected attention from the emotional impact of school entry on first graders and their families. In their collection of current research in beginning reading, Resnick and Weaver (1979) undertook to address "the specific issues that are dominant in today's debates about early reading" (vol. I, p. 1). Among the altogether 48 contributions in the three-volume collection, there in not a single one which addresses affective aspects of the acquisition of literacy. A possible reason for this neglect may be that after a long era of intensive preoccupation with emotional aspects of schooling in the 1930s and 1940s there is a feeling that this theme has been exhausted. Still the pendulum may have swung too far in the other direction.

Experts believe that "the child's first experience of primary school may be crucial and determinant of later success" (Wall, 1975, p. 251), and that even for well-adjusted children the transition to the more demanding school environment may lead to "mild anxiety and insecurity" (Wall, 1975, p. 252), especially as school entry occurs at a time in the individual's development when the equanimity of later school years has not yet been achieved (White, 1970; Wall, 1975).

Data gathered by Bloom (1976) in 15 countries showed that an individual's attitude to specific school subjects, to school in general, and especially his or her "academic self-concept" are largely influenced by cumulative experiences of success or lack thereof. In this context early experiences are especially important. As Bloom believes that learning outcomes can be greatly influenced by altering instructional approaches, he strongly suggests that when help is needed it should be provided during the early stages of new learning experiences rather than later on. Berliner's (1981) finding, that failure "even when it is only occasional" (p. 220) has a negative impact on younger student's attitudes, lends added support to Bloom's argument.

First graders, as well as those close to them, often link school entry specifically to learning to read. One consequence of the centrality of schooling in today's society is that parents, relatives, siblings, kindergarten teachers, and even casual acquaintances tend to talk to children frequently about their impending school entry. School entry thus turns into an event of great importance to which many children look forward with some trepidation, possibly partly because they fear that they may not be up to the demands with which they will be faced according to all they hear. In a study of kindergartners' expectancies in regard to school, Strauss (1977) found that children were unexpectedly apprehensive about their ability to cope with future school tasks. Case histories bear out Strauss's results. Here is one which recently came to my attention. The little boy in question, son of academic parents, refused from the very first day to go to school. For several weeks he had to be daily coaxed to school and led by hand into class. It turned out that the boy, who had been in a kindergarten with an intensive reading readiness program, assumed that the first grade teacher would expect him to be able to read. However, the child, who was both intelligent and sensitive, was well aware that he could not yet read. This discrepancy caused him great anxiety and led to his refusal to go to school. The case of Roger, described by Anderson and Dearborn (1952), is another good example of anxieties about reading which can beset school beginners. Roger refused to participate in any kind of reading activity and, in fact, told his teacher to her face that he was not going to learn to read. It turned out that Roger had an older friend whom he admired greatly. The older boy had already completed first grade and had warned Roger not to have anything to do with reading. He himself, it appeared, had "encountered nothing but failure in the subject" (p. 283).

In short, anxieties linked to school entry and especially to the scholastic aspects of school may be more prevalent than is generally realized.[7] Therefore it seems of the utmost importance that experiences connected with school entry and initial reading be as encouraging and devoid of stress as possible, and that uncertainties about children's ability to cope successfully with school requirements—both on the part of children themselves as well as on that of their families—be prevented.

Vernon (1971), on of Britain's best-known psychologists whose work influenced generations of reading researchers and practitioners, held that even quite intelligent children sometimes fail to realize "the symbolic nature of written language" (p. 77), namely, the connection between printed letter shapes and phonetic units. According to her, this state of confusion is the most "fundamental and basic characteristic of reading disability" (Vernon, 1957, p. 71). Moreover, once a child has become "confused" remediation is extremely difficult, often requiring extraordinary efforts and much individual attention over long periods of time (Vernon, 1957, 1971).

Yet, this kind of confusion can be prevented. Current reading theory views reading acquisition as a cognitive process in the course of which the learner discovers the connection between the technical aspects of reading and meaningful reading acts (i.e. Gibson & Levin, 1975). While most experts agree with this formulation they differ on the role of instructing adults in facilitating the discovery process. One school of thought holds that we are dealing here with an internal process happening within the child, and that beginners have to arrive at necessary insights on their own. Others feel that well designed instructional sequences and direct help provided by teachers can bypass difficulties and lead children step by step to necessary insights.

Implicit in the view that it is the child himself who has to discover

---

[7] This is also borne out by a study which showed that middle-class mothers are aware of and sensitive to children's need for reassurance at school entry (Hess & Shipman, 1965).

what reading is all about is the assumption of a lengthy process during which children amass pertinent information which finally enables them to infer the crucial connections. Thus a relatively long period of learning precedes the attainment of the breakthrough "Aha" experience which occurs for each child at a different point in time. However, it would seem that a long transitory period can lead to many problems and that crucial insights should occur as early in the learning process as possible. In some of the non-English programs used as examples in earlier chapters, the attainment of a full understanding of the way reading is linked to printed pages came about already in the first or at most second week of instruction, when learners knew no more than two or three letters. There is no reason to assume that the same could not be achieved also in English, all the more so as the data presented in Chapter Seven demonstrated that in several respects English poses fewer problems for beginning readers than some other languages. What we propose then is: (a) to make sure that from the very first day of school a child would encounter a carefully graded succession of learning tasks, each of which could be mastered without difficulty; and (b) to design these tasks in such a way that the learning child would attain crucial insights about the nature of reading behavior within a matter of days and with a minimum of prerequisite skills. Conversely, drawing out the introductory stage and basing initial functional reading experiences on a large quantity of previously acquired knowledge would, according to this view, prolong the period of uncertainty and increase the chances of failure and of possible negative side effects liable to accompany failure.

Let us see what translating these insights into practice would mean.

INTEGRATING MEANING-ORIENTED AND DECODING-ORIENTED BEGINNING READING INSTRUCTION

Present-day informed opinion about reading holds that reading is neither purely bottom-up nor top-down. Facile readers proceed by an interactive process drawing on elements from both (Rumelhart, 1977; Lesgold & Perfetti, 1981). In doing so, facile readers are not consciously aware to what extent they engage in one strategy or the other. Anyway, this changes from moment to moment according to the needs of the situation and the reader's expertise and experience. Attempting to guide beginners right from the beginning to the use of interactive reading strategies does not mean that beginners can be catapulted straight away into facile readers' modes of behavior. In the Austrian approaches which we used as examples, knowledgeable adults orchestrated learning experiences in such a way that they made beginners adopt interactive strategies. Accordingly, curriculum designers were those who decided what the nature of very initial learning experiences should be.

This seemingly brings us back to the old question whether teaching methods per se make a difference. Chall (1983b) feels that the reluctance to accept that methods of instruction differ in effectiveness is due to a tendency to confuse method—that is, clear-cut theoretical constructs about instructional alternatives—with publishers' packaged educational programs.

Consequently, many studies which supposedly compare "methods" are in fact comparisons of the achievements of children exposed to different sets of commercial materials. Commercial beginning reading programs are typically composed of numerous items developed by teams of experts (Aukerman, 1971, 1981), and encompass a myriad of professional decisions. Thus potential advantages or disadvantages of method per se tend to be overshadowed by many other operant factors which impinge on experimental results—for instance, the quality of an accompanying teachers' manual.

Also in the overall controversy about "decoding-oriented" versus "meaning-oriented" instruction, finer distinctions among methods were often overlooked. To this day, many theoretical treatments of decoding-oriented instruction imply an "analytic" (whole words are taught first, and letter-sound correspondences are inferred from them) approach. However, recent studies seem to indicate that children exposed to synthetic (phoneme-grapheme correspondences are taught directly and combined to form words), or as Chall (1983b) calls it "direct-synthetic" teaching tend to do better than children who learned with "indirect-analytic" phonic programs (p. 16).

In some countries synthetic teaching seems to predominate. The Soviet Union (Vasresensky, 1959), France (Ruthman, 1973), and Finland (Kyöstiö) are among the better known examples.

One reason researchers sometimes tend to be indifferent to the finer distinctions between analytic and synthetic strategies of beginning reading instruction is the popular contention that these distinctions are not that important because in the long run all good teaching will incorporate elements from both (Fry, 1977). There is much in this argument. Instruction which starts with stories, sentences, phrases, or words goes on at some stage to syllables, graphemes and letters. Conversely, when the initial units are letters, graphemes, or syllables, learning will proceed sooner or later to words, sentences, and contentful texts. The currently fashionable practice of labeling beginning reading programs as "analytic-synthetic" or "eclectic" illustrates that authors and publishers recognize this, and that they feel that indicating that they combine both is a positive attribute of their wares.

What is problematic about this line of reasoning is that it avoids the crucial question: which of the two overall approaches leads to better results and is one of them appreciably easier for school beginners than the other? Further, this line of reasoning does not face the fact that at some point every first grade teacher and author of beginners' materials will have to decide how to start off, namely what to introduce first—a text, word, syllable, or single letter?

Accumulating evidence seems to indicate recurrently that synthetic instruction leads to better results (i.e., Chall, 1983b;). However, in the past, synthetic teaching also seems to have aroused most opposition. Discussion was mostly in theoretical terms and supposedly factual substantiation of expressed opinions was not always adequate. A passage in an at one time widely popular text is a good example: "Any method which begins by teaching the child to examine each word, to analyze it into component phonograms, to sound each phonogram, to combine these sounds to get the word, places a premium on lip movement and unnecessary audible aids, and promotes slow, ponderous reading, which develops into habits that defy later efforts at correction. Our objection to synthetic methods is based on their teaching practices which develop these very undesirable reading habits" (Klapper, 1926, p. 24). The "suggested reading" list at the end of the chapter includes among others works by Dearborn, Gray, Huey, and Judd, implying a research base for expressed opinions.

A further argument against synthetic methods was that they required children to learn many abstract facts. These included recognizing graphic symbols, some of which were easily confused, learning to associate symbols with their respective names and sounds, and worst of all, mastering complicated pronounciation rules. No wonder that it was believed that the average school beginner would find all this more difficult than learning to directly associate letter strings with meaningful, age-appropriate words.

There can be little doubt that these listed difficulties represent just concerns, especially when one remembers that they do accurately describe instructional practices which were used in many schools. However, as we have seen before, the fact that particular teaching practices are used within the context of a specific approach does not necessarily mean that they are an intrinsic element of that approach. In Chapter Six we learned that the dichotomy—abstract, meaningless by implication, dead letter symbols versus contentful vital words—is avoidable. For generations gifted educators have possessed the ability to make single letters come to life imbued with meaning. To this day I remember not only the stories about fat Aunt O, sprightly jumpy I, the brother and sister sharing an apple M and many of their fellows, but even the colored chalk illustrations of these folks which our male(!) first grade teacher drew on the blackboard in Vienna more than 50 years ago.

Similarly, some American synthetic programs both of the past (i.e., Pollard, 1889; see Huey, 1908, pp. 281–84) as well as of the present (for instance Craig's 1977 Super Sounder System) rely on fanciful stories which not only turn letters and graphemes into meaningful entities, but provide also rationales for many of the apparent inconsistencies of symbol-sound correspondences in English. Furthermore, there is no clear-cut evidence that school beginners have difficulty in learning single letters.

Quite on the contrary, studies have repeatedly shown that young children are able to discriminate, match and learn single letters far better than letter-strings or words (Calfee, Chapman, & Venezky, 1972; Shankweiler & Liberman, 1976; Calfee, 1977; Feitelson & Razel, 1984). In addition Venezky and Shiloach (1972) demonstrated that individual speech sounds as well as sound-picture associations can be taught successfully already at kindergarten age. There is also evidence that learning letter-sound correspondences has a positive effect on preschoolers' and school beginners' ability to transfer to the decoding of new words (Jeffrey & Samuels, 1967; Vandever & Neville, 1976; Carnine, 1977). It is on this account that a way of teaching which proceeds from phonemes and their transcriptions to words may also be an effective strategy for dealing with what is presently believed to be one of the main difficulties of beginning readers, namely phonemic segmentation and the ability to recognize phonemes embedded in words (Liberman, 1973; Liberman et al., 1974; Liberman et al., 1977; Wallach, Wallach, Dozier, & Kaplan, 1977; Wallach and Wallach, 1979).

From the preceding paragraphs it appears that on many counts a synthetic approach would seem to be easier for young school beginners than an analytic one. If this were true, why has it not been recognized more widely? One possible reason may be that scholars seem to feel that even if letters were in fact learned more readily than words, this would not really matter because, in reading, single letters have to be combined to form words and this process—called blending—is beset by great difficulties. Thus, possible advantages of a synthetic approach would be offset by the extreme difficulties connected with learning to blend.

CAN LEARNING TO BLEND BE SIMPLIFIED?

That there is a positive relationship between blending ability and reading achievement has been established repeatedly (i.e., Chall, Rosewell, & Blumenthal, 1963; Balmuth, 1972). Further, there is evidence that "blending is a learned skill which develops during the early primary years" (Richardson, Di Benedetto, & Bradley, 1977, p. 330), and some suggestion that "the nature of the instructional approach may affect the development of the blending skill" (Richardson, et al., 1977, p. 328). Scholars also seem agreed about the nature of the difficulties commonly attributed to blending. The crux of the problem is that blending is not simply a process of slurring together sounds of letters which follow each other, but that blending requires the reader to adapt sound correspondences of single letters to the way these letters are sounded when part of a word.

It is the way this skill is practiced by facile readers and acquired by beginners which seems to baffle researchers most. Describing an instructional program which claims to include blending, Gibson and Levin (1975) remark that "the process remains mysterious and artful" (p. 315). Venezky (1972) states "we have no explanation for how a fused unit emerges from independent units, given that the independent units can be articulated separately, and that the articulatory instructions for some fused forms are significantly different from those for the independent units which form them. That is, even if the separate units could be articulated with zero pause between them, the result would not be a fused unit" (p. 17). It is here that historic developments described in Chapter Two become pertinent. Discussions of issues on the reading scene seem greatly influenced by the time- and situation-bound teaching conventions with which discussants happen to be familiar. Blending is closely related to phonemic-synthetic teaching, which, as we saw in Chapter Two, did not catch on in the United States. Consequently, available treatments of blending are mainly speculative. In order to realize how blending is achieved in practice in phonemic synthetic teaching, an observer from abroad would not only have to be fully conversant with the language of instruction at the site visited, but would also have to be present at a very specific point in time, namely, when blending is first introduced. As long as both these conditions have not been met, knowledge about how blending is achieved in non-English-speaking countries will remain scant.

We shall now try to understand why blending is often considered such a stumbling block.

The tendency to attribute difficulties to blending is due in part to the model most often employed in discussions of blending as well as to a number of additional factors. We shall single out four of these and then return to the problem of theoretical model.

First, there is a tendency to regard blending as a post-initial skill, developed only *after* primary skills have already been fully mastered. In other words the expectation seems to be that learners initially acquire letter-sound relationships, and that only when these have become fully established does the learner progress to blending.

Secondly, blending is conceived as an *oral process*. Thus, blending is most often described in terms of sounds and efforts at arriving at the correct pronounciation of a word by way of combining the sounds of single letters.

Thirdly, there is the oft-mentioned special problem of the nonpredictable nature of English orthography. How, so the argument goes, can one teach a child to sound and blend successive graphemes when the pronounciation of many words has but little to do with such a process?

Fourth, there is the matter of trying to describe the acquisition of complex skills by way of detailed analysis of subroutines. The old joke about the centipede, which, after having been asked with which leg it starts off, was unable to ever walk again, may not be inappropriate in this context. Similarly, when each of the prerequisite subskills of blending is identified and described in detail, the complexity of the resulting system may well seem overpowering, and the question of how this process can ever be attained by an average school entrant unanswerable. Probably the same might happen were one to try to analyze how other complex learned skills are acquired. Driving or playing tennis might be useful examples, especially as some of us may still remember salient points in our learning history of these. What comes nearly immediately to mind in this respect is the role played by modeling, as well as an appreciation of the need for drill to the point of automacity.

Further, we might remember that whoever instructed us judiciously integrated portions of our actually performing partial basic routines with coaching in a new subskill. Subsequently, the new skill was grafted onto the other routines and perfected before we advanced to the next step. We would also realize that a learning model in which each skill is introduced and perfected in isolation and subskills are combined in actual performance only in the final stage would hardly be adequate.

As we discussed the fourth issue first, let us continue backwards and now take up the third, namely, blending and the special case of English. It will be remembered that we assume all along that, in the initial stages of a beginners' program, words and texts will be spelling-pattern controlled. Regularities will also be further enhanced by subtle diacritical markings. Given these conditions, blending in English should not pose problems not encountered also in other languages. In the few cases when an irregular word has to be introduced already at this stage, children would simply be told that it is an exception. Probably it would work best if the teacher would then model sounding it out.

Let us now return to the first issue. Over many years and in several language settings, we had the good fortune to be able to observe and later to try out a variety of options. What emerged was that school entrants seemed to do best when letters were not overlearned in isolation. Instead, each time a new grapheme was introduced, it was blended immediately with graphemes that had been learned before, to create meaningful words. Thus, only the very first letter, usually a vowel, was ever learned by itself. For example, let us assume the first letter was short "i". Short "i" would be introduced by way of a meaningful sound association (see Chapter Six). Children could act out the story of the sound association. They could also practice writing "i" on the blackboard, in the air, with their fingers on their desks, and finally on paper. In the next few days there might be opportunities to form "i"s from wire, pipe cleaners, play-dough, lentils pasted on cardboard, and so forth.

In the meantime, a second letter, say, "n" may have been introduced, again via a meaningful sound association (see Chapter Six). Also this time children could act out the story and practice writing "n" in the air. However, within a very few minutes, much *before* the class would usually split up for individual practice, there is a challenge: "You remember 'i' which we learned the other day? Let's see what happens when we put 'i' and 'n' next to each other." The teacher writes "in" on the blackboard. "Now let's read this—i-n, in! Who knows what 'in' is?" Then and there the discussion would veer to the meaningful word "in". Children could provide examples of objects that can be *in* other objects. The teacher could take up these examples and draw-write several "in" stories on the board (see Figure 9.1).[8] The teacher would then suggest that children follow suit and create "in" stories of their own. Producing "in" stories by writing and drawing or by pasting letter or word cards which spell "in" next to pictures cut from magazines could remain a major occupation for a few days to come. However, simultaneously, perhaps the very day after "in" was first introduced, the teacher might also say, "Yesterday we saw what happened when we put "i" and "n" next to each other. Let's now see what happens if we do it the other way round." The teacher writes and has children sound "ni-ni—Nini". "Would you like to see a picture of Nini?" This would be an opportunity to introduce a main character for many following stories. According to cultural and neighborhood circumstances, "Nini" could be a rag doll or teddy bear, an alley cat, sparrow, turtle, or rat, or a fanciful fictional being like those chil-

---

[8] This and the following examples were developed ad hoc around the family dinner table. A professional team, working for many months would have considered many contingencies which were neglected here. It has to be remembered that, even in consistent orthographies like Hebrew and Arabic, developing an initial version of a structured learning approach is a matter of years and necessitates constant try-outs in actual classroom situations. The graphics were contributed by Dror G. Feitelson.

Figure 9.1.   Tentative example of blending and meaningful reading with only two letters.

dren enjoy in comics or Dr. Seuss's books. Humerous stories about "Nini in . . ." would now be the order of the day (see Figure 9.2).

Children's writing and reading experiences at this initial stage could be enlivened by providing them with mimeographed "IN" cards. Chil-

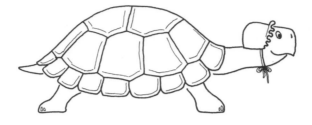

NINI

 IN **IN**

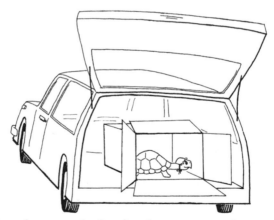

Figure 9.2. Tentative example showing that even at two letters texts need not be confined to repetitive single syllable word patterns.

dren could paste these cards next to their own drawings or in between pictures cut from magazines. Teachers could also use "IN" and "NINI" flash cards in order to train unitary word perception and speed up reading. In addition to word cards children could also receive single letter cards each time they learn a new letter. These would be stored in a permanent letter file or box and serve for word "building" or, better still, "discovery." We shall return to "word discovery" presently.

When a third letter is learned, once again the introduction of the meaningful sound and the symbol or symbols representing it would be followed within a very few minutes by attempts to combine the new letter with those learned before. In case the third letter was "o", "o-n" combined to "on" would be the result. Now children could invent both "in" and "on" stories, leading to a profusion of contentful writing. When children are allowed to experiment with the letter cards in their files or boxes, some would probably also arrive at "no", possibly recognizing and pronouncing "no" correctly even without special marking to indicate that this "o" is long (see Chapter Seven). "Ono", a matching character to "Nini", would, on the other hand, have to be suggested by the teacher as it is a made-up word and not in children's vocabulary. "Nino", "Ino", and "Ini" could become additional fictional characters, adding zest to the store of possible action stories. Many opportunities for unitizing reading of meaningful words composed of known elements would ensue (i.e., Figures 9.3—9.7).

With each new letter all at that stage possible blends and words could be elicited, provided the words are regular and known to children. Thus when, let us say, "r" is introduced as fourth letter, all kinds of combinations could be tried out—"ro", "ri", "ir", "or", "Ron", "Nir", "nor", "Rori", "Roni". The single letter cards children receive each time they learn a new letter would enable them to combine the new letter with previously learned ones in various juxtapositions. In this way they could "discover" words they know. Also, when children propose meaningless combinations or combinations that are words but not in their vocabulary, teachers would never set themselves up as arbiters of what a word is. Instead, a dictionary would be consulted with the proposer in eager anticipation. Experience in Israel showed that this procedure is a great equalizer as also children with a poor vocabulary can come up with an accredited "discovery." By now, the basic idea of blending letter strings into meaningful words should already be well understood. However, the practice of introducing additional letters slowly, one by one, each time deriving all, at that stage, possible blends would continue.

Before we go on to the next issue let us briefly touch on an intriguing question. In our description just now we seemed to suggest that blending should be an integral part of letter introduction right from the beginning. Does this imply that learning letters in isolation, not accompanied by immediate practice in blending, might be disadvantageous and should not be encouraged? Our experience would seem to show that this is so. Hopefully, research will provide a more definite answer before too long.

The time has now come to return to the second issue, namely, that blending is usually conceived as an oral process. It is here that we also had best discuss the generally accepted model of blending and its implications. In their review article Richardson et al. (1977) present the

Figures 9.3–9.7.   Tentative examples of meaningful passages created from two to three regularly sounded letters.

following model of blending which was also proposed by previous investigators (i.e., Silberman, 1963; Bateman, 1967; Richardson & Bradley, 1974).

1. *Visual analysis.* The reader organizes the component letters spatially in left-to-right order.

2. *Sound-symbol correspondence.* The reader orally produces the phonic sound corresponding to each of the component letters in a temporal order that matches the spatial order.
3. *Blending.* The reader *orally* [my emphasis, D.F.] produces an ordered blend of the sounds.

ONO

Figure 9.4

Figure 9.5

Richardson et al. (1977) feel that this model represents blending as well as the process children can and should be taught in order to be able to sound out novel words. By implication this is also the model most discussants of blending seem to have in mind. Resnick and Beck (1976), who went into the matter more deeply, differentiate between this "the final blending" procedure and their proposed "successive blending" routine (p. 185). The main difference between the two is that, in the "final blending" procedure, blending is only attempted after the sounds of all graphemes have been derived and stored in memory. In "suc-

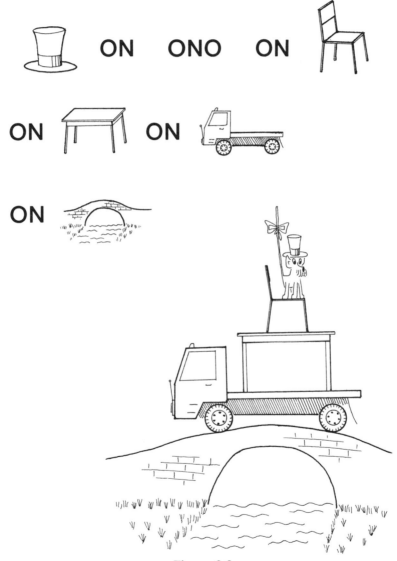

Figure 9.6

Figure 9.7

cessive blending," on the other hand, sounds are synthesized successively as the reader goes along, thereby substantially reducing memory load. The example used by Resnick and Beck (1976) to clarify the difference between the two procedures is "final blending"—/k/ /a/ /t/ /s/ cats— versus "successive blending"—/k/ /a/ /ka/ /t/ /kat/ /s/ /kats/ cats—(p.

185). We would hope that a child who had learned blends concurrently with single letters would be saved an additional step. The way such a child would proceed would be /ka/ /t/ /kat/ /s/ /kats/ cats. In addition, we would have made sure the initial "c" was marked so that the child would know instantly that here "c" assumed the sound "k".

Altogether "cat" may not be a good choice of word for the initial stages of learning to blend. Before having to tackle stop consonants like hard "c" or "t" learners should have ample opportunity to gain experience with words composed of more easily "blendable" letters. In addition, choice of words ought not to be dictated solely by considerations of phonemic accessibility. Content would be another major criteria. In this respect, too, "cats" would have little to recommend it.

Before we proceed it may be well to remember that "a substantial body of evidence indicates that even for young children, word decoding automatically leads to semantic activation *when the meaning of the word is adequately established in memory*" (Stanovich, 1986, p. 372). Thus the oft-voiced apprehension that phonological decoding may take place without extracting meaning, leading school beginners to becoming "word callers," is unfounded.

The tongue-in-cheek examples on the preceeding pages were meant to illustrate also that children's early reading experience need not be limited to one syllable words or to repetetive word patterns. Certain types of two- or three-syllable words may well be easier to blend than the proverbial "cat" or "pan". Research investigating specific instructional questions like these is desperately needed and should not be too difficult to execute.

We can now return to the issue from which we set off, namely, whether blending ought to be conceived as an exclusively *oral* process. We are here in complete accord with Lesgold and Perfetti (1981) who suggest a skill acquisition model based on "differences between expert adult readers and novice children" (p. 402). Lesgold and Perfetti (1981) postulate that a beginner must learn to map print to *speech sounds* [my emphasis, D.F.], but that increase in skill involves "learning to bypass the print-to-speech connection by acquiring a print-to-meaning connection" (p. 402).

Providing children with extensive practice in unitizing words out of their component parts in the very early stages of learning could probably considerably facilitate and accelerate the transfer to direct accessing of meaning. Thus, even before most grapheme-sound correspondences are introduced, children would be already using print-to-meaning connections (see examples). This situation is very different from children reading so-called sight words as here the underlying strategy of what it is they are doing is entirely clear and can be recapitulated in case of need. Also, as children become accustomed to accessing meaning internally from very early on processing an unknown word may proceed orally, silently, or by a combination of both according to individual preference. Experience shows that in the very beginning children do tend to resort to some murmured or silent mouthing but that surprisingly early they are able to transfer to a wholly internalized process. Sounding out and blending as an oral strategy is thus used mainly in interaction with an adult when the internal process failed. It is the *quality* of help a beginning reader receives in such instances that is of crucial importance.

THE QUALITY OF INSTRUCTION

A rather recent development in educational research has been a growing interest in what happens inside classrooms and how effective what happens is (i.e., Good & Brophy, 1978; Rosenshine & Berliner, 1978; Rosenshine, 1979; Durkin, 1979; Berliner, 1981; Cazden, 1981; Calfee & Piontkowski, 1981; Duffy & Roehler, 1982a, 1982b; Rosenshine & Stevens, 1984). So far this interest has led to the identification of several factors which seem to be positively related to learning outcomes.

Fairly consistently results of studies indicate that the time children spend actively engaged in learning tasks (Denham & Lieberman, 1980) as well as structured direct instruction (i.e., Calfee & Piontkowski, 1981) seems to be important. Researchers also criticize prevalent classroom practices in reading instruction because teachers seem to be mainly occupied with shepherding pupils through commercial programs instead of engaging in preplanned, goal directed instruction (Durkin, 1979; Brophy, 1981; Duffy & McIntyre, 1980; Duffy & Roehler, 1982c).

Duffy and Roehler (1982,b) compared detailed descriptions of two second grade teachers engaged in so-called "direct teaching." The different ways in which these two teachers went about their tasks substantiates Duffy and Roehler's (1982b) argument that the general shared understanding implied in recent use of the term direct instruction "can mask a multitude of qualitatively divergent classroom styles" (p. 36).

While attempts to identify and categorize salient characteristics of effective reading comprehension instruction have been underway for some time (i.e., Tierney & Pearson, 1981; Langer & Smith-Burke, 1982; Duffy, Roehler, & Mason, 1984; Flood, 1984), comparable efforts in the area of decoding are in an earlier stage.

Pearson's (1986) use of the term "explicit instruction" and his outline of teaching steps emphasize the importance of the *way* in which teachers structure learning encounters. Like him, we believe that careful sequencing and step-by-step progression combined with the teacher actively directing attention, clarifying, illuminating, modeling, and coaching will bring forth desired insights and acquisition of skills.

One way in which early decoding instruction is different from later reading comprehension instruction is that it has to be much more tightly structured and it needs to be completely consistent. It is to this point that we shall now address ourselves.

In the early stages, learning to decode is being able to unerringly and automatically derive known words from conventional graphic symbols. The speedier and the more accurately this is performed the better (Perfetti, 1985). Unfortunately, it is here that the conventions of research sometimes interfere with those of pedagogy. Research is at all times an open-ended process. There is always the possibility that the results of new investigations will prove former truths obsolete. Therefore, researchers tend to refrain from finally committing themselves and try to leave openings for new and unforeseen developments. However, when given the task of training a young child in the performance of a routine skill, it seems unfair to transfer the burden of our uncertitude to the learner. Here, definite decisions will have to be made about the best way to proceed, given the informed expertise available at any one point in time. Thus, once certain alternatives have been adopted, others will inevitably have to be rejected. Let us now see what this might mean in regard to several focal issues in initial reading instruction.

THE CASE OF LETTER NAMES

In preceding sections we reached the conclusion that a good way to teach initial decoding skills is to introduce school beginners to meaningful sounds and their grapheme equivalents, and to show them how they can apply this knowledge in order to construct words. Also, like La Berge (1979), we assume that even in early learning encounters children can gain considerable skill in automatizing and unitizing their responses to letter symbols. Clearly, then, we would refrain from doing anything which could jeopardize the acquisition of these automatic responses.

This leads us to the oft-debated issue about possible advantages or disadvantages of introducing beginning learners to letter names. More precisely the question is not: *whether* to introduce letter names? But rather: *when* to introduce them? Should beginners learn letter names before they learn grapheme-sound correspondences? Or would beginners be better served if letter names were introduced concurrently with or perhaps only after symbol-sound correspondences have become established? Let us briefly review arguments and factual evidence in support of these different options.

Attitudes to learning letter names seem to have been influenced by changing educational fashions. In the heyday of "Look-and-Say," when the alphabet method was severely criticized, the consensus of expert opinion, according to Gray (1956), was "that knowing the forms and names of the letters was of little help in recognizing new words" (p. 78). Therefore, experts seemed to feel that there was no point in teaching children to recognize or name letters *before* starting to learn to read (Hildreth, 1949; Anderson & Dearborn, 1952). The proper time for beginning to learn the names of the different letters was believed to be "at about the time they [children] begin word analysis and discussion of word structure so that they can talk with the teacher about the letters that make up a particular word" (Hildreth, 1949, p. 86). At the same time children were also to learn that the names of letters are different from their sounds and the alphabetical order of the letters. Given the conventions of those days, it is probably safe to assume that Hildreth believed that she was talking mainly of children in their second year of instruction.

Practices in regard to introducing letter names changed radically in the wake of studies which showed that knowing letter names at school entrance was a strong predictor of success in learning to read (i.e., Wilson & Flemming, 1938; Durrell, 1958; Gavel, 1958). This finding, which has since been replicated many times, led to a belief that teaching children letter names *before* they start to learn to read could ensure their success. A strong focus on early teaching of letter names in many beginning reading programs as well as in materials intended for preschoolers, ensued. A proliferation of commercial toys and games were further consequences of this trend, which continues.

More recently additional studies which specifically probed possible causal relationships between letter-name knowledge and learning to read (i.e., Muehl, 1962; Samuels, 1972; Jenkins, Bausell, & Jenkins, 1972) failed to uncover such a link. Children who had been taught letter names did not learn to read better than children who had no prior teaching (Venezky, 1975; Samuels & Pearson, 1980). Nor was instruction in letter names superior to other forms of reading pretraining (Ohnmacht, 1969; Johnson, 1970).

Lately there seems to be increasing evidence that learning letter names may not only be helpful but may in fact *interfere* with learning to read (Gibson & Levin, 1975). One accepted reason for suggesting that children learn letter names first is that letter names supposedly help children access letter sounds (Durrell, 1980). However, Venezky (1975) showed that in English there are only nine letters whose names begin with their sound. Furthermore, it is precisely the letters most useful in beginning instruction, namely, the continuants (s, r, m, etc.) and short vowels whose names do not begin with their sound (Venezky, 1975). In these cases "when children interpose the letter name in moving from the grapheme to the sound equivalent, they receive a false cue" . . . (Goldberg, Hebard, Rozensher, Kershner, & Osborn, 1977, p. 7).

According to the Soviet psychologist Elkonin (1957–59; in English, 1963) "To know the names of the letters is not to know their sound values." Moreover, "when children of 6 to 7 years already know the names of many letters *before* [my emphasis, D.F.] they can read they'll try to simply put together the names of letters." This, Elkonin (1963) feels, "is one of the worst habits with which many children enter school . . . and it is necessary to teach them afresh" (p. 170). It would seem that here is an area in which extensive research efforts are most urgently required. In case Elkonin's apprehensions were to prove justified, widely accepted beliefs and practices would have to be revised. For not only would we have to accept Venezky's (1975) conclusion that there is no experimental support for letter-naming instruction, but we would be faced with the possibility that letter-name instruction in the pre-initial or initial stages of beginning reading might be downright harmful. The fact that the self-discovery of reading by privileged children does not seem to be hampered by prior knowledge of letter names (Chomsky, 1971; Read, 1971; Bissex, 1980) can at the present state of knowledge hardly be considered as convincing counterevidence or as applicable to children growing up in very different circumstances.

CAPITAL AND LOWER-CASE WRITING

In most present-day beginning reading programs, capital and lower-case letters are introduced concurrently. Probably the reason for this is a wish to make children's reading experiences from the very beginning as naturalistic as possible. However, this advantage comes at a price. For as we have seen in Chapter Four, it means that from the very first children will have to learn at each step to associate phonemes with nearly twice the number of graphemes needed were they to learn either upper- or lower-case letters only. We also saw that in times past educators seemed very much aware of this problem and arbitrarily used only one type of script, even when as a result the learner was exposed to incorrectly spelled words. Evidently they believed that leading the learner to insights about the nature of reading acts was of prime importance and should be achieved as speedily and with as little hardship as possible. Therefore, they felt that it was preferable to introduce a second type of letters only when the main mystery had already been solved and reading had been achieved in a simplified medium. The same line of thinking seems to guide present-day educators in Finland where beginners' materials are printed in all capitals (Kallio & Merenkylä, 1974; Pikkanen, Louhi, Niskanen, & Totro, 1975; Kyöstiö, 1980).

It would seem that clearly conceived instructional alternatives like the present one should become targets for educational research. If it turned out that limiting initial reading materials to either upper- or lower-case letters only would indeed appreciably reduce difficulties encountered by average or below-average school entrants, such research could have immediate applicability. Furthermore, a definite answer to the question which of the two—capitals or lower-case letters—are learned more easily, would also be of considerable importance.

Prevalent opinion seems to be that if one had to decide on only one of the two the choice would be lower-case letters since they predominate in everyday reading matter (Mackay et al., 1979). However, the limited objective evidence available at present seems to go counter to common sense.

Investigations of children's letter perception used either all capitals or all lower-case letters but did not compare performance on both (i.e., Gibson, Osser, Schiff, & Smith, 1973; Gibson, Shapiro, & Yonas, 1968; Nodine & Evans, 1969; Nodine & Lang, 1971; Calfee, Chapman and Venezky, 1972). Available data are therefore mainly a series of classic studies of highly proficient readers by Tinker and his associates (Tinker & Paterson, 1928; Tinker, 1931; Tinker & Paterson, 1939; Paterson & Tinker, 1940). Tinker and Paterson (1928) found that facile readers read texts set exclusively in lower-case letters significantly faster than texts in all-capitals. However, from a distance, capital letters as well as words in all capitals were recognized accurately from farther away than lower-case ones (Tinker, 1931). Furthermore, there were many more "misreadings" in lower-case than in all-capital printing. Out of a total of 105 words presented to subjects in Tinker's (1931) study, this *difference* [my emphasis, D.F.] amounted on the average to 18.9 words.

Tinker's results indicate that even facile, experienced readers who, in other studies, read familiar lower-case writing much faster than all-capital print, find capital letters and all-capital words more discernible than lower-case letters or words. The fact that highway signs the world over (wherever the Roman alphabet is used) are lettered in all capitals seems to indicate that the superior discernibility of capitals has been substantiated. It would seem reasonable to assume that graphic symbols which are more discernible, that is, have more features which help to distinguish them from each other, are also learned more easily en masse than symbols which tend to be confused. Relatively simple studies could provide definite answers to this question. The Finnish practice of introducing beginners to all-capital script first seems to indicate that Finnish educators believe that capitals are learned more easily than lower-case letters.

One important possible advantage of introducing beginners to capitals first could be that the "bugaboo of teachers" (Gibson & Levin, 1975, p. 239), namely, the well-known difficulties usually associated with the letters "b," "d," "q" and "p", could perhaps be markedly reduced or even prevented altogether.

The reason for school entrants' tendency to confuse "b" and "d" and "p" and "q" is believed to be that there are no distinctive features differentiating these letters. In fact they are mirror images of each other and differ only in orientation. Prereaders whose previous experience has mainly been with solid objects may not spontaneously realize the importance of orientation in dealing with letters (Calfee, Chapman, & Venezky, 1972; Gibson & Levin, 1975).

Given the fact that we are dealing here with what is often held to be an especially persistent problem on the beginning reading scene, it would seem that research directed at possible solutions would be worth the effort. Specifically what needs to be investigated is whether indeed introducing beginners in the first instance only to the more distinctive B and D; P and Q and then advancing at a later stage via strongly bonded intra-letter associations (i.e., B → b; P → p) to lower-case letters would cause less difficulty than starting off with lower-case letters and have the learner exposed to the confusing letter pairs from the beginning.

Learning experiences are affected by many factors besides curriculum content. Classroom organization is an additional area of importance.

GROUP INSTRUCTION AND THE MONITORING OF DECODING ABILITY

In contrast to initial reading instruction in Britain, which is largely individualized, children in the United States are most often grouped during reading periods (Smith, 1963, 1965; Chall, 1967; Heilman, 1967; Karlin, 1975; Harris & Sipay, 1975; Fry, 1977; Calfee & Drum, 1978; Anderson, Mason, & Shirey, 1984). One aspect of grouped instruction in Stage 1 is that teachers monitor children's growth in reading ability in a group situation. Typically, one child is asked to read aloud while the other members of the group follow in their own books. A chief problem in this situation is that teachers cannot tune in solely to the child whose progress they are supposedly checking because they have to remain alert to the other children in the group in order to keep them interested and involved. Consequently, when the child whose turn it is falters or mispronounces, teachers tend to ask another child to supply the word or words the child reading found difficult. Alternatively, they supply it themselves (i.e., Johnson, 1982). In both cases, teachers miss the chance to find out exactly what it is the child found difficult. Nor is there an opportunity to work on the problem till it is cleared up. On the other hand, were teachers to act differently, they might lose the attention of the rest of the children.

There are several issues which strike one in the "catch-22" kind of situation we have just described. First, there is the child who failed to come up with the correct word. Not only did no learning take place which could have helped him perform better the next time, but it was also brought home to that child that other children have the key to what seems a mystery to him. As we have seen all along, it is exactly this kind of experience school beginners should be spared.

Second there is the undeniable fact that beginners can hardly provide good models of reading behavior to their peers. What point is there, then, in making them listen to each other? Actually, the poor quality of most beginners' oral reading is what turns group reading sessions, at this stage, mainly into exercises in discipline because the reading children hear cannot hold their attention in its own right.

There can be little doubt that in Stage 1 teachers need to be aware at all times of how each of their charges is faring. It would seem that the best and perhaps only sound way to ascertain children's progress is by individual monitoring. Experienced teachers can ascertain children's knowledge in a variety of ways. Examining daily written output is a good example and is, in fact, practiced by many teachers. Listening to individual children read connected text from books is another option. Our experience has been that once first grade teachers decide to forego group reading sessions they find time to hear each child at least twice a week. When the number of children is less than the typical Israeli 35 to 40 per class, or where there are teachers' helpers, children could be heard even more frequently.

A further advantage of monitoring children's progress in a teacher-pupil têt-atête session rather than in a group situation is that, in group situations, teachers often fail to notice children's specific difficulties because other children may help a reading child out without the teacher being aware of it (Au & Mason, 1982).

Monitoring children's progress is only one aspect of reading instruction. Deciding that individual monitoring may be especially effective does not therefore imply that it would be advantageous to individualize instruction completely. Especially in its initial stage, learning to read includes certain rote learning tasks like learning to recognize letter symbols and acquiring phoneme-grapheme associations. "Drill makes the master" is not an empty proverb. Like in sports and many other areas, a fair amount of exercises is practically a must in the early stages of reading. When dealing with six-year-olds drill does not, however, have to be conceived as boring, overly repetitious, or empty of content. In a collective situation drill can become a favorite pastime in the guise of a variety of games. It is mainly in whole-class teaching that teachers seem to develop the knack of arousing enthusiasm in regard to reading games. Group or individual teaching situations, on the other hand, seem to provide less opportunity for transforming drill into exciting games. This is because when only part of the class is involved available time is much shorter. Further, there is need to consider the remainder of the children who are working on other tasks and should not be disturbed. Venezky and Shiloach (1972) found that for kindergartners learning to associate letter-symbols with speech sounds, whole-class instruction proved more effective than individualized teaching. Venezky and Shiloach (1972) attribute this result in part to the possibility that children in the whole-class treatment were exposed to a greater number of repetitions than children taught individually or in small groups. A second factor which Venezky and Shiloach feel may have influenced their outcome was the use of a song, which was not included in the two other treatments. This seems to substantiate the points raised above. In the whole-class treatment there was: (a) more time; (b) more children could be called upon (providing a greater number of repetitions); (c) a song could be used without disturbing others.

In addition, teachers, not unlike actors, may tend to prepare better and to behave more spiritedly when assured of a largish audience. On the other hand, knowing in advance that one will have to repeat the "performance" over and over again may cut down on the vividness of each single presentation. Venezky and Shiloach's (1972) study was conducted in Israel and used the Israeli technique of creating strong associative bonds between sounds and the graphemes representing them by way of narrative stories and letter posters (Feitelson, 1965; see also Chapter Six). In the light of research which demonstrated positive relationships between teachers' enthusiasm and learning outcomes (Rosenshine, 1970; Armento, 1978; Land, 1980; Bettencourt, Gillet, Gall, & Hull, 1983) it stands to reason that the dramatic effect teachers create in telling letter stories will affect learning outcomes.

THE EFFECT OF DIFFERENTIAL PACING

Grouped reading instruction of first graders in the United States means in many cases ability grouping. Ability grouping was introduced in the

1920s (Smith, 1965) and continues to be the predominant mode of class-room organization for reading instruction (Calfee & Drum, 1978; Anderson, Mason, & Shirey, 1984). The usual practice in regard to grouping is that children are sorted into ability groups at the *beginning* [my emphasis, D.F.] of the school year and then proceed through a "predetermined curriculum for the remainder of the year" (Calfee & Drum, 1978, p. 232). Also, Barr (1974), who is perhaps the foremost authority on grouping and pacing in reading instruction, draws attention to the fact that teachers tend to establish organizational frameworks for instruction early on in the school year. Moreover, "class organization once established is highly stable and continues in essentially the same form throughout the remainder of the school year" (p. 550). One problem created by the early assignment to groups which then proceed at different rates is that children's "reading status . . . may be determined to a great extent from the beginning months of first grade" (p. 549). What seemed especially worrisome was that in Barr's study in which children's progress was measured in terms of the number of sight-words acquired, grouping seemingly penalized low aptitude pupils. Comparing children in grouped classes and in ones in which pacing was homogeneous, Barr (1974) found that grouping increased differences in achievement within the same class. However, the increase in variance in grouped classes was not only a result of high ability students having an opportunity to learn more sight-words than their peers in whole-class instruction. Children in the slower groups of a suburban middle to upper-middle class white neighborhood school, which was one of those studied, learned considerably less than nongrouped children in a similar school only five blocks away. Barr concludes that grouping and especially the practice of having lower groups proceed at a slow pace does not appear to solve learning problems of low aptitude pupils. On the contrary, it increases them. By second grade the gap between children in slow groups and children in other groups may have grown so wide that "teachers may have difficulty adjusting instruction appropriately" (p. 549). Barr's choice of population makes her results especially instructive in that they show that even a relatively privileged home background did not compensate children for the disadvantage of having been assigned to a slow group.

To conclude, it seems that organizational frameworks are another set of variables which have to be borne in mind in planning instruction. Organizational frameworks which may be particularly well suited for certain types of learning activities may be unsuited for others. In view of Venezky's and Shiloach's findings, we feel that in Stage 1 whole-class presentation of new material may be especially advantageous. This would seem to fit in well with homogeneous pacing provided a way was found so that especially able students would not be held back unnecessarily. We saw in Chapter Five that children's own writing could well provide a venue for high-level performance of more gifted children. Children's independent reading could serve the same end.

In the early weeks and months of instruction attainments have to be supervised runningly. We found that one-to-one teacher-pupil sessions seemed best suited to that end. Checking on children's progress individually at least twice a week could make teachers aware of any difficulty a child was having in its very initial stage. This would enable the teacher to immediately institute corrective action and so prevent the emergence of a more serious problem.

We shall return to a fuller discussion of the pros and cons of various forms of classroom management in Chapter Eleven. Before that, let us take a step back in time and try to find out what kinds of skills children must possess in order to be able to cope successfully with the demands of the onset of formal reading instruction.

CHAPTER 10

Before Reading

In this chapter we shall steer clear of the controversial question of at what age reading instruction had best start. Instead we shall concentrate on what it is that should happen before the onset of formal reading instruction irrespective of *when* that is.

Reading readiness is a term which first gained popularity in the United States in the late 1920s (Smith, 1965; Venezky, 1976).

Initially it was conceived as a fixed developmental stage before which there is little point in starting formal instruction. Harris and Sipay (1975) express this view when they define reading readiness as "a state of general maturity which, when reached, allows a child to learn to read without excess difficulty" (p. 19).

In the pre-Sputnik era of the 1930s and 1940s, when emotional well-being and social adjustment of pupils were greatly emphasized, a preferred policy in regard to lack of readiness was to postpone onset of formal instruction. Accordingly, the term reading readiness was mainly associated with assessment devices aimed at aiding educators in deciding when a child was ready to start to learn to read.

Great efforts were invested in trying to identify factors which would prove good predictors of success in learning to read. Among the factors which became popular and were frequently included in reading readiness test batteries were: mental age, various aspects of language proficiency, visual discrimination ability, health indices, acuity of hearing and vision, laterality, and emotional and social maturity (i.e., Tinker & McCullough, 1962; Austin, 1973).

One issue which occupied researchers a great deal was the question of prerequisite mental age. In the wake of a very widely quoted study (Morphett & Washburn, 1931) there developed a consensus that a mental age of about six and a half years would ensure better results than attempts to initiate reading instruction before that stage of mental development was reached (Tinker & McCullough, 1962).

In time, developers of beginning reading materials responded to the supposed interim period between the time a child entered first grade and the point at which he/she was considered ready to start to learn to read by providing pre-primers and readiness books to be used during the "readiness period" (Smith, 1965, p. 277). Pre-primers had many of the characteristics of typical primers except that stories were even shorter, and fewer words were used. Readiness materials featured picture stories about the characters whom pupils would meet in their pre-primers and primers, activities which would improve children's language proficiency, and exercises in directionality, visual discrimination, left to right progression, and the like.

In the 1960s the belief in a predetermined developmental threshold of reading ability was undermined by the results of several experimental studies in which preschoolers were taught to read at much younger ages than was previously thought possible (Moore, 1961; Fowler, 1962; Brzeinski, 1964; Durkin, 1970). These studies coincided with the initiation of Headstart and an increased awareness of the role of social background variables for school achievements (Seitz, 1977). Contrary to earlier times, the recognition of the importance of social factors was now viewed as a challenge to action rather than as a determinist factor.

Consequently, the term readiness came to be used primarily in relation to exercises and instructional materials designed to improve skills supposedly necessary for learning to read.

The belief that children could be prepared for learning to read by way of pretraining in isolated skills activated during reading led to a profusion of programs designed to introduce preschoolers to the letters of the alphabet and reading-related terminology, and to train them in visual and auditory discrimination, directionality, ability to segment speech into words and words into their components, and the like.

The new conceptions of reading readiness had a dramatic effect on kindergarten curricula. While a national study showed that in 1961–1962, slightly more than a quarter of the school systems that maintained kindergartens taught reading to some children, by 1967–1968, 83.9% of the systems sampled in a National Education Association (NEA) survey provided experiences in reading (Austin, 1973). Moreover, the latter study indicated that 41.1% were using "largely *structured* methods—instruction through *formalized* classroom procedures" (Austin, 1973, p. 503).

The great involvement in reading preparatory work was, in its early phases, so all pervasive that in some cases it spread also to other countries, irrespective of local needs or conditions. In Israel, for instance, a great rush to publish workbooks modeled on overseas ones resulted sometimes in the retention of original left-to-right sequencing in discrimination and directionality exercises, while both Hebrew and Arabic are written and read from right to left.

The intense preoccupation with reading readiness is not common to all countries. In both Britain—where children enter school at age five—and Denmark—where entry is at seven—educational experts caution against basing decisions in regard to onset of reading instruction on test results (Jansen, 1973; Bullock, 1975). Further, in both countries dominant opinion seems to be that reading instruction had best proceed by engaging in reading activities per se, and that "artificially segmented" pretraining by "formal pencil-and-paper tasks" should be avoided (Jansen, 1973, p. 290). Also in several other countries included in Downing's (1973) comparative study of reading instruction, there is little mention of readiness testing, or reading preparatory formal exercises. In summing up this section of his book, Downing (1973) refers back to a long ignored research conclusion by Gates (1937), who had found that the age at which children are able to learn to read depends on the nature of the program by which they are taught.

On the other hand, conceiving reading readiness as a definite assessable stage of development presupposes that curricular and teaching approaches are fixed and unchanging (Harris, 1969; MacGinitie, 1969). During the relatively long sway of undiluted "look and say" this was in fact the case in great parts of the American school system. Smith (1965), who examined beginners' materials of popular reading series from 1935 to 1965, found great similarity among series and little substantial change during this 35 year period.

The notion that readiness to undertake learning tasks depends on the level of difficulty of particular tasks and that level of difficulty can be changed deliberately by teachers is today gaining recognition (Downing & Thackray, 1971; Downing, 1973).

Previous chapters provided examples of ways in which this belief can be implemented. Descriptions of a variety of teaching strategies illustrated how particular learning tasks could be drastically simplified. By implication one result of the use of such strategies could be that the need for a readiness period or readiness work would be greatly reduced or eliminated altogether. Furthermore, in a few cases it was even hinted that specific readiness exercises, for instance, learning to name isolated letters, may be not only redundant but even outright harmful.

Before dismissing the notion of reading readiness altogether, however, we should examine the possible benefits of pretraining reading-related skills. The main thrust of prereading work in recent years has been in the area of decoding. The evidence we shall examine deals therefore with this aspect of reading preparatory exercises.

HOW BENEFICIAL ARE DECODING-ORIENTED PREREADING PROGRAMS?

Lists of skills included in programs designed to prepare kindergartners for the tasks they will have to face when learning to read often include some or many of the following: visual-motor perception, fine motor coordination, visual motor coordination, figure-ground discrimination, spatial relations, color discrimination, perceptual constancy, visual memory, visual discrimination, visual sequencing, auditory discrimination in addition to skills having to do with gross motor development, instruction in body concepts, and the like (i.e., Meyers & Ball, 1974).

Among the many programs aimed at training these and related abilities, the "Frostig Program for Development of Visual Perception" (Frostig & Horn, 1968) had a particularly great impact on classroom practices. Consequently it attracted also a predominant share of the attention of would-be evaluators of the results of reading preparatory work (i.e., Harris, 1969; Hartman & Hartman, 1973; Hammill, Goodman, & Wiederholt, 1974). By and large, these studies failed to establish significant correlations between visual perception and reading achievement, or positive effects of Frostig's and other visual perception training programs. In fact the reverse was sometimes true. Rosen (1964) found that about 300 first graders who had daily an additional half hour's reading instruction improved more in reading than a matched sample who had devoted an identical amount of time to Frostig exercises. Gibson and Levin (1975) who reviewed additional studies on the effects of discrimination pretraining, concluded that most of the advocated techniques did not prove advantageous. Moreover, they felt that letter discrimination "normally proceeds quite well spontaneously, and that confusion of single letters is seldom an important source of difficulty in learning to read" (p. 246). Hence, they strongly imply that pretraining on perception, letter naming, and other skills whose usefulness for learning to read has not been unequivocally established is at best superfluous. In fact even the Frostig, Lefever, & Whittlesey (1961) test of visual perception which had predated the Frostig Program and had been the source of its rationale, proved on re-examination to be a poor predictor of reading achievement (Olson, 1966; Rosen & Ohnmacht, 1968; Pick, 1970).

The reading research community has adopted these conclusions so overwhelmingly that, in recent authorative collections of research (i.e., Resnick & Weaver, 1979; Pearson, 1984) no studies dealing with the pretraining of perception and other skills formerly believed to foster readiness for learning to read were included. There would be little sense in restating this were it not that phasing out well-established educational practices sometimes proves, even more, difficult than getting them adopted in the first place.

Although Gates (1922) showed 66 years ago that there is no "general" ability to perceive, programs designed to train perception per se continue to flourish. Durkin (1974b) attributes the tendency of teachers to spend time on "unnecessary and even erroneous instruction" (p. 13) to their unquestioning use of commercial teaching materials and acceptance of the instructions contained in the manuals which come with these materials. According to Durkin (1974b) this tendency is so strong that it persists even when the prescribed instructional sequences make little or no pedagogical sense or are clearly outdated. Durkin found that sometimes teachers observed by her were aware of the inadequacy of particular routines they were using, but continued to use them out of a combination of "insufficient self-confidence and a naive trust in commercial materials" (p. 17).

In the present case the problem is especially severe, because research findings in reading may not easily reach kindergarten and preschool teachers. On the other hand readiness programs tend to be well advertised and aggressively promoted. The lack of direct day-to-day professional contacts between kindergarten teachers and elementary school staff may further contribute to efforts on the part of the former to prove themselves by "preparing" their charges as best they can for school. A diversified, elaborate commercial program which promises to do just that is therefore enticing. Classroom practices in a few Boston kindergartens described in Chapter Two can serve as further corroborating evidence of how preoccupied with reading many kindergarten teachers have become.

This is a good starting point for the next issue we wish to discuss, namely the dangers of reading preparatory work which is not thoroughly coordinated with instructional strategies children will encounter when learning to read.

CONFUSIONS ARISING FROM UNCOORDINATED TEACHING EFFORTS

The following case history was reported by the parents of a little boy, whom we shall call Raymond. Raymond's father is a university professor.

Like most faculty children at that institution, Raymond attended a private preschool, run by the university. The school has a varied and many-sided curriculum and a long waiting list. Raymond, who entered when he was four and one-half years old, adjusted quickly. Because of his art work, which teachers found exceptionally good, he became used to being extravagantly praised, and to having his work exhibited conspicuously. During his first months in school Raymond learned to label his work by himself RAYMOND, and to recognize the names of his closest friends. Teachers habitually used all capital letters for children's names and classroom labels. About the middle of the school year Raymond's class was asked to participate in an experimental project of the university, designed to teach reading at early ages. Children started to have daily group sessions in which reading was taught from mimeographed booklets provided by the project. Booklets were along so-called linguistic principles, and in lower-case letters only. Teachers now used lower-case letters exclusively in all their writing, but did not discard many of the old labels displayed in rooms. Raymond learned to write his name in the new way—raymond—but made no efforts to learn to recognize also the names of his friends. Children were assigned to groups by reading achievements, and teachers, parents, and adults involved in the project showed keen interest in their rate of progress. Raymond, who was among the oldest children in his class, did surprisingly poorly in reading, and found himself in the second lowest group. The booklets provided by the project were numbered, so that children were well aware of their progress compared to that of their peers. By the end of the school year Raymond was still working on the second booklet while some of his classmates were on the fourth. He also knew the names of several letters. All the booklets provided that year were on a very initial level and contained altogether only a few letters and extremely limited nonappealing content of the "can dan fan nan?" type.

The next year Raymond went to the kindergarten which is part of the university-administered elementary school. He again had a very good teacher with many years' experience, who was well known for her success in preparing her pupils for school. Actually, a great part of the work in her room is usually devoted to early reading activities, some of it along Language Experience lines. She also has very sound science and math programs. There were a wide variety of books in class. The teacher used both capital and lower-case letters intermingledly in her own writing and expected the same from her charges. Raymond now learned to write his name Raymond. He also participated eagerly and well in the math and science programs but shirked reading activities, despite considerable pressure by the teacher. The gap between him and other children in his class, some of whom were already able to decode easy texts, grew steadily wider. Due to Raymond's perceptive parents, he got professional help in time to prevent serious difficulties. Yet even at such a relatively early stage, his problems necessitated relatively prolonged treatment.

It is hard to know what percentage of children with so-called reading disabilities suffer from no more than a personal history somewhat like Raymond's, only without adequate help being secured early enough. Remedial specialists tend to attribute reading failure to a combination of interacting causative factors (i.e., Rosewell & Natchez, 1964) and to emphasize the urgent need to deviate as much as possible from sufferers' earlier learning experiences (i.e., Fernald, 1943; Roswell & Natchez, 1964). This may indicate an often unadmitted awareness that earlier educational history was somewhere at fault. Inconsistencies in teaching approaches, especially at sensitive stages like the onset, may perhaps be more often a contributing factor to reading disabilities than is generally recognized. Raymond's case is a good example in that it highlights concomitant conditions in which inconsistencies are particularly likely to occur, namely, when children move from one educational framework to another, and when basic school skills are taught by practitioners who were not specifically trained to teach them.

What this means in terms of the ongoing debate about when reading instruction per se should best begin is that teaching approach and children's development and preparedness are not the only factor which have to be taken into account. Other important factors which need be considered are whether overall circumstances are such that they will allow a child to continue in the setting in which instruction was initiated until basic reading processes are fully mastered, and further, to what extent adults who will be teaching have had adequate experience and training. Unless provisions in regard to these conditions are entirely favorable, it would seem that pretraining of decoding-related skills is too liable to result in haphazard accumulation of partial bits of information to be justified.

If some current practices aimed at increasing children's readiness to learn to read are ineffectual or even counterproductive, is there then no way in which children can be prepared for reading? Is it not wasteful not to try to make use of the considerable time young children are nowadays apt to spend in educational settings before they start school in order to develop skills that may help them cope better with future learning tasks? It is to this issue that we shall turn now.

USES AND ABUSES OF PRESCHOOLERS' TIME

First let us clearly reiterate where we stand. It was not argued that facile readers do not employ many cognitive and technical skills that have in recent years been identified through insightful and painstaking research efforts. What was questioned was only whether *pretraining* these skills out of context is the best way to prepare preschoolers for the learning tasks they will encounter at the onset of formal reading instruction. The evidence in Chapter Nine showed that introducing skills in preplanned sequence so that at each stage they can be applied functionally in conjunction with all that has been learned before, seems a more promising approach. A further concern which was raised in the last paragraph was that trying to pretrain subskills or even to start reading instruction proper in preschool often results in fragmented and uncoordinated teaching efforts which may in the long run prove more confusing than helpful. On both these counts it would seem that direct teaching of isolated prereading skills had best wait until formal reading instruction starts.

A third point which was mentioned only in passing and to which we shall now return at greater length was that typically reading preparatory workbooks address themselves mainly to developing skills which will be of help in decoding processes. Yet in recent years, the reading research community seems agreed that it is in the area of comprehension and not decoding that the chief difficulty resides (Vellutino, 1977; Teitel, 1980). Using preschoolers' time in order to prepare them chiefly for decoding may thus not be in their best interest. Furthermore, doing so could in a way prove discriminatory against children whose homes are not book-oriented.

Child rearing traditions of majority culture middle-class parents tend to lay a firm foundation for book appreciation and reading comprehension (Chomsky, 1972a; Bissex, 1980, Heath, 1982; Snow, 1983). Concentrating in preschool frameworks on pretraining decoding skills could thus unintentionally widen the gap in future school achievements between children from school-oriented and nonschool-oriented homes. Middle-class children whose preschool teachers engaged mainly in developing decoding-related skills (which prepare essentially for first grade learning tasks) would continue to be exposed in their homes to stimulating experiences which would be conducive to improved performance also in later grades. On the other hand, minority culture children whose school preparedness depends to a much greater extent on what is offered in preschools might emerge prepared solely for first grade. Consequently they might fall behind in later years when decoding has already been achieved by all and it is comprehension which becomes a prime factor for successful school performance. This is, in fact, exactly the situation described in studies comparing school achievements of children from different social and/or cultural backgrounds in various countries (Kyöstiö, 1973, 1980; Thorndike, 1973; Chall & Jacobs, 1984; Lewy & Chen, 1974).

Against this background it seems pertinent to ask whether it would not be preferable to use precious preschool years in order to prepare children for the kind of learning tasks they will face throughout their school careers, instead of for skills they will master anyway in the early grades?

Learning difficulties in school subjects have been attributed to many causes. Among them is the discrepancy between the language of school text books and other resource materials and everyday speech with which learners are familiar. Mosberg (1978) claims that "one of the most serious problems in reading research and in teaching reading is the lack of clear distinctions between what are reading and what are essentially language problems" (p. 163). For many children and adults existing oracy skills are inappropriate to written language. In these cases so-called reading problems could be solved by identifying and teaching skills necessary for dealing effectively with written language (Mosberg, 1978). Experimental studies pursued at the University of Haifa showed that it may be possible to familiarize children with book language before they are able to read on their own.

In technologically highly developed societies young children are extensively exposed to written language through lists, labels, television, and junk mail (Goodman & Altwerger, 1981; Heath, 1983; Taylor, 1983). However, studies revealed pervasive social class and cultural differences in the amount and nature of parents' story book reading to their preschool aged children (Heath, 1982, 1983; Schieffelin and Cochran-Smith, 1984; Teale, 1986). Feitelson & Goldstein (1986) found that about 60% of kindergarteners in neighborhoods where children tend to do poorly in school did not own a single book. On the other hand, kindergartners in neighborhoods where children tend to do well in school owned on the average more than 54 books each. Also daily reading to children had started in about half of the families in these neighborhoods before children were two years old, and in 86% of all families before children were three.

In most languages, speech addressed to young children lacks many of the complexities and sophisticated grammatical forms found in written texts (Cazden, 1972; Tizard, 1980; Perera, 1984). One would assume that through being read to by "mediating" (Heath, 1982; Cochran-Smith, 1984) adults preschoolers would acquire at least a passive knowledge of literary language. In fact, kindergartners who were read to regularily in classroom settings improved not only on comprehension but also on measures of active use of language. In addition they sometimes used typical "book language" in conversing with each other during free play periods (Eshel, 1979; Feitelson, Goldstein, Eshel, Flasher, Levin, & Sharon, 1984; Reshef, 1984).

Ingesting literary language may not be the only way in which reading to preschoolers may affect their future performance at school.

Books intended for young children frequently include themes that are outside young children's everyday experiences. When reading adults interpret these to their listeners, elaborating beyond the text where needed (Heath, 1982; Cochran-Smith, 1984), reading sessions may substantially enrich children's accumulating information base. Comprehension involves the integration of new information with preexisting schemata (Pearson, Hansen, & Gordon, 1979; Langer & Nicolich, 1981; Langer, 1984). Therefore, knowledge acquired through being read to may in turn improve children's ability to comprehend additional texts as appropriate schemata will be available when needed (Steffensen, Joag-Dev, & Anderson, 1979; Adams and Bruce, 1982). In the Haifa studies, kindergartners and first graders who were read to regularly for four to six months outperformed control groups on measures of reading (for kindergartners, listening) comprehension (Eshel, 1979; Feitelson et al. 1984; Feitelson, Kita, & Goldstein, 1986).

Heath (1982) suggests, that because knowledge that is acquired in reading sessions is acquired by way of language, children should also possess adequate terminology to discuss this knowledge in class, and answer teachers' questions about it.

A further way in which reading to children may increase their ability to cope with literary texts in the future is that through listening to stories children may become familiar with story structure (Applebee, 1980). Their resulting expectations in regard to stories could help them cope successfully when they encounter new ones (Stein, 1979). These expectations were largely borne out when first graders living in a neighborhood with a high percentage of multiproblem families, who were read several volumes of a series story, did well on retelling a picture story (Feitelson, Kita, & Goldstein, 1986).

Another result that stood out in all the studies of reading to kindergartners was the increase in children's attention span for hearing stories (Feitelson et al. 1984; Reshef, 1984).

To sum up, informed opinion as well as the results of experimental studies seem to indicate that a particularly good way to use the years *before* children enter school may be to emulate what middle-class parents seem to have been doing intuitively all along, namely read intensively to their children.

In general this approach seems to fit in well with the attitude of developmentalists. Kohlberg (1968) expresses himself strongly against teaching specific, by implication fragmented, bits of knowledge, despite the temptation to do so linked to the fact that the results of specific teaching can be easily assessed. Similarly Bloom (1976), in expounding on what he calls "cognitive entry behaviors" (p. 30) of learning tasks shows that general cognitive entry behaviors such as verbal ability and reading comprehension appear to influence later school learning more than *specific* cognitive behaviors, which are prerequisites for specific learning tasks (p. 69).

Reading to preschoolers does not require the kind of training, needed in order to teach school skills such as math or decoding. It is also on this account that reading to children would seem well suited for use by volunteers and practitioners who lack formal training for teaching decoding.

When preschoolers' time is viewed as valuable resource which has to be utilized to best advantage, there is need to dwell in passing also on another area of childhood activity which has lately come in for renewed attention, namely play in general and—even more so—make-believe play.

A growing appreciation for the role of play in the development of important cognitive skills and behavioral traits (Vygotsky, 1967; Bruner, 1972; Bruner, Jolly & Sylva, 1976; Sutton-Smith, 1979; Singer & Singer, 1980; Vandenberg, 1980; Pellegrini, 1983) has led to concern about the implications of studies which showed that in present-day societies environmental conditions sometimes restrict play (Hetzer, 1929; Ammar, 1954; Feitelson, 1954; LeVine & LeVine, 1963; Smilansky, 1968). Since studies which investigated play incidence found that high SES preschoolers usually have more play opportunities than low SES ones (Freyberg, 1973; Saltz, Dixon, & Johnson, 1977) the conclusions we reached in regard to reading to young children may apply also here. Using preschool time for prereading exercises instead of for play will be less disadvantageous for high SES children who have ample opportunity to play also outside preschool than for children whose homes do not provide a play-conducive environment.

The results of two studies which compared the effectiveness of reading readiness workbooks and informal play materials on furthering prereading skills cast further doubt on the benefits children supposedly derive from workbook exercises. In a carefully controlled experiment with 90 kindergartners, Church (1974) found that when children were retested a year later, those who had done workbook exercises were not superior to their mates who had engaged in play with form boards, puzzles, blocks building and the like on a visual perception measure and on a standardized reading achievement test. In Klebanov, Gruper, & Diab's (1983) study children in three groups who played with construction toys outperformed those who had done paper and pencil worksheets on assembling sentences from letter-blocks. More important still is that Church's comment—"while a few children found the work books enjoyable, many had to be continually encouraged or reprimanded to continue work" (p. 364)—applies to both studies. In the Klebanov et al. (1983) study children in the work sheet groups from widely divergent backgrounds (Arab village, new immigrant development town, oldtimer urban) could be induced to continue participation only by the promise that soon they too would be allowed to play. On the other hand children in the toy groups enjoyed their sessions, and tended to want to stay on rather than return to class. Paper and pencil prereading exercises may thus not only be no more effective than manipulative play with certain kinds of toys, but may even lead to an altogether negative attitude to such tasks. Thus, instead of preparing children for school they may unwittingly set them against it.

During play with construction toys children are free to interact with each other. They also tend to be actively engaged and can try different venues to their goal. Successful completion is self-evident and intrinsically rewarding. Reading preparatory worksheets on the other hand means that children have to work solitarily, to follow imposed directions, and that any evaluation of their efforts will have to be provided by adults.

When one believes that school beginners can learn to read within their first year at school, using preschool time in order to prepare children mainly for first grade may be wasteful. In some instances it may also be counterproductive. A more useful approach might be to use preschool time in order to develop skills and aptitudes which would be of use throughout children's school careers. The provision of ample play opportunities, access to books, and intensive regular reading to children may be ways to upgrade school performance also in the later grades.

It is to the early part of these later grades, namely, to the immediate post-initial stage of reading instruction that we shall now turn.

CHAPTER 11

Stage 2—From Decoder to Book Consumer

In the acquisition of many skills there comes a magic moment when all that has been drilled fuses together in smooth performance. A bicycler is able to ride without the aid of holding hands or training wheels, a swimmer can swim the length of the pool, and a tennis player can slam across a serve with force and accuracy. In professional jargon we would say that subroutines have been mastered and have become automatic; they can now be perormed without conscious attention. Attaining this stage allows the performer to enjoy the exhilaration of achievement and, in the long run, also the continuing dividends of a new competence. The present chapter deals with the stage in a reader's development that parallels these processes.

It is now that the new reader progresses from initially established decoding routines to automaticity and the ability to engage in reading for its own sake. Chall (1979) appropriately names this stage "confirmation, fluency, ungluing from print" (p. 41). Emphasizing similarities to the acquisition of other skills will be an aid in making a more convincing case for our main concern, namely the assumption that it is essential that newly proficient readers will engage in much reading, and that a good way for this to happen is for them to enjoy what they are doing. The emphasis here is on "newly" for we also assume that once essential decoding skills have been mastered, the transition from decoding simplified texts to hooked consumption of books should occur as quickly as possible—certainly before a negative attitude to reading as something boring, relegated only to prescribed periods in school, has had time to gain foothold (Southgate, Arnold, & Johnson, 1981).

In ascribing crucial importance for later reading development to the early occurrence of Stage 2 we are in agreement with Chall (1979, 1983c), Southgate, Arnold, & Johnson (1981) and others. Relying on data of Bloom (1964) and Kraus (1973), Chall (1979) shows that pupils who have fallen behind by third grade are likely to continue to experience failure throughout their whole school careers. She also believes that it is at this early stage that the gap between children from non-school-oriented homes and their peers from intellectually stimulating ones, widens. Southgate and her colleagues (1981), whose data were obtained in Britain, also stress the vital importance of the immediate post initial stage for turning children on to reading. For if children have not established the reading habit by the time they enter what in America would be fourth grade, there is great likelihood that they will join the ranks of those who were found not to have read a single book on their own in the course of a month. Furthermore, the percentage of children who did not read for pleasure increased from 13% of sampled 10-year-olds to 36% by the age of 14 (Whitehead, Capey, Maddren, & Wellings, 1977). Stage 2 is thus a crucial turning point, radically different from the stages that preceded it, as well as from those that follow.

Chall (1979) calls her Stage 3 "Reading for Learning." At this stage reading becomes a tool, in the service of different subject-matter areas. Chall (1979) feels that for many children the skills needed in Stage 3 will have to be taught specifically in school. Stage 3 may also be the appropriate time for introducing children to literary devices and other tools useful in dealing with literary texts. Therefore, it is at this and the following stages that educators will benefit most from results of the immense research efforts directed in recent years to metacognitive processes related to reading comprehension.

Stage 3 is beyond our present concerns. It was brought up only in order to highlight pertinent differences between it and Stage 2. We believe that Stage 2 in reading acquisition is one of those interim periods during which newly learned skills are practiced and integrated till they become in time stepping stones towards higher levels of performance (i.e. Lesgold & Perfetti, 1981). Skill development literature generally suggests that such plateau periods are essential prerequisites for further learning growth (Samuels, 1978). In other words, we assume that unless new readers are given adequate opportunities to engage in intensive reading bouts in the course of Stage 2, developments ideally envisioned for later stages may be impeded. That this is more than idle speculation is shown by the consistent finding that children who fall behind in the early grades seldom catch up (Bloom, 1976; Chall, 1979).

The overriding aim in regard to children in Stage 2 is therefore to entice them to become readers. This may require the discarding of long-time favorite classroom practices. Because we live at a time when alternative ways of spending time enjoyable are more widely available to children than ever before, it would seem that above all one would have to make sure that reading is experienced as a highly pleasurable activity in which one would like to engage of one's own volition, and that negative experiences connected with reading be avoided. We shall focus on two main issues—"what?" and "how?" Namely, what kind of reading materials will make children want to read? And how could reading sessions be conducted and organized so that children will enjoy them?

CHARACTERISTICS OF READING MATERIALS DESIGNED TO EXPAND POST-INITIAL PROFICIENCY AND LURE CHILDREN TO READING

Maintaining Literary Quality

One of the many challenging findings of a four-year study conducted by University of Manchester scientists (Southgate, Arnold, & Johnson, 1981) on reading practices in the first two grades of British Junior Schools (seven- and eight-year-olds) was that teachers used basic reading-scheme books to a much greater extent than had been assumed. Similarly on the American reading scene basal readers continue to be very widely used (Aukerman, 1981). This is surprising since for many years critics have claimed that the use of basals does not promote reading as a lifetime habit (i.e., Jacobs, 1953; Lazar, 1957).

Wiberg and Trost (1970) compared the content of first grade primers and the contents of free choice library selections made by 45 first grade students throughout a whole year. The total number of selections during that time was 1,371. There was a very marked discrepancy between the two. In primer stories activities were neutral and redundant without much content significance and variation. Family attachment and younger siblings were emphasized. Library selections on the other hand were very diversified and could not be easily stereotyped. The two main clusters which could be established were: "(1) fun, fantasy-promoting, highly creative imagery, plot and characterization, and (2) adventuresome, age appropriate or relevant to a more advanced age, informative, life-oriented realism" (p. 797).

The fact that stories in readers for the early grades tend to lack suspense, realistic characterizations, variety in the selection of topics, themes which appeal to children's imagination or challenge their feelings of self-worth, and that they are overly bland and shallow has been criticized by nearly every author who wrote on the subject (i.e. Blom, Waite, & Zimet, 1970; Zimet, 1972; Chall, 1976; Beck, McKeown, Mc-Caslin, & Burkes, 1979; Bettelheim & Zelan, 1982; Southgate, Arnold, & Johnson, 1981).

Advocates of basals sometimes claim that while these and other weaknesses may have existed in the past, they have been rectified in recent editions of the better-known programs (Aukerman & Aukerman, 1981). However, a sample story provided in the *Teacher's Manual* of a popular basal hardly bears out this contention. Here it is:

"The Peter Rabbit Play"

Jeff jumped from his bed. This was the day for the Peter Rabbit play at school. And Jeff's teacher was going to let him play Peter Rabbit. Jeff dressed very fast that morning. He got something to eat. Then he ran from his apartment. Soon he was at school with all the other boys and girls.

"Boys and girls," said the teacher.

"You won't forget what to do in the play, will you? Jeff, what are you in the play?"

"I won't forget," said Jeff. "I am Peter Rabbit and I am bad. I run away from the rabbit house. I get hungry, and so I go into Mr. McGregor's garden. I eat and eat and eat."

"What comes next?" said the teacher.

Billy's hand went up. "I run after Peter Rabbit," he said. "I am Mr. McGregor, and I yell at him. I don't like rabbits eating things in my garden."

"Then what?" said the teacher.

"I jump into a big can," said Jeff. "But the can has water in it, and I get all wet. So I jump from the can when Mr. McGregor is not looking. He won't get his hands on me! I run away as fast as my legs can go."

"And then?" said the teacher.

"I go back to my mother," said Jeff. "And my mother gets after me. And, boy do I get it from her!"

"I am the mother," said a tall girl. "Peter was very bad. He has to go to bed hungry. The other rabbits get something to eat but not poor Peter. Bad rabbits must go to bed hungry."

"Very good," said the teacher.

"Now, rabbits, get the ears and put them on."

The children went to a box and got the rabbit ears they had made. The teacher looked at the children.

"Billy," she said, "are you a little mixed up? You are the man, Mr. McGregor. You don't need rabbit ears."

"What am I thinking of?" said Billy. He put the ears back into the box.

Then the children from the next room came to see the play.

The play was good, and the children liked it.

It was fun when Peter hid in the can.

It was fun when Mr. McGregor yelled.

But the best fun came when Mr. McGregor put on rabbit ears.

(Teacher's edition, Level 7 of the *Young American Basic Reading Program*; In Aukerman and Aukerman, 1981, pp. 405–406).

What is it that puts one off in stories like these? In great part it is their contrived nature. The accompanying teachers' manual to "The Peter Rabbit Play" story (Aukerman & Aukerman, 1981, pp. 404–407) shows clearly that the main instructional goal of the envisaged lesson was to train specific decoding and language skills. In other words what is happening in this case is that language skills are being taught via texts in schoolbooks. Many experts have argued that when instead of meeting the real thing, namely, fiction written by artists out of their own inclination, children are exposed to stories which were crafted for instructional purposes, they may not discover, "what reading is and what it is for" (Britton, 1977).

We do not wish to enter the question whether this may be legitimate in Stage 3 and beyond, when reading serves also for instructional purposes, and when hopefully children have already discovered the joys of reading. However, Stage 2, is precisely the time when children should become enthusiastic about reading. Endangering this main purpose for the sake of other goals which, at this stage, are of secondary importance hardly seems wise. Especially when, as in the present case, a closer examination of the skills, which according to the Teachers Manual "The Peter Rabbit Play" was supposed to train, reveals that they could have been introduced equally well if not even better by other strategies.

"The Peter Rabbit Play" is also a handy example in order to point out additional problems which sometimes arise when pedagogic considerations decide choice of texts in children's readers. When authors and compilers are strongly concerned with specific learning goals, other important considerations may unwittingly escape attention.

"The Peter Rabbit Play," for example, cannot be fully understood without previous knowledge of Beatrix Potter's "The Tale of Peter Rabbit," which not all children have. Also notable in this example is the fact that the child who got "mixed up" and whose mistake was the "best fun" of the story happened to be Billy, who in the illustrations is shown to be the single black child in class, a reinforcing of ethnic stereotypes that the authors surely did not consciously intend.

The fact that it seems to be difficult to give attention to the very many diverse elements of scholastic reading programs is also brought out by Beck at al.'s (1979) finding that, even in widely used programs, accompanying pictures sometimes conflict with texts they were meant to illustrate.

One reason why it may be difficult to develop truly effective reading programs, devoid of the kind of mishaps just described, is that they are altered so very frequently. According to Aukerman (1981) American reader series must be revised every five years or less so that they can be used in states where reading series compete for "state adoption" every fifth year. "A series with a copyright date older than five years would not be considered for adoption" (p. 12).

To an observer from abroad this practice appears highly questionable on both artistic as well as pedagogic grounds. The enduring quality of good children's fiction is a matter beyond dispute. Is not the very use of the term classic for the best of it an acknowledgement of the continuing appeal of these works? Nor are good children's stories so numerous that one can easily forego the use of any of them. Assuming that compilators of a reading series have come up with an age-appropriate selection of works of real literary merit, what point would there be in having to discard them after only five years? It may well be that many of the faults commonly attributed to typical basal fare are due to the fact that stories in basals have to be crafted under time pressures and with very many specifications in mind. Few would claim that such circumstances are conducive to literary creation. A good conclusion to our argument could be a reminder of the time when the Swedish Ministry of Education commissioned a famous author to write a geography book and Selma Lagerlöf's *Niels Holgerson* was the result. What would have been gained, one might well ask, had the five-year rule applied there?

Also on pedagogical grounds, having to renew school books every five years seems self-defeating. Developing a well-conceived, experience-based instructional approach is a very lengthy process. Ideally, once such a program has been completed, all that should be needed would be continued improvements of rather minor details in accord with changing needs and accumulating feedback from the field. The long successful histories of the *Blue-backed Speller* or McGuffey's *Eclectic Readers* are illustrations of such an approach and indicate how eminently practical it seemed to be.

Perhaps we ought to adopt the view of Greene and Petty (1959) that when a book has had frequent revisions, this shows that the authors did not invest enough initial effort in fully conceiving and developing their instructional approach.

In many countries long continued use of texts modified only slightly from time to time is the rule rather than the exception. Bettelheim and Zelan (1982) mention an Austrian primer which was reprinted 22 times without changes.

Data collected by Southgate and her associates (Southgate, Arnold, & Johnson, 1981) between 1975 and 1977 also show that a considerable portion of the readers in use in schools in the Manchester area at that time, had been published in the 1950s or before. Also the innovative "Breakthrough" approach to initial reading (Mackay, Thompson, & Schaub, 1979) which has gained wide popularity in Britain, shares the pattern of slow careful evolvement. The project began in 1964, followed by a first edition in 1970 with so far only a single revision in 1979.

The Problem of Vocabulary Control

In the previous section we discussed the often restated view that authentic children's literature, unemcumbered by ulterior aims, is much more likely to turn on seven- and eight-year-olds to reading than typical school book fare (i.e. Zimet, 1972; Southgate, Arnold, & Johnson, 1981; Bettelheim & Zelan, 1982). Publishers have been influenced by these trends and works by recognized authors are now included in many reading series (Aukerman, 1981). However, the tendency to introduce selections from original writings of established authors is often counteracted by the belief in a need for so-called "vocabulary control." Consequently, original pieces are relegated mainly to readers intended for the intermediary and higher grades of elementary school, while material with literary merit for the beginning grades, if included at all, is sometimes heavily edited.

The small size of the vocabulary used in some American readers for the early grades has been the subject of much adverse comment (i.e. Trace, 1961, 1965; Spalding & Spalding, 1969; Chall, 1977, 1983b). Critics have also pointed out that stringent vocabulary control results in truncated unnatural sentences which in turn impede children's ability to understand what they read (Smith, 1983). Thus a measure which was introduced in order to facilitate reading by beginners may in fact make it more difficult. Altogether the issue of vocabulary control seems to be beset by confusion.

To introduce clarity it is first of all important to realize that "the rationale for 'vocabulary control' in primers, and first and second grade reading textbooks, is based not on the limited *meaning* [my emphasis, D.F.] vocabularies of the children, but on their limited facility with recognizing. . . . .words in print" (Lorge & Chall, 1963, p. 154). The chief aim of vocabulary control in the early grades is not to make texts more easily understood. In fact, as was already mentioned, vocabulary control per se may have the opposite effect.

Vocabulary control came into its own when beginning reading instruction was conceived as drilling instant recognition of "sight words." During the nearly 40 years this approach to reading instruction predominated in the United States, decoding skills were introduced only very gradually in second and third grade. Children's ability to "read" was thus confined for a relatively long period to texts made up of words which they knew. Hence the need for strict vocabulary control.

However, when as at present, learning to decode starts in most cases simultaneously with the onset of formal instruction, and especially when graphemes are introduced sequentially according to language patterns, progress is no longer in terms of single words. Consequently, vocabulary control of reading texts becomes unnecessary. What will have to be exercised instead is control by graphemes and language patterns— namely at each step texts will contain only those graphemes and language patterns which have already been introduced. The pages of the Viennese primer in Chapter Seven can serve as pertinent example. They show how the addition of each new grapheme makes accessible *many* additional words. Obviously, as learning proceeds, texts become less restricted, till ideally, once all possible patterns have been mastered, restrictions can be dropped altogether. It is here that the special problems of English once again come to the fore.

We have seen in Chapter Seven that even in regard to languages in which symbol-sound relationships are highly predictable, the inventory of "phonemic reading facts" learners have to master in order to be able to correctly pronounce every word they may come across will differ from language to language. Supposedly, the smaller the number of "phonemic reading facts" in a particular language the more quickly readers will be able to complete Stage 1 and proceed to Stage 2. In orthographies like Russian, Finnish, or German where the inventory of essential "phonemic reading facts" is relatively small and visual characteristics of graphic symbols do not create special problems for average school beginners, it is often assumed that children will have learned to decode after only six to seven months of formal instruction. In English, on the other hand, the task may appear much larger. Nor does it seem quite possible to conceive of a definite point when it can be considered "completed." Does this mean that reading matter need indeed be restricted well into second or third grade, and that original literature cannot be included before that? The answer to this question may prove less complicated than it looks at first hand. We have seen in Chapter Seven that beginners' programs which emphasize the regularities of English orthography have been able to come up with remarkably compact sets of reading facts. Further, the authors of several of these programs stress that they assume that learning to decode will be completed within the first year of formal instruction (i.e. Spalding & Spalding, 1969; Carus, Anderson, Webber, Thomas, & Lebo, 1979). On the other hand, it certainly does seem true that contrary to other languages in English the process can never be considered *quite* completed. It is always possible that a reader will come across a word that he/she will mispronounce were he/she to follow only regular pronunciation rules. It is here that teachers' reactions in Stage 2 will have to be entirely different from those appropriate in Stage 1. All through Stage 1, and also later whenever readers have difficulty in decoding regularly spelled words, teachers will help them decode with the aid of numerous instructional devices available in classrooms. In Stage 2, however, a major aim is not to obstruct reading processes unnecessarily. Therefore, whenever it can be assumed that a difficulty stems from the idiosyncrasies of a particular word and not from lack of mastery of decoding strategies, insistence on going into esoteric rules for pronouncing non-regular words would seem counterproductive. A preferable strategy in such cases would probably be to supply the word speedily, with a short remark that it is irregular. Results of a recent study by Meyer (1982), who found no difference between word analysis and word-supply correction procedures in regard to poor readers who were in an intensive synthetic-phonics remedial program would seem to support this line of action. Furthermore, most probably the problem will arise anyway mainly when children engage in oral reading. In the next section, when we proceed to the question of "how" we shall see that in Stage 2 *silent* reading predominates. Also as children's silent reading becomes more proficient it gradually takes on characteristics of reading processes of fluent readers. Accordingly, children become increasingly able to access words directly, without recourse to phonological sounding rules (Lesgold & Perfetti, 1981).

When called upon to read aloud, learners who have reached this state usually pronounce most words correctly according to regional and social class usage (Chomsky, 1979b). That knowledge of sounding rules per se is not all that matters at this stage is evident from listening to the reading of non-native speakers of English, who tend to intonate and pronounce differently from native speakers of English even when, like, for instance, Henry Kissinger, they happen to have an excellent command of written English.

Circumstantial Factors Affecting Motivation

Typical classroom readers generally contain collections of stories, poems, and informational pieces. In recent years readers are often designated by level rather than by grade (Aukerman, 1981) in order to prevent stigmatizing children who progress at slow rates. Even when books are not overtly marked by grade, most publishers of present-day American basal series tend to provide approximately two books for each grade level beyond first grade (Aukerman, 1981). In less affluent countries, a single book will frequently serve for the entire school year.

Southgate, Arnold, and Johnson's (1981) study shows that British practices are somewhat different. There, the majority of what in the

States would have been second graders included in the study read three to four "teaching books" a year. The overall range of books read with the help of the teacher was between one and 27. By the third grade the range had widened to between one and 58 books. Moreover, the number of books children had read with the teacher were not always all the books they had read in class. Especially in the older age group (paralleling American third grade) children who had read the final book of the program were allowed to have "free choice" books to read on their own (Southgate, Arnold, and Johnson, 1981, p. 119). According to the recording procedures used in the study these additional books would not have been included in the list of books read with the teacher, that is, the number quoted above.

Southgate, Arnold, & Johnson (1981) found that children's records of the books they had read with their teachers were more accurate than expected. Southgate and her colleagues attribute this to the fact that "completing a 'teaching book' was generally regarded as a highlight for both the teacher and pupil, and the process of recording it gave satisfaction to both" (p. 115). If this is the case it seems surprising that school-book publishers do not afford learners this pleasure more often. Southgate, Arnold, and Johnson (1981) mention that generally the most widely used "teaching books" were of "substantial" size with about 200 "well filled" pages so that completing one was apt to take several months (p. 119).

By contrast younger British children, namely, those still in infant schools, typically go through a great number of short soft-bound booklets in a single year. This obviously enables children to enjoy the pleasurable experience of having completed a book much more frequently. In addition, they have the repeated thrill of starting out on a new one.

Continuing to work on one and the same book for what must seem to second and third graders a very long stretch of time, may, on the other hand, dim its appeal. According to Clay (1979) school book publishers in New Zealand, have initiated a changeover to "the Little Book approach" in the interest of children's morale and motivation (p. 155), thereby enabling children to experience joy in accomplishment more often.

Continued use of one reading book may also lead to an additional problem. The better readers in a group may browse through a book in their hands and read many or all the stories in it *before* they are read in class. Consequently, when these stories are eventually read in class, these erstwhile eager readers may be bored and lose interest.

If a great number of short books seem advantageous in Stage 1, why abandon that practice in Stage 2 just when the motivational aspects of reading may be even more important than before?

Once again it would seem that decisions of this kind ought not to be left to chance and local conventions alone. Relatively simple research paradigms could provide substantiated information about possible advantages and disadvantages of different options in regard to number and size of class readers at different learning stages. Actually, the possible disadvantages of typical classroom readers are compounded by an additional factor. In British Infant School booklets there is only one self-contained story in each booklet. On the other hand, classroom readers the world over usually contain what Southgate, Arnold, and Johnson (1981) refer to as "disjointed collections of short stories and other items" (p. 122). The problem here is twofold. First, the pieces gathered together bear no intrinsic relation to each other in either content or style. This means that every few pages the neophyte reader will be called upon to, as it were, change gears and adjust both to the personal way different authors have in telling their tale and in using language, as well as to a switch about in content matter. Factual informative pieces intermingle with fairy tales, and stories depicting events generations apart follow upon each other. Second, the literary genre the beginner will encounter in these circumstances more than any other are short stories, which are harder to follow than more fully developed narratives. In fact, in their intended effects, authors of short stories often assume considerable literary sophistication on the part of their audience.

Recent research (Feitelson, Kita & Goldstein, 1986) showed that what could perhaps be called the opposite of the short story, namely, series, in which the same set of characters continue their adventures from volume to volume, have especially strong appeal for young readers. Continuity in story setting and unchanging narrative and language style may thus be qualities to look for when the goal is to hook beginners on reading.

It is intriguing to speculate that not too long ago compilers of reading texts seem to have been well aware of this aspect of children's tastes in reading matter. Even if the accounts of the doings of the proverbial and often ridiculed fictional families which filled the pages of many bestselling reading programs of the 1940s, 1950s and 1960s fell far short of authentic children's literature, they were still exercises in continuity. This does not mean that there is need to return to the "fabricated" school readers of the past. Massive exposure to enticing real books seems much preferable and has in fact been advocated many times (i.e. Jacobs, 1953; Lazar, 1957; Veatch, 1959; Sartain, 1960; Stauffer, 1960; Duker, 1966, 1969). Although "series stories" are not generally considered to have much literary merit (Harris and Hodges, 1981), it would seem that this genre should be included and even emphasized in Stage 2, because of the undeniable great attraction this format has for young readers.

Suggesting that teachers would do best to let six-, seven-, and eight-year-olds "enjoy real books" raises the question whether children in the early grades are able to tackle original writings? Were not graded class-room-readers created in the first place partly in response to the need to provide children with transitory reading matter, which would help them develop skills so that eventually they could advance to real books? This brings us to the second main topic of this Chapter: the "how" of reading activities in Stage 2. For it may well be that it is within the means of carefully developed instructional strategies to overcome the gap between Stage 2 children's skills and the level of difficulty of fiction which appeals to them.

THE "HOW" OF STAGE 2 READING ACTIVITIES

Aided and Unaided Reading

Southgate, Arnold, and Johnson's (1981) study of post-initial reading practices in British schools provides in-depth insights into the twin aspects of classroom life. Their data show what it is teachers as well as pupils do during instructional time, and how the one impinges on the other. One of their more startling findings was that in the classrooms they studied there was no consistent relationship between the levels of children's attainments and the level of difficulty in the texts they were reading. "Different teachers provided children of the same ages and levels of reading attainment with very different levels of reading books" (p. 121). Thus, eight-year-old average readers might be reading at one end books intended for a reading level of 5.0 to 5.6 and at the other ones for 10.0 to 10.11. What was especially striking was that many more children were reading with the help of their teachers books that were too easy for them rather than the other way around. Consequently, the research team poses the question whether it is a profitable use of teachers' time to have them help children read books which they could have easily read on their own.

Southgate and her colleagues have come up here with a very pertinent distinction, namely the differences between children's aided and unaided reading, both of which should occur in class. Graded and simplified reading matter can have its uses, as long as it is intended primarily for children's private reading. However, during so-called "directed reading," namely when reading activities are led by the teacher, the aim is to expand and upgrade children's skills. Consequently, this would seem an appropriate time to help children make the transition to regular fare. Before we turn to the complex issue of what it is that should take place during teacher-led instruction, let us first conclude our discussion of children's unaided reading.

The fact that in many modern schools other activities have usurped the place of reading, and that consequently children may not always have enough opportunity to read has been repeatedly documented (i.e. Durkin, 1979; Cazden, 1981; Mason, 1982). These findings and a growing concern about lack of models of adult readers in the home, as well as non-development of leisure time reading habits has led to a variety of attempted countermeasures. "Sustained silent reading" (ssr), namely fixed periods during which entire schools—pupils as well as staff—engage in undisturbed private reading is one of them (i.e. Mork, 1972; Evans & Towner, 1975; Gambrell, 1978; McCracken & McCracken, 1978; Moore, Jones, & Miller, 1980; Hong, 1981).

Advocates of ssr tend to emphasize the interrelatedness of all the elements of ssr, and to argue that the approach should be implemented holistically. However, such an all-or-nothing policy could, in the long run, result in many children missing reading experiences they might have had if at least some aspects of ssr had been implemented. The notion of everyone in a school reading at one and the same time may smack of overregimentation and therefore arouse antagonism, which could lead to a decision not to adopt ssr altogether. Ssr also hardly resembles naturalistic leisure time behavior. In terms of participating children it could conceivably turn into just another teacher-imposed activity, to be gotten through speedily, but not to be engaged in of one's own free will.

Making private reading an activity of choice, for instance during unoccupied time, when tasks have been completed, or as one of several alternatives during free activity periods, would ensure that undisturbed reading of one's own, according to personal preference, could acquire the flavor of something to be looked forward to, linked to relaxation and enjoyment. Decoding considerations, which limited choice of books children could read for fun in Stage 1 will most probably not be necessary in Stage 2. "Easy" in terms of books for unaided reading will thus mainly mean that most words are predictable or alternatively very common, that language and syntax are simple, themes fully developed, prerequisite knowledge kept to a minimum or incorporated in the tale, and that illustrations—if provided—fit in with the text (Beck et al., 1979).

Fortunately, in English-speaking countries with their vast readership, books of this kind are commercially available. In small countries the situation is more difficult and teachers may find it necessary to create their own easy books. In Israel, for instance, teachers sometimes buy English, French, or Italian titles with attractive illustrations, and substitute Hebrew or Arabic texts by simply pasting over the original print.

It has to be remembered that Stage 2 children's eagerness to engage in unaided reading for fun, and their ability to do so, will depend to a considerable degree on the reading-related experiences they had in Stage 1 and before formal instruction started. This is the time that information and acquaintance with book language and literary devices children acquired through being read to prior to entering school and in first grade will come in useful. Concurrent classroom experiences in regard to reading will also be of great importance. It is to these that we shall turn now.

Grouping and Its Concomitants

Grouped reading instruction, which became fashionable in the first half of this century, continues to be very widely practiced (Smith, 1965; Chall, 1967; Calfee & Drum, 1978; Durkin, 1979; Hiebert, 1983).

How does grouped reading typically work? What seems to be happening most often is that the teacher will be reading with one group, while children belonging to other groups carry out tasks which they were assigned beforehand. Once the portion allotted for that day is completed the teacher will take on another group. In Stage 2 many teachers continue to view group reading sessions as an effective way to train decoding (Mason & Osborn, 1982). Therefore, after a short introduction in which the teacher draws attention to the content of the passage children are about to read, and sometimes also points out decoding or language features which will be encountered, children are asked to take turns in reading the passage aloud (Aukerman, 1981; Cazden, 1981). This practice is often referred to in professional jargon as "round-robin" style reading, because it suggests the "image of a nest of baby birds wherein the one that gets fed next is the one holding its head highest and making the most noise" (Harris & Hodges, 1981, p. 283). An inordinate amount of attention to turn taking, often at the expense of more important matters, is only one of the problems besetting round robin style reading (McDermott, 1978; Cazden, 1981).

A second concern is that round-robin reading may have a negative effect on children's attitude to reading. Even under the best of circumstances, namely when the text is engrossing in its own right (Bruce, 1981), children are sufficiently proficient to be able to read it, and their previous encounters with reading were positive so that they are motivated to want to do so, they are unable to follow their inclination and read on, at their own speed, because of the necessity to "keep place" with the child reading aloud. Also, instead of being introduced to the text via undisturbed perusal or alternatively through the text being presented by a competent reader, the text is distorted by being read in start-and-stop fashion by far from perfect readers who are moreover interrupted by teacher corrections. Not only is there thus great likelihood that interest in what the text has to offer may be nipped in the bud; but it is also probable that the necessity to keep to the rate of an orally reading peer, who is moreover only a beginner, may be disadvantageous to emerging proficiency in speedy silent reading. Also, for the less able readers in the group, the distortions introduced by the child who is reading aloud are liable to add to and compound the difficulties they are experiencing anyway. In short, just at the point when it would seem of the utmost importance that the child develop efficient silent reading strategies, increase speed of reading, and come to enjoy reading for its own sake, round robin reading would seem to affect all three negatively.

Another issue which has increasingly drawn attention is whether grouping is altogether a good way to use pupils' and teachers' time. Cazden (1981) has shown that even in a group working directly with the teacher, children will not be engaged in reading all the time. Valuable time is sometimes spent on allocating turns, attempts to focus children's attention, poorly conceived or poorly presented explanations, and explanations that are not in keeping with children's level of understanding or the needs of the moment. The vignettes illustrating Cazden's argument show that the complexity of the situation, namely that the teacher was trying to make a given text understood in an interactive group situation, may have added considerably to the difficulty, and hence to the amount of time used.

Even more problematic, and also treated in the literature more extensively, is the fact that grouped reading instruction means unavoidably that children will be in direct contact with their teacher for only part of the time. At other times children will be working on their own. It is in the way they are kept busy at such times that British and American classroom practices differ markedly from each other. In British schools work children do on their own is largely self-directed, though clearly inspired and guided by the teacher. By the time they are in Stage 2 many children will already follow a personal project. Consequently, a particular child's reading and writing activities, art work, and craft creations will often be linked to a theme he/she is keenly interested in and knowledgeable about. There are also many additional kinds of writing, such as, composing stories or poems, reporting on family and other events, keeping personal diaries/journals, and the like.

In many American schools, on the other hand, seatwork in the early grades means that children fill out workbook assignments or ditto sheets. A major problem with workbook exercises is that the difficulty of the task at hand is compounded by the way the task is presented. Thus instead of children being able to start to work on their own, they often need initial explanations and guidance from their teacher. Durkin

(1979) and lately Mason (1982) have already pointed to the danger that eventually more effort and time is spent on administering workbook assignments than on direct teaching of reading comprehension.

Also, workbook assignments may not only not be an especially effective way to train reading comprehension, but worse still, they may cause children to actively dislike reading. Especially telling in this respect are Durkin's (1984) results in a study of poor black children who were successful readers:

> Consistently, the interviewees came across as children who did a great deal of reading, knew what kinds of books they liked, and appreciated teachers who let them read what they wanted to read. Equally clear was their disdain for workbooks and the need to write answers to questions about content in textbooks. The distinction between reading and what is done with reading in school was well expressed by one girl who, when asked to explain what she meant when she said that she liked school reading 'half of the time,' said that the half she liked was 'reading stories' whereas the half she didn't like was 'doing the questions and doing the workbook' (p. 26).

The evidence seems to show that grouping in beginning reading does not seem to have particular advantages in either Stage 1 or Stage 2. Why then is grouping so widely practiced? When one combs the literature for an answer to this question an interesting fact emerges. In general the reading community does not seem to have been especially interested in research results reporting purported advantages, disadvantages, or lack of impact of grouping studies per se (i.e. Goldberg, Passow, & Justman, 1966; Sharon, 1980; Webb, 1982). Instead grouping is considered in relation to the problem of individual differences.

School entrants may differ very much in ability, and previous experiences. Many researchers seem to feel that the best way to cope with these differences would be to individualize instruction, and allow each child to progress at the rate best suited to his/her needs. However, as this is usually not considered feasible, the next best alternative is to instruct children in more or less homogeneous groups. Ability grouping is thus conceived as a substitute for much more desirable individualization.

Arguments used to justify grouping are in this case actually arguments in favor of individualization as opposed to whole class instruction. It is not so much that grouping per se is good, but that it is preferable to whole class instruction in lieu of unobtainable individualization.

This line of argument seems flawed. Our examination so far showed that ability-grouped instruction in reading is beset by serious problems of its own. It also seems to retain some of the less desirable characteristics of both whole-class teaching *and* individualization. What one could suggest instead would be to try to elucidate the more effective elements of each of the two options, and experiment with various ways in which these could be integrated according to learners' needs at different stages in the learning process. For instance, we saw already that in Stage 1 it might be best to use a whole-class approach when introducing new materials, and for daily drill work, while children's progress would be monitored entirely individually. Corrective work ensuing from monitoring could, according to circumstances, take place in individual, group, or whole-class settings. In this scheme there would be no place for children hearing other children's oral reading except during drill, when all are intent on gamelike tasks. Any sustained oral reading of children would be solely in one-to-one settings with teachers or tutors. In addition to learning new material, Stage 1 children would also be read to daily in a collective setting, and have ample time to read on their own according to individual interests and pace from very easy reading matter which would be freely available.

Let us now see how combining different options of classroom organization would work in Stage 2.

STAGE 2 READING

Free Access to Books: Individual

The declared aim of Stage 2 is to catapult erstwhile beginners into reading extensively on their own, and coming to regard reading above all as enjoyable. The key to fulfilling these aims lies with the teacher and what the teacher actually does in class. Letting children have free access to easy books and making them feel that reading is recreation rather than a drudge is only one side of the picture. Equally important are the many ways by which teachers will concurrently endeavor to upgrade children's reading skills and draw them to reading.

Reading to Children: Collective

In Stage 2, reading to children continues to be an excellent way to work towards these twin aims. Most researchers agree that teacher-led discussion of a jointly experienced text can cover most elements of effective reading comprehension instruction (Bormouth, 1969; Golinkoff, 1976; Durkin, 1979; Mason, 1982).

One of the advantages of having a live teacher rather than a workbook serving as mediator between children and the text they are trying to comprehend is that teacher explanations can be adapted specifically to prior knowledge and level of ability of a particular group of children.

One of the differences between class reading activities in Stage 2 and in later years is that in higher grades texts are often chosen for their artistic or informational value. When this is the case, it is necessary to establish clear distinctions between the text itself and the classroom treatment of the text. Further, there will be a desire to familiarize the reader with the text, sometimes to the point of practically internalizing it. To that end, the text may be read and reread several times, additional dimensions may be elucidated, and a more profound in-depth understanding groped for. In Stage 2, on the other hand, explanations should probably interfere as little as possible with children's direct experiencing and enjoyment of the text. Having the teacher read to children may, in fact, eliminate the need for at least part of the explanations, as judicious use of teacher's voice and intonation can serve in their place.

Also in choice of books read to children, Stage 2 is somewhat different from both earlier and later stages. Earlier on, books read by the teacher are clearly on a considerably higher level than books children could attempt on their own. Again, in the intermediate grades, teachers may choose to introduce children to works of acknowledged artistic merit by way of reading to them. Consequently, books read by the teacher will, once again, be rather different from those children read by themselves. During Stage 2, on the other hand, it might make good sense to introduce mainly easier, series-format stories. Feitelson, Kita, and Goldstein (1986) found that once series characters and story setting had become somewhat familiar, even children whose homes typically lacked children's books asked their parents to buy them additional titles in the 15-volume series their teacher had started to read to them in class.[9]

By selecting books which have especially strong appeal for six- to 8-year-olds, and which are only slightly beyond their range of ability, teachers may induce them to attempt the crucial transition to reading "real books." A full realization of the importance of this step could ensure that teachers devote ample time to daily reading to children, and do not mistakenly think that now that children can read on their own it is a misuse of class time to read to them.

Improving Overall Language Proficiency Including Writing: Alternatively Whole Class and Individual

Reading comprehension is highly dependent on overall language proficiency. Emphasizing that reading activities in Stage 2 should be enjoy-

---

[9] The special suitability of series-format stories for Stage 2 readers is in keeping with Mandler and Johnson's (1977) and Mandler's (1978) results that the recall of seven- or eight-year-olds is more dependent on familiar schemata than recall by adults.

able does not mean that there is reason to forego instruction in language skills per se. Improving language competency will, in turn, affect both active use of language and reading comprehension.

Several years ago I happened to visit a second grade class in Vienna on the first day of school after the summer break. The teacher, who had taught the same class also in first grade, asked individual children about what they had done during the vacation. Once the whole class had become active and interchanges were lively, she suddenly asked the boy who had last recounted his adventures to step forward. Then and there, she had other children retell his doings while referring to him by the personal pronoun "he." She then proceeded to do the same with a little girl. The lession now turned into a spirited session in forming sentences with personal pronouns. There can be little doubt that lessons like the one just described are apt to have a positive impact on reading comprehension, especially when they are part of a carefully preplanned graded language curriculum which also includes writing. It will be remembered from Chapter Five that graded language instruction is also one way toward a gradual elimination of spelling mistakes in children's writing. Letting children write freely without being corrected in the early phases of reading instruction does not mean that spelling is of no concern. It is only that strategies for achieving correct spelling are different.

Monitoring: Individual

Also in Stage 2 teachers will want to continue to monitor each child's progress. However, monitoring in Stage 2 will be different from monitoring in Stage 1. Reading instruction in Stage 1 focused on sequential introduction of decoding skills. Hence the aim of individual monitoring was mainly to make sure that all children had indeed mastered what had just been learned. To this end, monitoring sessions with each child were frequent but brief. Despite the short duration of individual monitoring sessions, each included also a short discussion of the content of the passage the child had read.

In Stage 2 we assume that basic decoding skills have already been mastered. The aim of the very short decoding component included in each monitoring session is thus mainly to alert teachers to the rate of acquisition of more esoteric decoding skills. Therefore, contrary to what would happen in Stage 1, decoding difficulties discovered in individual monitoring sessions in Stage 2 will not always be treated on the spot. Sometimes they will serve mainly as an indication to the teacher of topics which need to be brought up in class. The main part of monitoring sessions in Stage 2 will be devoted to hearing children read from their personal book and to making sure that they have grasped the story line and understood the text. Monitoring sessions also give teachers an opportunity to guide children to further books and to suggest follow-up activities.[10] In order to allow enough time for all this, monitoring sessions in Stage 2 will be of longer duration than in Stage 1, but will occur less frequently.

Additional Reading Activities: Varied Organizational Frameworks

The activities described so far do not cover all a teacher of Stage 2 children will want to do in regard to reading. Teachers' manuals suggest many additional reading-related pursuits suitable for children at this level of reading development such as staging plays, organizing collections, following written cooking or assembly instructions and the like.

Of all of these we shall discuss only peer tutoring, because tutoring is not usually thought of in relation to young children.

Tutoring, when it involves monitoring slightly younger children's reading, participating with them in reading games, or reading to them, can turn into a useful vehicle for exercising young tutors' own freshly acquired skills. Feitelson, Eshel, Sharon, and Goldstein (1987) found that second graders who had read to kindergartners three times a week for about four months ourperformed their classmates on technical reading, reading comprehension, and active use of language. In another study 30 second graders read to first graders while another 30 second graders monitored first graders reading to them. Both groups also played reading games with their tutees. Pairs met five days a week for three weeks. Second graders kept daily records of the progress of the first graders with whom they worked. They also showed much initiative in helping first graders cope with difficulties and in finding or inventing suitable games for them (Feitelson & Shamir-Dolev, 1985).

School personnel connected with the project, which had been initiated by an outsider, commented on the positive effects of the project on second graders' motivation and self-confidence. Another by-product of the project was that participating second graders read at least five booklets a week more than they would have otherwise. Several of them even volunteered to take booklets home in advance in order to be able to prepare for reading them aloud. The reason we have described this

---

[10] Readers of this book who are familiar with so-called "individualized reading" will realize that individual monitoring in Stage 2 resembles in some respects the teacher-pupil conferences (Heilman, 1967) which are one of the features of individualized reading.

project in some detail is that it is an example of still another way in which the advantages of whole class teaching can be combined effectively with those of individualization. Irrespective of their personal role, all participating children were intensely busy on highly individualized tasks throughout the half-hour a day devoted to the project. Yet all children engaged in their tasks at one and the same time, and, as just mentioned, only one-half-hour a day of class time was expended on the project.

In summing up, there may be need to emphasize explicitly one aspect of Stage 2 reading which was implicit throughout this chapter. Selections in conventional reading programs are usually carefully adjusted to children's rate of progress. By contrast, the approach proposed here assumes that concurrent exposure to reading matter of different levels of difficulty will expedite the breakthrough to readership which is the goal of Stage 2. Teacher-directed reading from texts which are difficult enough to tax children's capabilities are thus only one of the varied reading activities Stage 2 children will engage in. Simultaneously they will have access to very easy stories which they can read on their own purely for enjoyment. Books read to children by adults would, on the other hand, veer in the opposite direction and tend to be appreciably more difficult than even the stories read by children in teacher-directed sessions. Moreover, their quality and level of difficulty could change during Stage 2, in keeping with changing needs. In the beginning, books could still be chosen with the aim of enticing children to plunge into reading on their own. Later on, when this aim was largely attained, teachers could use periods in which they read to children in order to upgrade children's literary taste and as a way of introducing them to works of lasting worth.

It is at this point, with the beginning reader well on the way to become a consumer of books, that we shall let our argument rest.

References

Adams, M. J. 1981. What good is orthographic redundancy? In *Perception of print*, eds. O. J. L. Tzeng and H. Singer. Hillsdale, NJ: Erlbaum.

Adams, M. and B. Bruce. 1982. Background knowledge and reading comprehension. In *Reader meets author / bridging the gap: A psycholinguistic and sociolinguistic perspective*, eds. J. A. Langer and M. T. Smith-Burke. Newark, DE: International Reading Association.

Allen, R. V. 1964. The language experience approach. In *Teaching young children to read*, ed. W. G. Cutts. Washington, DC: U.S. Department of Health, Education and Welfare. (Reprinted in *Perspectives on elementary reading*, ed. R. Karlin, 1973. New York: Harcourt, Brace Jovanovich.)

Ammar, H. 1954. *Growing up in an Egyptian village*. London: Routledge and Kegan Paul.

Anderson, I. H., and W. F. Dearborn. 1952. *The psychology of teaching reading*. New York: Ronald.

Anderson, R. C., J. Mason, and L. Shirey. 1984. The reading group: An experimental investigation of a labyrinth. *Reading Research Quarterly* 20:6–38.

Anderson, R. C., and P. P. Pearson. 1984. A schema-theoretic view of basic processes in reading comprehension. In *Handbook of Reading Research*. ed. P. D. Pearson. New York: Longman.

Antesperg, J. B. von. 1741. *Das Josephinische Erzherzogliche A.B.C. oder Namenbüchlein*. Vienna: Fleyinger. (Reprinted: 1980, Dortmund: Harenberg).

Applebee, A. N. 1980. Children's narratives: New directions. *The Reading Teacher*. 34:137–142.

Armento, B. J. 1978. *Teacher behavior and effective teaching of concepts*. Paper presented at the Annual Meeting of the American Association of Colleges for Teacher Education, February, Chicago. (ERIC Document Reproduction Service, No. ED 153949).

Arnold, S. L. 1899. *Reading: How to teach it*. Newark, NJ: Silver Burdett.

Ashton-Warner, S. 1963. *Teacher*. New York: Simon and Schuster.

Askov, E. N., and J. W. Lee. 1980. The language experience approach in the content area classroom. *The Journal of Language Experience*, 2:13–20.

Au, K. H., and J. M. Mason. 1982. *A microethnographic approach to the study of classroom reading instruction: Rationale and procedures.* Champaign, IL: Center for the Study of Reading. Technical Report No. 237.

Aukerman, R. C. 1971. *Approaches to beginning reading.* New York: Wiley.

——— 1981. *The basal reader approach to reading.* New York: Wiley.

Aukerman, R. C., and L. R. Aukerman. 1981. *How do I teach reading?* New York: Wiley.

Austin, M. 1973. United States. In *Comparative reading.* ed. J. Downing. New York: Macmillan.

Avinor, M. 1980. The Karmelitic script—a writing system for Hebrew. *Hebrew Studies* 20–21:167–178.

Balmuth, M. 1972. Phoneme blending and silent reading achievement. In *Some persistent questions on beginning reading.* ed. R. C. Aukerman. Newark, DE: International Reading Association.

Balmuth, M. 1982. *The roots of phonics: A historical introduction.* New York: McGraw-Hill.

Barnitz, J. G. 1978. *Interrelationship of orthography and phonological structure in learning to read.* Champaign, IL: Center for the Study of Reading, Technical Report No. 57.

Barr, R. 1974. Instructional pace differences and their effect on reading acquisition. *Reading Research Quarterly* 9:526–554.

Bateman, B. 1967. Reading: A controversial view research and rationale. *Curriculum Bulletin,* No. 278. Eugene, OR: School of Education, University of Oregon.

Beck, I. L., M. G. McKeown, E. S. McCaslin, and A. M. Burkes. 1979. *Instructional dimensions that may affect reading comprehension: Examples from two commercial reading programs.* Pittsburgh: University of Pittsburgh Learning Research and Development Center.

Beck, I. L., and D. D. Mitroff. 1972. *The rationale and design of a primary grades reading system for an individualized classroom.* Pittsburgh: University of Pittsburgh Learning Research and Development Center.

Berliner, D. C. 1981. Academic learning time and reading achievement. In *Comprehension and teaching: Research reviews.* ed. J. T. Guthrie. Newark, DE: International Reading Association.

Bettelheim, B., and K. Zelan. 1982. *On learning to read: The child's fascination with meaning.* New York: Knopf.

Bettencourt, E. M., M. H. Gillet, M. D. Gall, and R. E. Hull. 1983. Effects of teacher enthusiasm training on student on-task behavior and achievement. *American Educational Research Journal* 20:435–450.

Biemiller, A. J. 1970. The development of the use of graphic and contextual information as children learn to read. *Reading Research Quarterly* 6:75–96.

Biglmaier, F. 1973. Germany. In *Comparative reading.* ed. J. Downing. New York: Macmillan.

Bissex, G. L. 1980. *Gnys at wrk: A child learns to write and read.* Cambridge, MA: Harvard University Press.

Björnsson, C. H. 1983. Readability of newspapers in 11 languages. *Reading Research Quarterly* 18:480–497.

Blom, G. E., R. R. Waite, and S. G. Zimet. 1970. A motivational content analysis of children's primers. In *Basic studies on reading*. eds. H. Levin, and J. P. Williams. New York: Basic Books.

Bloom, B. S. 1964. *Stability and change in human characteristics*. New York: Wiley.

———— 1976. *Human characteristics and school learning*. New York: McGraw-Hill.

Bloom, S. 1966. Israeli reading methods for their culturally disadvantaged. *Elementary School Journal* 66:304–310.

Bloomfield, L. 1942. Linguistics and reading. *Elementary English Review* 19:125–130; 183–186.

Blumenthal, A. L. 1970. *Language and psychology*. New York: Wiley.

Bond, G. L., and R. Dykstra. 1967. The cooperative research program in first grade reading instruction. *Reading Research Quarterly* 2 (4) (entire issue).

Bormuth, J. R. 1969. An operational definition of comprehension instruction. In *Psycholinguistics and the teaching of reading*. eds. K. S. Goodman, and J. T. Fleming. Newark, DE: International Reading Association.

Brauer, E. 1947. *The Jews of Kurdistan*. Jerusalem: The Palestine Institute of Folklore and Ethnology. (Hebrew).

Britton, J. N. 1977. Language and the nature of learning: An individual perspective. In *The teaching of English*, ed. J. R. Squire. Chicago: University of Chicago Press.

Brophy, J. E. 1983. Fostering student learning and motivation in the elementary school classroom. In S. Paris, G. Olson, and H. Stevenson (Eds.), *Learning and motivation in the classroom*. (pp. 283–305). Hillsdale, NJ: Erlbaum.

Brown, R. 1958. *Words and things*. Glencoe, IL: The Free Press.

Bruce, B. 1981. *A new point of view on children's stories*. Champaign, IL: Center for the Study of Reading, Reading Education Report No. 25.

Bruner, J. S. 1972. The nature and uses of immaturity. *American Psychologist* 27:687–708.

Bruner, J. S., A. Jolly, and S. Sylva, eds. 1976. *Play—its role in development and evolution*. London: Penguin.

Brzeinski, J. E. 1964. Beginning reading in Denver. *The Reading Teacher* 18:16–21.

Bullock, A. Sir. 1975. *A language for life*. Report of the Committee of Inquiry appointed by the Secretary of State for Education and Science. London: Her Majesty's Stationery Office.

Buswell, G. T. 1937. *How adults read*. Supplementary Educational Monographs, No. 45. Chicago: University of Chicago Press.

Calfee, R. C. 1977. Assessment of independent reading skills: Basic research and practical applications. In *Toward a psychology of reading*, eds. A. S. Reber, and D. L. Scarborough. Hillsdale, NJ: Erlbaum.

Calfee, R. C., R. Chapman, and R. Venezky. 1972. How a child needs to think to learn to read. In *Cognition and learning in memory*, ed. L. W. Gregg. New York: Wiley.

Calfee, R. C., and P. A. Drum. 1978. Learning to read: Theory, research, and practice. *Curriculum Inquiry* 8:184–249.

Calfee, R. C., and D. Piontkowsky. 1981. The reading diary: Acquisition of decoding. *Reading Research Quarterly* 16:346–373.

Carnine, D. W. 1977. Phonics vs. look-say: Transfer to new words. *The Reading Teacher* 30:636–640.

Carus, M., T. G. Anderson, H. R. Webber, N. Thomas, and J. D. H. Lebo. 1979 *The Headway Program*. La Salle, IL: Open Court.

Cattell, J. McK. 1885. Über die Zeit der Erkennung und Benennung von Schriftzeichen, Bildern und Farben. *Philosophische Studien* 2:635–650. (Reprinted in translation in *James McKeen Cattell: Man of Science*, ed. A. T. Poffenberger. 1947. York, PA: Science Press.

———— 1886a. The time it takes to see and name objects. *Mind* 11:63–65.

———— 1886b. The inertia of the eye and brain. *Brain* 8:295–312.

———— 1890. Mental tests and measurements. *Mind* 15:373–380.

Cazden, C. B. 1972. *Child language and education.* New York: Holt, Rinehart & Winston.

———— 1981. Social context of learning to read. In *Comprehension and teaching: Research reviews*, ed. J. T. Guthrie. Newark, DE: International Reading Association.

Chall, J. S. 1967. *Learning to read: The great debate.* New York: McGraw-Hill.

———— 1977. *Reading 1967–1977: A decade of change and promise.* Bloomington, IN: Phi Delta Kappa Fast Back 79.

———— 1979. The great debate: Ten years later, with a modest proposal for reading stages. In *Theory and practice of early reading*, eds. L. B. Resnick, and P. A. Weaver. Vol. 1. Hillsdale, NJ: Erlbaum.

———— 1983a. *Learning to read: The great debate.* Updated edition. New York: McGraw-Hill.

———— 1983b. Literacy: Trends and explanations. *Educational Researcher* 12:3–8.

———— 1983c. *Stages of reading development.* New York: McGraw-Hill.

Chall, J. S., and V. A. Jacobs. 1984. Writing and reading in the elementary grades: Developmental trends among low SES children. In *Composing and Comprehending.* ed. J. M. Jensen. Urbana, IL: National Conference on Research in English.

Chall, J. S., F. Rosewell and S. H. Blumenthal. 1963. Auditory blending: A factor in success in beginning reading. *The Reading Teacher.* 16:113–118.

Chall, J. S., and C. Snow. 1982. A study of family influences on literacy acquisition in low-income children in grades 2 through 8. Paper presented at the Annual Meeting of the American Educational Research Association, March. New York City.

Chomsky, C. 1970. Reading, writing and phonology. *Harvard Educational Review* 40:287–309.

———— 1971. Write first, read later. *Childhood Education* 47:296–299.

———— 1972a. Stages in language development and reading exposure. *Harvard Educational Review* 42:1–33.

———— 1972b. Write now read later. In *Language in early childhood education*, ed. C. Cazden. Washington, D.C.: National Association for the Education of Young Children.

———— 1975. How sister got into the grog. *Early years* 6:36–39, 78–79.

———— 1976. Invented spelling in the open classroom. In *Child language—1975*, ed. W. von Raffler-Engel. Milford, CT: International Linguistics Association. Special Issue of *Word* 27:499–518.

———— 1979a. Approaching reading through invented spelling. In *Theory and practice of early reading*, Vol. 2, eds. L. B. Resnick, and P. A. Weaver. Hillsdale, NJ: Erlbaum.

———— 1979b. Language and reading. In *Applied linguistics and reading*, ed. R. E. Shafer. Newark, DE: International Reading Association.

Chomsky, N., and M. Halle. 1968. *The sound pattern of English*. New York: Harper & Row.

Church, M. 1974. Does visual perception training help beginning readers? *The Reading Teacher* 27:361–364.

Clark, M. M. 1976. *Young fluent readers*. London: Heinemann.

Clay, M. M. 1979. *Reading: The patterning of complex behaviour*. Auckland, New Zealand: Heinemann.

———— 1980. Early writing and reading: Reciprocal gains. In *Reading and writing for the child with difficulties*, eds. M. M. Clark, and T. Glynn. Educational Review: Occasional Publications, No. 8. University of Birmingham.

Cochran-Smith, M. 1984. *The making of a reader*. Norwood, NJ: Ablex.

Cohen, A. 1975. First and second graders' use of graphic and contextual cues in reading. Unpublished master's thesis, Department of Psychology, Hebrew University of Jerusalem. (Hebrew).

Cohen, A. 1980. Recreational reading among Israeli junior-high school pupils. *Reading Circles* 7:5–34. (Hebrew).

Craig, R. 1977. *Super sounder system*. Enid, OK: Mimeographed.

Cremin, L. 1961. *The transformation of the school*. New York: Knopf.

Cubberley, E. P. 1920. *The history of education*. Boston: Houghton Mifflin.

Davis, E. A. 1937. *The development of linguistic skill in twins, singletons with siblings, and only children from ages five to ten years*. Minneapolis: University of Minnesota.

Davis, L. G. 1963. *k-a-t spelz cat*. New York: Carlton.

———— 1965. *the davis speller*. New York: Carlton.

Dearborn, W. F. 1906. *The psychology of reading*. New York: Science Press.

Deci, E. 1975. *Intrinsic motivation*. New York: Plenum.

Denham, C. and A. Lieberman, eds. 1980. *Time to Learn*. Washington. DC: U.S. Department of Education.

Deutsch, M. 1965. The role of social class in language development and cognition. *American Journal of Orthopsychiatry* 35:78–88.

Diack, H. 1960. *Reading and the psychology of perception*. Nottingham, UK: Skinner.

Diesterweg, F. A. W. 1846. The schools of Germany before Pestalozzi. From an address delivered in Berlin, at the celebration of the centennial of the birth of Pestalozzi. Initially translated in *American Journal of Education* 4:343–345. (Reprinted In *Readings*, ed. E. R. Cubberly, 1920. Boston, MA: Houghton Mifflin.

Downing, J. 1965. *The initial teaching alphabet reading experiment*. Chicago: Scott Foresman.

_____ 1970. Children's concepts of language in learning to read. *Educational Research* 12:106–112.

_____ , ed. 1973. *Comparative reading.* New York: Macmillan.

_____ 1978. Learning to read in different languages—universals and specifics. Paper presented at the Seventh World Congress on Reading. August. Hamburg, F.R.G.

_____ 1979. *Reading and reasoning.* New York: Springer.

Downing, J., and D. Thackray. 1971. *Reading readiness.* London: University of London Press.

Duffy, G. G., and L. McIntyre, 1980. *A Qualitative analysis of how various primary grade teachers employ the structured learning component of the direct instruction model when teaching reading.* Research Series No. 80, Institute for Research on Teaching. East Lansing, MI: Michigan State University.

Duffy, G. G., and L. R. Roehler, 1982a. An analysis of the instruction in reading instructional research. In *New inquiries in reading research and instruction.* (Thirty-first yearbook of the National Reading Conference). eds. J. Niles and L. Harris. Rochester, NY: National Reading Conference.

_____ 1982b. Direct instruction of comprehension: What does it really mean? *Reading Horizons* 23(1):35–40.

_____ 1982c. The illusion of instruction. *Reading Research Quarterly* 17:438–445.

Duffy, G.., L. R. Roehler and J. Mason. eds. 1984. *Comprehension instruction: Perspectives and suggestions.* New York: Longman.

Duker, S. 1966. Needed research on individualized reading. *Elementary English* 43:220–225.

_____ , ed. 1969. *Individualized reading: Readings.* Metuchen, NJ: Scarecrow.

Durkin, D. 1959. A study of children who learned to read prior to first grade. *California Journal of Educational Research* 10:109–113.

_____ 1961. Children who learned to read at home. *Elementary School Journal* 62:15–18.

_____ 1966. *Children who read early.* New York: Teachers College Press.

_____ 1970. A language arts program for pre-first grade children: Two-year achievement report. *Reading Research Quarterly* 5:534–565.

_____ 1974a. A six-year study of children who learned to read in school at the age of four. *Reading Research Quarterly* 10:9–61.

_____ 1974b. Some questions about questionable instructional materials. *The Reading Teacher* 28:13–17.

_____ 1979. What classroom observations reveal about reading comprehension instruction. *Reading Research Quarterly* 14:481–533.

_____ 1984. *Poor black children who are successful readers: An investigation Urban Education* 19:53–76.

Durrell, D. D. 1940. *Improvement of basic reading abilities.* Yonkers, NY: World Book.

_____ 1958. Success in first grade reading. *Journal of Education* 140:2–6.

_____ 1980. Letter-name values in reading and spelling. *Reading Research Quarterly* 16:159–163.

Dyson, A. H. 1982. The emergence of visible language: Interrelationships between drawing and early writing. *Visible Language* 16:360–381.

———— 1983. The role of oral language in early writing processes. *Research in the Teaching of English.* 17:1–30.

Ehri, L. C. 1980. The role of orthographic images in learning printed words. In *Orthography, reading and dyslexia,* eds. J. F. Kavanagh, and R. L. Venezky. Baltimore: University Park Press.

Elkonin, D. B. 1957–9/1963. The psychology of mastering the elements of reading. (Originally Moscow: 1957–9.) Translated in *Educational Psychology in the U.S.S.R.,* eds. B. Simon and J. Simon. London: Routledge & Kegan Paul.

Engleman, S., and E. C. Bruner. 1974. *Distar reading: An instructional system.* (Second edition.) Chicago: Science Research Associates.

Erdman, B., and R. Doge. 1898. *Psychologische Untersuchungen über das Lesen, auf experimenteller Grundlage.* Halle; Niemeyer. (German).

Erika Fibel nach der Normalwörter-Methode mit einem Vorkursus. 1899. Bearbeitet von Lüneburger Lehrern. 9 Auflage. Harburg: Verlag von Gustav Elkan. (German).

Eshel, M. 1979. *Improving language skills of low SES kindergartners through tutoring.* Unpublished master's thesis, University of Haifa (Hebrew).

Evans, H. M., and J. C. Towner. 1975. Sustained silent reading: Does it increase skills? *The Reading Teacher* 29:155–156.

Farnham, G. L. 1887. *The sentence method of teaching reading, writing and spelling. A manual for teachers.* Syracuse, NY: Bardeen. (Second edition).

Feitelson, D. 1954. Childrearing practices in the Kurdish community. *Megamot* 5:95–105. (Hebrew).

———— 1965. Structuring the teaching of reading according to major features of the language and its script. *Elementary English* 42:870–877.

———— 1980. Relating instructional strategies to language idiosyncracies in Hebrew. In *Orthography, reading, and dyslexia,* eds. J. F. Kavanagh, and R. L. Venezky. Baltimore: University Park Press.

Feitelson, D., Z. Goldstein, M. Eshel, A. Flasher, M. Levin, and S. Sharon. 1984. *Effects of listening to stories on kindergartener's comprehension and use of language.* Unpublished manuscript.

Feitelson, D., M. Eshel, S. Sharon, and Z. Goldstein. 1987. *Effects of disadvantaged second graders reading to kindergartners on reading and language skills of children in both age groups.* University of Haifa. Unpublished manuscript.

Feitelson, D., and Z. Goldstein. 1986. Patterns of book ownership and reading to young children in Israeli school-oriented and nonschool-oriented families. *The Reading Teacher* 39:924–930.

Feitelson, D., B. Kita, and Z. Goldstein. 1986. Effects of listening to series-stories on first graders' comprehension and use of language. *Research in the Teaching of English* 20:339–356.

Feitelson, D., and M. Razel. 1984. Word superiority and word shape effects in beginning readers. *International Journal of Behavioral Development* 7:359–370.

Feitelson, D., and Y. Shamir-Dolev. (1985). Second graders tutor first graders in reading. (Unpublished manuscript.)

Feitelson, D., S. Weintraub, and O. Michaeli. 1972. Social interactions in hetero-geneous preschools in Israel. *Child Development* 43:1249–1259.

Fellman, J. 1979. The teachers did it: A case history of the revival of the mother language. In *Mother tongue or second language: On the teaching of reading in multi-lingual societies,* ed. D. Feitelson. Newark, DE: International Reading Association.

Fernald, G. 1943. *Remedial techniques in basic school subjects.* New York: McGraw-Hill.

Fernald, G. M., and H. Keller. 1921. The effect of kinesthetic factors in the development of word recognition in the case of non-readers. *Journal of Educational Research* 4:355–377.

Fishbein, J., and R. Emans. 1972. *A question of competence: Language, intelligence and learning to read.* Chicago: Science Research Associates.

Flesch, R. 1955. *Why Johnny can't read—and what you can do about it.* New York: Harper & Row.

Flood, J. ed. 1984. *Promoting reading comprehension.* Newark. DE: International Reading Association.

Fowler, W. 1962. Teaching a two-year-old to read: An experiment in early childhood learning. *Genetic Psychology Monographs* 66:181–283.

Freyberg, J. 1973. Increasing the imaginative play of urban disadvantaged kin-dergarten children through systematic training. In *The child's world of make-believe,* ed. J. L. Singer. New York: Academic Press.

Fries, C. C. 1962. *Linguistics and reading.* New York: Holt, Rinehart & Winston.

Frith, U. 1979. Reading by eye and writing by ear. In *Processing of visible language,* eds. P. A. Kolers, M. E. Wrolstad, and H. Bouma. (volume 1). New York: Plenum.

———, ed. 1980a. *Cognitive processes in spelling.* London: Academic Press.

——— 1980b. Reading and spelling skills. In *Scientific foundations of developmental psychiatry,* ed. M. Rutter. London: Heinemann.

Frith, U., and C. Frith. 1980. Relationships between reading and spelling. In *Orthography, reading and dyslexia,* eds. J. F. Kavanagh, and R. L. Venezky. Baltimore: University Park Press.

Frostig, M., D. W. Lefever., and J. R. B. Whittlesey. 1961. A developmental test of visual perception for evaluating normal and neurological handicapped children. *Perceptual and Motor Skills* 12:383–394.

Frostig, M., and D. Horn. 1968. *Frostig program for development of visual perception.* Chicago: Fallett.

Fry, E. B. 1964. A diacritical marking system to aid beginning reading instruc-tion. *Elementary English* 41:526–529; 537.

——— 1977. *Elementary reading instruction.* New York: McGraw-Hill.

Gage, N. L. and Berliner, D. C. 1984. *Educational Psychology* (Third Edition). Boston: Houghton Mifflin.

Gambrell, L. B. 1978. Getting started with sustained silent reading and keeping it going. *The Reading Teacher* 32:328–331.

Gates, A. I. 1922. *The psychology of reading and spelling.* New York: Teacher College Contributions to Education No. 129.

——— 1937. The necessary mental age for beginning reading. *Elementary School Journal* 37:497–508.

_____ 1953. _Teaching reading._ Washington, DC: National Education Association "what research says to the teacher pamphlet."

Gates, A. I., and E. Boeker. 1923. A study of initial stages in reading by pre-school children. _Teachers College Record_ 24:469–488.

Gates, A. E., and G. A. Taylor. 1923. The acquisition of motor control and writing by pre-school children. _Teachers College Record_ 24:459–468.

Gavel, S. R. 1958. June reading achievement of first-grade children. _Journal of Education_ 140:37–43.

Gibson, E. J., and H. Levin. 1975. _The psychology of reading._ Cambridge, MA: MIT Press.

Gibson, E. J., H. Osser, W. Schiff, and J. Smith. 1963. An analysis of critical features of letters tested by a confusion matrix. In _Final Report on a Basic Research Program on Reading._ Cooperative Research Project No. 639, Cornell University and U.S. Office of Education.

Gibson, E. J., F. Shapiro, and A. Yonas. 1968. Confusion, matrices for graphic patterns obtained with a latency measure. In _The analysis of reading skill: A program of basic and applied research._ Final Report, Project No. 5-1213, Cornell University and U.S. Office of Education.

Gillooly,.W. B. 1971. The influence of writing-system characteristics on learning to read. In _Final Report: The literature of research in reading with emphasis on models,_ ed. F. B. Davis. New Brunswick, NJ: Rutgers University Graduate School of Education.

Goddard, N. 1974. _Literacy: Language-experience approaches._ London: Macmillan.

Goldberg, M. L., A. J. Hebard, S. G. Rozensher, B. Kershner, and J. Osborn. 1977. _Early decoding and encoding strategies project._ Final Report, Phase II. New York: Teachers College Columbia University.

Goldberg, M. L., A. H. Passow, and J. Justman. 1966. _The effects of ability grouping._ New York: Teachers College Press.

Golinkoff, R. M. 1976. A comparison of reading comprehension processes in good and poor comprehenders. _Reading Research Quarterly_ 11:623–659.

Good, T., and J. Brophy. 1978. _Looking in classrooms._ New York, NY: Harper and Row.

Goodman, K. S. 1964. The linguistics of reading. _The Elementary School Journal_ 64:355–361. (Reprinted In _Reading instruction: Dimensions and issues,_ ed. W. K. Durr. Boston: Houghton Mifflin, 1967, 287–293).

_____ 1967. Reading: A psycholinguistic guessing game. _Journal of the Reading Specialist_ 6:126–135.

_____ 1969. Words and morphemes in reading. In _Psycholinguistics and the teaching of reading,_ eds. K. S. Goodman, and J. T. Fleming. Newark, DE: International Reading Association.

Goodman, Y. M., and B. Altwerger. 1981. _Print awareness in pre-school children: A working paper._ Occasional Papers No. 4. Program in Language and Literacy, College of Education. University of Arizona.

Goody, J., and I. Watt. 1972. The consequences of literacy. In _Language and social context,_ ed. P. P. Giglioli, Harmondsworth, UK: Penguin.

Goshen-Gottstein, E. R. 1981. Towards a social policy for families of multiple infants. _International Social Work_ 24:46–58.

Gough, P. B., C. Juel, and D. Roper/Schneider. 1983. Code and cipher: A two-stage conception of initial reading acquisition. In *Searches for meaning in reading, language processing and instruction*. ed. J. A. Niles and L. A. Harris. Rochester NY: The National Reading Conference.

Gray, W. S. 1949. Basic competencies in efficient reading. In *Reading in an age of mass communication*. National Council of Teachers of English. Committee on Reading at the Secondary School and College Levels. New York: Appelton-Century Crofts.

———— 1956. *The teaching of reading and writing*. Paris: UNESCO.

Greene, H. A., and W. T. Petty. 1959. *Developing language skills in the elementary school*. Boston: Allyn and Bacon.

Guthrie, J. T., ed. 1981. *Comprehension and teaching: Research reviews*. Newark, DE: International Reading Association.

Hall, M. A., S. A. Moretz, and J. Statom. 1976. Writing before grade one—a study of early writers. *Language Arts* 53:582–585.

Hammill, D., L. Goodman, and J. L. Wiederholt. 1974. Visual—motor processes; can we train them? *The Reading Teacher* 27:469–478.

Harris, A. J., and E. R. Sipay. 1975. *How to increase reading ability*. (6th edition). New York: McKay.

Harris, A. S. 1969. Visual and auditory modalities how important are they? In *Current issues in reading*, ed. N. B. Smith, Newark, DE: International Reading Association.

Harris, T. L. 1969. Reading. In *Encyclopedia of Educational Research*, ed. L. Ebel. (A project of the American Educational Research Association). New York: Macmillan.

Harris, T. L., and R. E. Hodges. 1981. *A dictionary of reading and related terms I.R.A.* Newark, DE: International Reading Association.

Harter, S. 1974. Pleasure derived from cognitive challenge and mastery. Child Development 45:661–669.

———— 1978. Effectance motivation reconsidered: Toward a developmental model. *Human Development* 21:34–64.

Hartman, N. C., and R. K. Hartman. 1973. Perceptual handicaps or reading disability. *The Reading Teacher* 27:684–695.

Hayes, R. B., and R. C. Wuest. 1968. A three-year look at i.t.a. In *ita as a language arts medium*, ed. J. R. Block. Hempstead, NY: i.t.a. Foundation at Hofstra University.

Heath, S. B. 1982. What no bedtime story means: Narrative skills at home and school. *Language in Society* 11:49–76.

———— 1983. *Ways with words: Language, life and work in Communities and classroom*. London: Cambridge University Press.

Heilman, A. W. 1967. *Principles and practices of teaching reading*. Columbus, OH: Merrill.

Hess, R. D., and V. C. Shipman. 1965. Early experience and the socialization of cognitive modes in children. *Child Development* 36:869–886.

Hetzer, H. 1929. *Kindheit und Armut*. Leipzig: Hirzel. (German).

Hiebert, E. H. 1983. An examination of ability grouping for reading instruction. *Reading Research Quarterly* 18:231–255.

Hildreth, G. 1949. Reading programs in the early primary period. In *The forty-

eight yearbook of the National Society for the Study of Education, ed. N. B. Henry. Chicago: University of Chicago Press.

———— 1963. Early writing as an aid to reading. *Elementary English* 40:15–20.

———— 1965. Lessons in Arabic. *The Reading Teacher* 19:202–210.

———— 1966. Armenian children enjoy reading. *The Reading Teacher* 19:433–445.

———— 1968. Reading with a rational alphabeth: The Russian system. *The Reading Teacher* 22:251–261.

Hodges, R. E. 1977. In Adam's Fall: A brief history of spelling instruction in the United States. In *Reading and writing instruction in the United States: Historical trends*, ed. H. A. Robinson. Newark, DE: International Reading Association.

Holland, J. G. 1979. Analysis of behavior in reading instruction. In *Theory and practice of early reading*, eds. L. B. Resnick, and P. A. Weaver. (Vol. 1). Hillsdale, NJ: Erlbaum.

Hong, L. K. 1981. Modifying SSR for beginning readers. *The Reading Teacher* 34:888–891.

Hoole, C. 1660/1912. *A new discovery of the old art of teaching school.* Syracuse, NY

Howlin, P. 1980. Language. In *Scientific foundations of developmental psychiatry*, ed. M. Rutter. London: Heinemann (Pp. 198–220).

Huey, E. B. 1898. Preliminary experiments in the physiology and psychology of reading. *American Journal of Psychology* 9:575–586.

———— 1900, 1901. On the psychology and psychology of reading. *American Journal of Psychology* 11:283–302; 12:292–313.

———— 1908. *The physiology and pedagogy of reading.* New York: Macmillan. (Reprinted 1968. Cambridge, MA: MIT Press).

Jacobs, L. B. 1953. Reading on their own means reading at the growing edges. *The Reading Teacher* 6:27–30.

Jansen, M. 1973. Denmark. In *Comparative reading*, ed. J. Downing. New York: Macmillan.

Javal, E. 1878. Sur la physiologie de la lecture. *Annales d'Oculistique* 81: 131–140. (French).

———— 1879a. Essai sur la physiologie de la lecture. *Annales d'Oculistique* 82:242–253. (French).

———— 1879b. Conditions de la lecture facile. *Comptes rendus de la Societe de Biologie* p. 8. (French).

Jeffrey, W. E., and S. J. Samuels. 1967. Effect of method of reading training on initial learning and transfer. *Journal of Verbal Learning and Verbal Behavior* 6:354–358.

Jenkins, J. R., R. B. Bausell, and L. M. Jenkins. 1972. Comparisons of letter name and letter sound training as transfer variables. *American Educational Research Journal* 9:75–86.

Johnson, R. J. 1970. The effect of training in letter names on success in beginning reading for children of differing abilities. Paper presented at the American Educational Research Association Meeting, Anaheim, CA.

Johnson, S. 1982. Listening and reading: The recall of 7-to-9-year-olds. *British Journal of Educational Psychology* 52:24–32.

Johnson, T. D. 1977. Language experience: We can't all write what we can say. *The Reading Teacher* 31:297–299.

Judd, C. H. 1918. *Reading: Its nature and development.* Supplementary Educational Monographs. Chicago: University of Chicago Press.

Kallio, E., and L. Merenkylä. 1974. *Peruskoulua Aapinen.* Helsinki: Valistus. (Finnish).

Kandel, I. L. 1926. University study of education. In *Twenty-five years of American education: Collected essays by former students of Paul Monroe,* ed. I. L. Kandel. New York: Macmillan. (Reprinted in *American education in foreign perspectives: Twentieth century essays,* ed. S. E. Fraser. New York: Wiley, 1969).

Karlin, R. 1975. *Teaching elementary reading.* New York: Harcourt, Brace & Jovanovich.

Kavanagh, J. F., and R. L. Venezky, eds. 1980. *Orthography, reading and dyslexia.* Baltimore: University Park Press.

Kehr, K. 1888. Geschichte des Leseunterrichts. In *Geschichte der Methodik des deutschen Volksschulunterrichts,* [History of reading instruction. In History of the methodology of German elementary-school instruction] ed. K. Kehr. Gotha: Thienemann. (German).

Kirkland, E. R. 1968. The effect of two different orthographies on beginning reading. In *i.t.a. as a language arts medium,* ed. J. R. Block. Hempstead, N.Y.: i.t.a. Foundation at Hofstra University.

Klapper, P. 1926. *Teaching children to read.* (Fourth edition revised and enlarged.) New York: Appleton.

Klebanov, A., E. Gruper, and M. Diab. 1983. Effects of two approaches to enhancing kindergartners' reading readiness. Unpublished manuscript, University of Haifa. (Hebrew).

Klein, M. L. 1980. Language games: An important component of the reading program. *Journal of Language Experience* 2:39–52.

Kohl, H. 1973. *Reading how to.* New York: Bantam.

Kohlberg, L. 1968. Early education. A cognitive-developmental view. *Child Development* 39:1013–1062.

Kolers, P. A. 1966. Reading and talking bilingually. *American Journal of Psychology* 79:357–376.

Kramer, R. 1976. *Maria Montessori.* New York: Capricorn.

Kraus, P. E. 1973. *Yesterday's children: A longitudinal study of children from kindergarten into the adult years.* New York: Wiley.

Kuenne, M. R. 1946. Experimental investigation of the relation of language to transposition behavior in young children. *Journal of Experimental Psychology* 36:471–490.

Kunschak, E., H. Rinner, H. Schraffl, und W. Vavra. 1978. *Frohes Lernen.* (1 Teil: Leselehrgang). Wien: Österreichischer Bundesverlag für Unterricht, Wissenschaft und Kunst. (German).

Kyöstio, O. K. 1977. *The child and his environment.* Oulu: (Finnish).

――― 1973. Finland. In *Comparative reading,* ed. J. Downing. New York: Macmillan.

――― 1980. Is learning to read easy in a language in which the grapheme-phoneme correspondence is regular? In *Orthography, reading and dyslexia,* eds. J. F. Kavanagh and R. L. Venezky. Baltimore: University Park Press.

La Berge, D. 1979. The perception of units in beginning reading. In *Theory and practice of early reading,* eds. L. B. Resnick and P. A. Weaver. (Vol. 3). Hillsdale, NJ: Erlbaum.

Laing, M. E. 1911. *Reading: A manual for teachers.* Boston: Heath.

Land, M. L. 1980. Joint effects of teacher structure and teacher enthusiasm on student achievement. Paper presented at the annual meeting of the Southwest Educational Research Association, San Antonio, TX. (ERIC Document No. ED 182 310).

Langer, J. A. 1984. Examining background knowledge and text comprehension. *Reading Research Quarterly* 19:468–481.

Langer, J. A., and M. Nicolich. 1981. Prior knowledge and its effect on comprehension. *Journal of Reading Behavior* 13:373–379.

Langer, J. A., and M. T. Smith-Burke, eds. 1982. *Reader meets author: Bridging the gap.* Newark, DE: International Reading Association.

Lazar, M. 1957. Individualized reading: A dynamic approach. *The Reading Teacher* 11:75–83.

Leigh, E. 1864. *Pronouncing orthography.* St. Louis.

Leong, C. K. 1978. Learning to read in English and Chinese: Some psycholinguistic and cognitive considerations. In *Cross-cultural perspectives on reading and reading research,* ed. D. Feitelson. Newark, DE: International Reading Association.

Lesgold, A. M., and C. A. Perfetti. 1978. Interactive processes in reading comprehension. *Discource Processes* 1:323–336.

Lesgold, A. M., and C. A. Perfetti. 1981. Interactive processes in reading: Where do we stand? In *Interactive processes in reading,* eds. A. M. Lesgold and C. A. Perfetti. Hillsdale, NJ: Erlbaum.

LeVine, R, A., and B. B. LeVine. 1963. Nyansanga: A Gusii community in Kenya. In *Six cultures,* ed. B. B. Whiting. New York: Wiley.

Lewy, A., and M. Chen. 1974. *Educational achievement of 4–6 grade students in the Israeli school system.* (Research Report.) Tel-Aviv: School of Education Tel-Aviv University. (Hebrew).

Liberman, A. M. 1977. An ethological approach to language through the study of speech perception. In *Human ethology,* eds. M. von Cranach, K. Foppa, W. Lepenies, and D. Plooq. Cambridge: Cambridge University Press, 682–704.

Liberman, I. Y. 1973. Segmentation of the spoken word and reading acquisition. *Bulletin of the Orton Society* 23:65–77.

———— 1982. A language-oriented view of reading and its disabilities. In *Progress in learning disabilities* (Vol. 5), ed. H. Myklebust. New York: Grune & Stratton.

Liberman, I. Y., D. Shankweiler, F. W. Fischer, and B. Carter. 1974. Explicit syllable and phoneme segmentation in the young child. *Journal of Experimental Child Psychology* 18:201–212.

Liberman, I. Y., D. Shankweiler, A. M. Liberman, C. Fowler, and F. W. Fischer.

1977. Phonetic segmentation and recoding in the beginning reader. In *Towards a psychology of reading: The proceedings of the CUNY conference*, eds. A. S. Reber and D. Scarborough. Hillsdale, NJ: Erlbaum.

Lippincott Basic Reading. 1975. Philadelphia: J. B. Lippincott Company.

Liu, S. S. F. 1978. Decoding and comprehension in reading Chinese. In *Cross-cultural perspectives on reading and reading research*, ed. D. Feitelson. Newark, DE: International Reading Association.

Lorge, I. and J. S. Chall. 1963. Estimating the size of vocabularies of children and adults: An analysis of methodological issues. *The Journal of Experimental Education* 32:147–157.

MacGinitie, W. H. 1969. Evaluating readiness for learning to read: A critical review and evaluation of research. *Reading Research Quarterly* 4:396–410.

Mackay, D., B. Thompson, and P. Schaub. 1979. *Breakthrough to literacy. Teacher's manual.* Harlow, Essex: Longman.

Malmquist, E., and H. U. Grundin. 1980. Cross-national studies on primary reading: A suggested program. In *Orthography, reading and dyslexia*, eds. J. F. Kavanagh and R. L. Venezky. Baltimore: University Park Press.

Malone, J. R. 1962. The larger aspects of spelling reform. *Elementary English* 39:435–445.

―――― 1965. The Unifon system. *Wilson Library Bulletin* 40:63–65.

Mandler, J. M. 1978. A code in the node: The use of story schema in retrieval. *Discourse Processes* 1:14–35.

Mandler, J. M., and N. S. Johnson. 1977. Remembrance of things parsed: Story structure and recall. *Cognitive Psychology* 9:111–151.

Mason, J. M. 1980. When do children begin to read: An exploration of four year old children's letter and word reading competencies. *Reading Research Quarterly* 15:203–227.

―――― 1982. *A description of reading instruction: The tail is wagging the dog.* Champaign, IL: Center for the Study of Reading. Reading Education Report 35.

Mason, J., and J. Osborn. 1982. *When do children begin "reading to learn"?* A survey of classroom reading instruction practices in grades two through five. Champaign, IL: Center for the Study of Reading. Technical Report No. 261.

Mathews, M. M. 1966. *Teaching to read: Historically considered.* Chicago: University of Chicago Press.

Mayer, M. 1965. Introduction. In *The Montessori Method*, M. Montessori. Cambridge, MA: Bentley.

Mazurkiewicz, A. J. 1968. Fourth year results—Bethlehem i.t.a. study. In *i/t/a as a language arts medium*, ed. J. R. Block. Hempstead, NY: The i.t.a. Foundation at Hofstra University.

McCracken, R. A., and M. J. McCracken. 1978. Modeling is the key to sustained silent reading. *The Reading Teacher* 31:406–408.

McDermott, R. P. 1978. Pirandello in the classroom: On the possibility of equal educational opportunity in American culture. In *Futures of exceptional children: Emerging structures*, ed. M. C. Reynolds. Reston, VA: Council for Exceptional Children.

McGuffey's first eclectic reader. 1879. (Revised edition). Cincinnati: American Book Company. (Facsimile, undated).

Menyuk, P. 1971. *The acquisition and development of language.* Englewood Cliffs, NJ: Prentice-Hall.

Messmer, O. 1904. *Zur Psychologie des Lesens bei Kindern und Erwachsenen.* [On the psychology of reading by children and adults]. Leipzig: Wilhelm Engelman. (German).

Meyer, L. A. 1982. The relative effects of word-analysis and word-supply correction procedures with poor readers during word-attack training. *Reading Research Quarterly* 17:544–555.

Meyers, E. S., and H. H. Ball. 1974. *The kindergarten teacher's handbook.* Los Angeles: Gramercy.

Mittler, P. 1973. Language development and mental handicaps. In *The child with delayed speech.* eds. M. Rutter and J. A. M. Martin. London: Heinemann.

Montessori, M. 1898. Miserie sociali e nuovi ritrovati della scienza. *Il Risveglio Educativo.* Milan, December 7 and December 17. (Italian).

―――― 1965. *The Montessori Method.* Cambridge, MA: Bentley. Originally Stokes, 1912.

―――― 1966. *The secret of childhood.* New York: Ballantine.

Moore, J. C., C. J. Jones, and D. C. Miller. 1980. What we know after a decade of sustained silent reading. *The Reading Teacher* 33:445–450.

Moore, O. K. 1961. Orthographic symbols and the preschool child. A new approach. *Proceedings of the Third Minnesota Conference on Gifted Children.* Minneapolis: University of Minnesota Press.

Mork, T. A. 1972. Sustained silent reading in the classroom. *The Reading Teacher* 25:438–441.

Morphett, M. V., and C. Washburne. 1931. When should children begin to read? *Elementary School Journal* 31:496–503.

Morris, J. M. 1959. *Reading in the Primary School.* London: Newnes.

―――― 1974. *Language in action.* London and Basingstoke: Macmillan.

―――― 1984. Phonics 44 for initial literacy in English. *Reading* 18:13–24.

Mosberg, L. 1978. A response: Comments on language by eye and by ear. In *The acquisition of reading,* eds. F. B. Murray and J. J. Pikulski. Baltimore: University Park Press.

Mraz, G. 1980. Nachwort, Das Josephinische Erzherzogliche A.B.C. oder Namenbüchlein. Johann Balthasar von Antesperg. In *Nachdruck des Widmungsexemplars von 1741 im Landesmuseum Johanneum in Graz.* Dortmund, Germany: Harenberg. (German).

Muehl, S. 1962. The effects of letter-name knowledge on learning to read a word list in kindergarten children. *Journal of Educational Psychology* 53:181–186.

Nelson, K. 1973. Structure and strategy in learning to talk. *Monographs of the Society for Research in Child Development* 38, Nos. 1–2 (Serial No. 149).

Nodine, C. F., and J. D. Evans. 1969. Eye movements of prereaders containing letters of high and low confusability. *Perception and Psychophysics* 6:39–41.

Nodine, C. F., and N. J. Lang. 1971. The development of visual scanning strategies for differentiating words. *Developmental Psychology* 5:221–232.

Nooraihan, A., and J. O. Urbano. 1967. *Guide in the use of Bumasa Tayo at Sumulat.* Los Santos, Philippines: De Los Santos Community School.

Ohnmacht, D. D. 1969. *The effects of letter-knowledge on achievement in reading in the first grade.* Paper presented at American Educational Research Association Meeting, Los Angeles.

Oliver, H., A. Nicholson, D. Jantzi, and G. Tanner. 1981. *Abc-dabra: A phonics course for beginning readers.* Toronto: The Ontario Institute for Studies in Education.

Olson, A. V. 1966. The Frostig Developmental Test of Visual Perception as a predictor of specific reading abilities with second grade children. *Elementary English* 43:869–872.

Open Court Educator, November 1980, 15(1), La Salle, IL: Open Court.

Opie, I., and P. Opie, eds. 1980. *A nursery companion.* Oxford: Oxford University Press.

Osborn, J. H. 1977. Skill hierarchies and decoding. In *A consideration of skill hierarchy approaches to the teaching of reading,* In J. M. Mason, J. H. Osborn, J. H. and B. V. Rosenshine. Champaign, IL: Center for the Study of Reading. Technical Report, No. 42.

Paterson, D. G., and M. A. Tinker. 1940. *How to make type readable.* New York: Harper.

Paulsen, F. 1920. *Das deutsche Bildungswesen in seiner geschichtlichen Entwicklung.* (3rd edition). Leipzig: Teubner. (German).

Pearson, P. D., ed. 1984. *Handbook of Reading Research.* New York: Longman.

———— 1986. *Must we teach what must be learned?* Invited address to closing plenary session of 11th World Congress on Reading. London: University of London, (July 31).

Pearson, P. D., J. Hansen, and C. Gordon. 1979. The effect of background knowledge on young children's comprehension of explicit and implicit information. *Journal of Reading Behaviour.* 11:201–209.

Pearson, P. D., and D. D. Johnson. 1978. *Teaching reading comprehension.* New York: Holt, Rinehart & Winston.

Pellegrini, A. D. 1983. Sociolinguistic contexts of the preschool. *Journal of Applied Developmental Psychology* 4:380–397.

Perera, K. 1984. *Children's writing and reading: Analysing classroom language.* Oxford: Blackwell.

Perfetti, C. A. 1977. Language comprehension and fast decoding: Some psycholinguistic prerequisites for skilled reading comprehension. In *Cognition, curriculum and comprehension,* ed. J. T. Guthrie. Newark, DE: International Reading Association.

———— 1985. *Reading ability.* New York: Oxford University Press.

Perfetti, C. A., and S. F. Roth. 1981. Some of the interactive processes in reading and their role in reading skill. In *Interactive processes in reading,* eds. A. M. Lesgold and C. A. Perfetti. Hillsdale, NJ: Erlbaum.

Pfungst, O. 1911. *Clever Hans.* New York: Holt.

Pick, A. D. 1970. Some basic perceptual processes in reading. *Young Children* 25:162–181.

Pikkanen, A., M. Louhi, V. Niskanen, and M. Totro. 1975. *A ja O Aapinen.* [A and O primer.] Helsinki: Soderstrom. (Finnish).

Pitman, J. 1968. The historical background of i.t.a. In *i.t.a. as a language arts medium,* ed. J. R. Block. Hempstead, NY: Hofstra University.

Pollard, R. 1889. *Synthetic method of reading and spelling.* New York: American Book Company.

Popp, H. M. 1975. Current practices in the teaching of beginning reading. In *Toward a literate society,* eds. J. B. Carroll and J. S. Chall. New York: McGraw-Hill.

Rabin, C. 1977. Spelling reform—Israel 1968. In *Advances in the creation and revision of writing systems,* ed. J. A. Fishman. The Hague: Mouton.

Read, C. 1971. Pre-school children's knowledge of English phonology. *Harvard Education Review* 41:1–34.

Reeder, R. R. 1900. *Historical development of school readers and of method in teaching reading.* New York: Macmillan.

Reid, J. F. 1966. Learning to think about reading. *Educational Research* 9:56–62.

Reshef, O. 1984. *Daily reading to kindergarten children as a way to improve verbal skills and comprehension.* Unpublished master's thesis, University of Haifa. (Hebrew).

Resnick, L. B., and I. L. Beck. 1976. Designing instruction in reading: Interaction of theory and practice. In *Aspects of reading acquisition,* ed. J. T. Guthrie. Baltimore, MD: Johns Hopkins University Press.

Resnick, L. B., and P. A. Weaver, eds. 1979. *Theory and practice of early reading.* Hillsdale, NJ: Erlbaum. (3 Vols.).

Rice, J. M. 1893. *The public-school system of the United States.* New York: Century. (Reissued—New York: Arno, 1969).

Richardson, E., and C. M. Bradley. 1974. ISM: A teacher-oriented method of reading instruction for the child-oriented teacher. *Journal of Learning Disabilities* 7:344–352.

Richardson, E., B. Di Benedetto, and C. M. Bradley. 1977. The relationship of sound blending to reading achievement. *Review of Educational Research* 47:319–334.

Rickoff, A. 1857. *Common schools of Cincinnati, Annual Report.* Cincinnati.

Roberts, W. R. 1910. *Dionysius of Halicarnassus.* London.

Rosen, C. L. 1964. An experimental study of visual perceptual training and reading achievement in first grade. *Perceptual and Motor Skills* 22:979–986.

Rosen, C. L., and F. Ohnmacht. 1968. Perception readiness and reading achievement in first grade. In *Perception and Reading.* Proceedings of the 12th Annual Convention of the International Reading Association. Newark, DE: International Reading Association.

Rosenshine, B. 1970. Enthusiastic teaching: A research review. *School Review* 78:499–514.

———— 1979. Content, time and direct instruction. In *Research on Teaching: Concepts, findings and implications,* eds. H. Walberg, and P. Peterson, Berkely: McCutchan.

———— 1980. Skill hierarchies in reading comprehension. In *Theoretical issues in reading comprehension,* eds. R. T. Spiro, B. C. Bruce, and W. F. Brewer. Hillsdale, NJ: Erlbaum.

Rosenshine, B. and D. C. Berliner, 1978. Academic engaged time. *British Journal of Teacher Education* 4:3–16.

Rosenshine, B. and R. Stevens. 1984. Classroom instruction in reading. In *Handbook of Reading Research,* ed. P. D. Pearson. New York: Longman.

Roswell, F., and G. Natchez. 1964. *Reading disability: Diagnosis and treatment.* New York: Basic Books.

Rumelhart, D. E. 1977. Toward an interactive model of reading. In *Attention and Performance 6:* Proceedings of the Sixth International Symposium on Attention and Performance, Stockholm, Sweden, ed. S. Dornic. Hillsdale, NJ: Erlbaum.

Ruthman, P. 1973. France. In *Comparative reading,* ed. J. Downing. New York: Macmillan.

Sakiey, E., E. Fry, A. Goss, and B. Loigman. 1980. A syllable frequency count. *Visible Language* 14:137–150.

Saltz, E., D. Dixon, and J. Johnson. 1977. Training disadvantaged preschoolers on various fantasy activities: Effects on cognitive functioning and impulse control. *Child Development* 48:367–380.

Samuels, S. J. 1972. The effect of letter-name knowledge on learning to read. *American Educational Research Journal* 9:65–74.

——— 1978. Application of basic research in reading. In *Psychology from research to practice,* eds. H. Pick, W. Herschel, A. Leibnitz, J. L. Singer, A. Steinschneider, and H. W. Stevenson. New York: Plenum.

——— 1979. How the mind works when reading: Describing elephants no one has ever seen. In *Theory and practice of early reading* (Vol. 1), eds. L. B. Resnick, and P. A. Weaver. Hillsdale, NJ: Erlbaum.

Samuels, S. J., and P. D. Pearson. 1980. Caution: Using research in applied settings. *Reading Research Quarterly* 15:317–322.

Sartain, H. W. 1960. A bibliography on individualized reading. *The Reading Teacher* 13:262–270.

Schank, R. C. 1982. *Reading and understanding: Teaching from the perspective of artificial intelligence.* Hillsdale, NJ: Erlbaum.

Schank, R. C., and R. P. Abelson. 1977. *Scripts plans goals and understanding.* Hillsdale, NJ: Erlbaum.

Schieffelin, B. B., and M. Cochran-Smith. 1984. Learning to read culturally: Literacy before schooling. In H. Goelman, A. A. Oberg, and F. Smith, eds. *Awakening to literacy.* Exeter, NH: Heinemann.

Schonell, F. J. 1966. *The psychology and teaching of reading* (5th ed.) London: Oliver & Boyd.

Seguin, E. 1846. *Traitement moral, hygiène et education des idiots et des autres enfants arrières.* (The moral treatment, hygiene and education of idiots and other backward children). (French).

——— 1866. *Idiocy and its treatment by the physiological method.* New York.

Seitz, V. 1977. *Social class and ethnic group differences in learning to read.* Newark, DE: International Reading Association.

Seuss, Dr. 1960. *Green eggs and ham.* New York: Random House.

———— 1957. *The cat in the hat.* New York: Random House.

Shankweiler, D., and I. Y. Liberman. 1976. Exploring the relations between reading and speech. In *Neuropsychology of learning disorders: Theoretical Approaches,* eds. R. M. Knights, and D. J. Bakker. Baltimore: University Park Press.

Sharan, S. 1980. Cooperative learning in small groups: Recent methods and effects on achievement, attitudes and ethnic relations. *Review of Educational Research* 50:241–272.

Sigel, I. 1970. The distancing hypothesis: A causal hypothesis for the acquisition of representational thought. In *Miami Symposium on the Prediction of Behavior, 1968: Effect of Early Experiences,* ed. M. R. Jones. Coral Gables, FL: University of Miami Press.

Silberman, H. F. 1963. *Reading and related verbal learning.* (SP-1105/001/01). Santa Monica, CA: System Development Corporation.

Singer, J. L., and D. G. Singer. 1980. *Television, imagination and aggression: A study of preschoolers' play.* Hillsdale, NJ: Erlbaum.

Smilansky, S. 1968. *The effects of sociodramatic play on disadvantaged preschool children.* New York: Wiley.

Smith, F. 1973. Twelve easy ways to make learning to read difficult. In *Psycholinguistics and reading,* ed. F. Smith. New York: Holt, Rinehart & Winston.

———— 1983. *Essays into literacy.* Exeter, N.H.: Heinemann.

Smith, N. B. 1963. *Reading instruction for today's children.* Englewood Cliffs, NJ: Prentice-Hall.

———— 1965. *American reading instruction.* (Second edition). Newark, DE: International Reading Association.

Snow, C. E. 1983. Literacy and language: Realationships during the preschool years. *Harvard Educational Review* 55:165–189.

———— 1984. Parent-child interaction and the development of communicative ability. In *The acquisition of communicative competence,* ed. R. L. Schiefelbusch and J. Pickar. Baltimore: University Park Press.

Southgate, V., H. Arnold, and S. Johnson. 1981. *Extending beginning reading.* London: Heinemann.

Spalding, R. B. with W. T. Spalding. 1969. *The writing road to reading.* (Second revised edition). New York: Morrow Quill Paperbacks.

Spiro, R. J., B. C. Bruce, and W. F. Brewer, eds. 1980. *Theoretical issues in reading comprehension.* Hillsdale, NJ: Erlbaum.

Stanovich, K. E. 1986. Matthew effects in reading: Some consequences of individual differences in the acquisition of literacy. *Reading Research Quarterly* 21:360–407.

Stauffer, R. G. 1960. Individualized and group-type directed reading instruction. *Elementary English* 37:375–382.

———— 1970. *The language-experience approach to the teaching of reading.* New York: Harper & Row.

Steffensen, M. S., C. Joag-Dev, and R. C. Anderson. 1979. A cross-cultural perspective on reading comprehension. *Reading Research Quarterly* 15:10–29.

Stein, N. L. 1979. How children understand stories: A developmental analysis.

In *Current topics in early childhood education*, ed. E. L. Katz. Norwood, NJ: Ablex.

Stevens, R., and B. Rosenshine. 1981. Advances in research on teaching. *Exceptional Education Quarterly* 12:1–9.

Stipek, D. J., and J. R. Weisz. 1981. Perceived personal control and academic achievement. *Review of Educational Research* 51:101–138.

Strauss, H. 1977. Kindergartners' expectancies in regard to school entry. In *The infant schools—An educational experiment and its conclusions*, eds. D. Feitelson and E. Rokach. Jerusalem: Ministry of Education. (Hebrew).

Strauss, H., J. Harrison, M. Gross, and P. Kedem. 1976. Evaluation of the experimental infant schools project. In *Final Report on the Infant School Experiment*, ed. D. Feitelson. Jerusalem: Ministry of Education. (Hebrew).

Sutton-Smith, B., ed. 1979. *Play and learning*. New York: Gardner.

Tanyzer, H. J., H. Alpert, and L. Sandel. 1968. The effects of transition from i.t.a. to T.O. and spelling achievement. In *i.t.a. as a language arts medium*, ed. J. R. Block. Hempstead, NY: i.t.a. Foundation at Hofstra University.

Tauber, A. 1965. Introduction. In *George Bernard Shaw on language*, ed. A. Tauber. London: Owen.

Taylor, D. 1983. *Family literacy: Young Children learning to read and write*. Exeter, NH: Heinemann.

Teale, W. H. 1986. Home background and young children's literacy development. In *Emergent literacy: Writing and reading*, eds. W. H. Teale, and E. Sulzby. Norwood, NJ: Ablex.

Teitel, B. 1980. *Language and perception as predictors of reading comprehension*. Unpublished Ph.D. dissertation, New York University. University Microfilms International No. 8028649.

Terman, L. M. 1943. Foreword. In *Remedial techniques in basic school subjects*, G. M. Fernald. New York: McGraw-Hill.

Thorndike, E. L. 1935. *The psychology of wants, interests and attitudes*. New York: Appleton-Century.

Thorndike, R. L. 1973. *Reading comprehension education in fifteen countries*. New York: Halsted.

Tierney, R. J., and P. D. Pearson. 1981. Learning to learn from text: A framework for improving classroom practice. In *Reading in the content area: Improving classroom instruction*, eds. E. Dishner, J. Readence, and T. Bean. Dubuque, IA: Kendall/Hunt.

Tinker, M. A. 1931. The influence of form of type on the perception of words. *Journal of Applied Psychology* 16:167–174.

Tinker, M. A., and C. McCullough. 1962. *Teaching elementary reading*. (second edition). New York: Appleton—Century—Crofts.

Tinker, M. A., and D. G. Paterson. 1928. Influence of type form on speed of reading. *Journal of Applied Psychology* 12:359–368.

Tinker, M. A., and D. G. Paterson. 1939. Influence of type form on eye movements. *Journal of Experimental Psychology* 25:528–531.

Tizard, B. 1980. Language at home and at school. In *Language in early childhood education*, ed. C. B. Cazden. (Revised edition). Washington, DC: The National Association for the Education of Young Children.

Trace, A. S. J. 1961. *What Ivan knows that Johnny doesn't.* New York: Random House.

———— 1965. *Reading without Dick and Jane.* Chicago: Regnery.

Vandenberg, B. 1980. Play, problem-solving, and creativity. In *New directions for child development: Children's play,* ed. K. H. Rubin. San Francisco: Jossey-Bass.

Vandever, T. R., and D. D. Neville. 1976. Transfer as a result of synthetic and analytic training instruction. *American Journal of Mental Deficiency* 80:498–503.

Vasresensky, V. D. 1959. Methods of teaching reading and writing to adults. *Fundamental and Adult Education* 11:154–173.

Veatch, J. 1959. *Reading in the elementary school.* New York: Ronald.

Vellutino, F. R. 1977. Alternative conceptualizations of dyslexia: Evidence in support of a verbal deficit hypothesis. *Harvard Educational Review* 47:334–354.

Venezky, R. L. 1970. *The structure of English orthography.* The Hague: Mouton.

———— 1972. Language and cognition in reading. In *Current trends in educational linguistics,* ed. B. Spolsky. The Hague: Mouton.

———— 1973. The letter-sound generalizations of first, second, and third grade Finnish children. *Journal of Educational Psychology* 64:288–292.

———— 1975. The curious role of letter names in reading instruction. *Visible Language* 9:7–23.

———— 1976. Prerequisites for learning to read. In *Cognitive learning in children: Theories and strategies,* eds. J. R. Levin, and V. L. Allen. New York: Academic Press.

Venezky, R. L., and Y. Shiloach. 1972. The learning of picture sound associations by Israeli kindergartners. In *Studies on prereading skills* in Israel, eds. R. L. Venezky, Y. Shiloah, and R. C. Calfee. Madison, W.I.: Technical Report 222, Wisconsin Research and Development Center Cognitive Learning.

Vernon, M. D. 1957. *Backwardness in reading.* London: Cambridge University Press.

———— 1971. *Reading and its difficulties.* London: Cambridge University Press.

Vogel, T. M. 1894. *Leben und Verdienste Valentin Ickelsamers.* [The life and achievements of Valentin Ickelsamer]. Leipzig (German).

Vygotsky, L. S. 1967. Play and its role in the mental development of the child. *Soviet Psychology* Vol. 3.

———— 1978. *Mind in society: The development of higher psychological processes.* Cambridge, MA: Harvard University Press.

Wall, W. D. 1975. *Constructive education for children.* London: Harrap.

Wallach, L., M. A. Wallach, M. G. Dozier, and N. E. Kaplan. 1977. Poor children learning to read do not have trouble with auditory discrimination but do have trouble with phoneme recognition. *Journal of Educational Psychology* 69:36–39.

Wallach, M. A., and L. Wallach. 1979. Teaching phoneme identification skills. In *Theory and practice of early reading,* eds. L. B. Resnick, and P. A. Weaver. (Vol. 3). Hillsdale, NJ: Erlbaum.

Warburton, F. W., and V. Southgate. 1969. *i.t.a.: An independent evaluation.* London: Murray & Chambers.

Wardhaugh, R. 1971. Theories of language acquisition in relation to beginning reading instruction. *Reading Research Quarterly* 7:168–194.

Watson, J. S., ed. 1875–76. *Quintillian's institutes of oratory.* London: I. 16.

Webb, J. R. 1855. *Webb's normal readers,* No. 1 to No. 4.

Webb, N. M. 1982. Student interaction and learning in small groups. *Review of Educational Research* 52:421–445.

Webster, W. G. 1866. Preface. In *The elementary spelling book, Being an improvement on the American Spelling Book by Noah Webster.* New York: American Book Company. (Facsimile-undated).

Webster's New Universal Unabridged Dictionary. 1983. Cleveland: Dorset and Baber.

White, R. W. 1959. Motivation reconsidered: The concept of competence *Psychological Review* 66:297–333.

White, S. H. 1970. Some general outlines of the matrix of developmental change between five and seven years. *Bulletin of the Orton Society* 20:41–57.

Whitehead, F., A. C. Capey, W. Maddren, and A. Wellings. 1977. *Children and their books.* London: Macmillan.

Wiberg, J. L., and M. A. Trost, 1970. Comparison between the content of first grade primers and the free choice library selections made by first grade students. *Elementary English* 47:792–798.

Wijk, A. 1959. *Regularized English: An investigation into the English spelling reform problem with a new, detailed plan for a possible solution.* Acta Universitatis Stockholmiensis 7. Stockholm: Almqvist & Wiksell.

———. 1972. How to teach reading by the aid of regularized Inglish. Paper presented at the United Kingdom Reading Association Ninth Annual Conference. Hamilton College Scotland. Reprinted in A. Wijk. 1977. *Regularized English/Regularized Inglish.* Stockholm: Almqvist and Wiksell. 14–24.

———. 1974. A suggestion for a reading scheme based on regularized Inglish. Lecture delivered at the United Kingdom Reading Association Eleventh Annual Conference. Edge-Hill College, Lancashire, Reprinted in A. Wijk 1977. *Regularized English/Regularized Inglish.* Stockholm: Almqvist and Wiksell. 25–40.

———. 1977. *Regularized English/Regularized Inglish: A proposal for an effective solution of the reading problem in the English-speaking countries.* Stockholm: Almquist and Wiksell.

Wijk, A., M. Cross, E. Oakensen, W. Reed, and B. Tudor-Hart. *Regularized Inglish reading skeme.* Teachers' Manual and Books Wun, Too, Three (mimeographed and undated).

Wilson, F. T., and C. W. Flemming. 1938. Correlations of reading progress with other abilities and traits in grade 1. *Journal of Genetic Psychology* 53:33–52.

Winch, W. H. 1904. *Notes on German schools: With special relation to curriculum and methods of teaching.* London: Longmans, Green.

Wir Können Schon Lesen. 1964. Herausgegeben von der Wiener Fibel-Kommission, Wien: Österreichischer Bundesverlag und Andere. (German).

Ylisto, I. P. 1977. Early reading responses of young Finnish children. *The Reading Teacher* 31:167–172.

Yomirui Newspaper, Books for babies. *Yomirui Shimbuu,* April 18, 1977. (Japanese).

Zimet, S. G. ed. 1972. *What children read in school.* New York: Grune & Stratton.

Author Index

Subject Index

641

641007